PRAISE FOR *THE THIRD INDUSTRIAL REVOLUTION*

"Mr. Rifkin clearly outlines the challenges facing our global community, and creates a vision for business leaders, government and citizens."

—John Chambers, chairman and CEO of Cisco

"The creative thinking of Jeremy Rifkin has been inspiring policy makers and citizens alike. This book shows the key role renewables and modern technologies can play in our transition to a low-carbon economy."

—José Manuel Barroso, president of the European Commission

"This is a remarkable piece of work from one of the foremost thinkers of our time . . . Rifkin has come up with a visionary and innovative economic development model that ensures the sustainability of our natural resources and ecosystems."

—Rajendra Pachauri, chairman of the United Nations Intergovernmental Panel on Climate Change

"A brilliant new economic paradigm to guide the human journey in the 21st century. Jeremy Rifkin's comprehensive Third Industrial Revolution vision, which is the centerpiece of Rome's long-term economic development plan, provides a blueprint for every city in the world to create a sustainable and prosperous society."

—Gianni Alemanno, mayor of Rome

"More than thought provoking . . . a call for action to policy makers and business leaders to embrace the opportunity of a society and economy driven by sustainable innovation and powered by renewable and distributed energy."

—Rudy Provoost, CEO of Philips Lighting

"A provocative strategy for transforming the global energy system. This book may help frame the social and economic solutions for the 1.5 billion poorest people who lack access to clean, reliable, and efficient energy services."

—Dr. Kandeh K. Yumkella, director-general of the United Nations Industrial Development Organization (UNIDO) and chairman of UN Energy

"Jeremy Rifkin's intellectual rigor, combined with lively and engaging prose, has produced a timely and important work on how to diversify our energy sources in order to create a world in which people can live well and within the limits of the planet."

—Björn Stigson, president of the World Business Council for Sustainable Development

"As the chairman of a global real estate services company, I'm convinced that Jeremy Rifkin's vision of rethinking buildings as green 'micro-power plants' is the future. But to do this, we need the courage to act quickly and lay the foundation for the Third Industrial Revolution. So let's get on with it."

—Bruce Mosler, chairman of Cushman & Wakefield Global Brokerage

"Very compelling . . . while many experts focus on how to transform our energy systems, few offer such a comprehensive economic vision and social road map as Jeremy Rifkin. The 'Energy Internet' will lift our world to a new plateau of economic growth, while at the same time addressing climate change and increasing our energy security . . . A must-read."

—Guido Bartels, chairman of the Global Smart Grid Federation

"An exciting vision for a post-carbon society. Rifkin embeds green transport inside a new high-tech Third Industrial Revolution infrastructure, reframing the very concept of human mobility. This could well be the future of transportation."

—Alan Lloyd, president of the
International Council on Clean Transportation

"The old ways of creating wealth just don't work anymore, and politicians the world over are struggling to cope with the convergence of financial meltdown, huge debt, rising commodity and energy prices, accelerating climate change, and food and water shortages. The Third Industrial Revolution presents us with a breathtakingly exciting alternative that will create the jobs, the profits, and the technological breakthroughs we now so urgently need."

—Jonathon Porritt, founder and director of Forum for the Future

"Jeremy Rifkin's Third Industrial Revolution sets forth a comprehensive, realistic, technically sound, market-driven model for transitioning the global economy into a more sustainable future. Rifkin's vision of 'Distributed Capitalism' strikes a powerful chord among leading CEOs in the design and construction industries who will be tasked with turning the theory and promise of a Third Industrial Revolution into reality."

—Mark Casso, president of the Construction Industry Round Table

"Erudite and highly entertaining . . . Jeremy Rifkin sees the reality of the Third Industrial Revolution overturning conventional economic theory, doing away with traditional political ideologies, and redefining capitalism itself. This is a book no serious thinker should miss."

—Stéphane Rambaud-Measson, president of Passengers at
Bombardier Transportation

THE
THIRD INDUSTRIAL
REVOLUTION

HOW LATERAL POWER IS TRANSFORMING
ENERGY, THE ECONOMY, AND THE WORLD

JEREMY RIFKIN

palgrave
macmillan

THE THIRD INDUSTRIAL REVOLUTION
Copyright © Jeremy Rifkin, 2011.
All rights reserved.

First published in hardcover in 2011 by PALGRAVE MACMILLAN® in the
United States—a division of St. Martin's Press LLC, 175 Fifth Avenue, New
York, NY 10010.

Where this book is distributed in the United Kingdom, Europe, and the
rest of the world, this is by Palgrave Macmillan, a division of Macmillan
Publishers Limited, registered in England, company number 785998, of
Houndmills, Basingstoke, Hampshire RG21 6XS.

Palgrave Macmillan is the global academic imprint of the above companies
and has companies and representatives throughout the world.

Palgrave® and Macmillan® are registered trademarks in the United States,
the United Kingdom, Europe and other countries.

ISBN: 978-0-230-34197-5

Library of Congress Cataloging-in-Publication Data

Rifkin, Jeremy.
    The third industrial revolution : how lateral power is transforming energy,
the economy, and the world/ Jeremy Rifkin.
        p.   cm.
    Includes index.
    ISBN 978-0-230-11521-7 (hardback)
    1. Energy development.   2. Power resources—Environmental
aspects.   3. Industries.   I. Title.

HD9502.A2R54   2011
333.79—dc22
        2011009609

A catalogue record of the book is available from the British Library.

Design by Letra Libre, Inc.

First PALGRAVE MACMILLAN paperback edition: January 2013

10 9 8 7 6 5 4 3 2 1

Printed in the United States of America.

"The European Union's priority task in the first half of the twenty-first century will be—to quote Jeremy Rifkin—'to lead the way to the Third Industrial Revolution.' Reducing CO_2 emissions is only part of the story: the time for a switch to a low-carbon economy has come.

This is no Utopia, no futuristic vision: in twenty-five years' time, we will be able to construct each building as its own 'mini power station' producing clean and renewable energy for its own needs, with the surplus being made available for other purposes.

These are the pillars of the 'Third Industrial Revolution,' which Jeremy Rifkin has described so powerfully: greater use of renewable energies, the construction of buildings which produce their own energy, and the transition to the use of hydrogen for energy storage.

What is at stake is the future of the European Union—and we should not be so complacent as to understand the word 'future' as meaning only something which comes after us!

We must not miss the opportunity to usher in the Third Industrial Revolution: it offers us a chance to put the European economy on a forward-looking and sustainable footing and, in that way, to secure its competitiveness in the long term."

—Hans-Gert Pöttering, president of the European Parliament, speaking at the European Union's second Citizens' Agora, June 12, 2008

CONTENTS

ACKNOWLEDGMENTS

I would like to thank Nicholas Easley, who heads up our global operations, for his stellar job in overseeing the Third Industrial Revolution master plans and his valuable editorial contributions to the book. I'd also like to thank Andrew Linowes, our programs director, for his rigorous stewardship of our day-to-day operations and for his many valuable editorial contributions to the book. I would also like to acknowledge our interns Flore De Sloover, Alma Velazquez, Valbona Tika, Lauren Bush, Bart Provoost, Divya Susarla, Bobby Samuel, Brian Bauer, Petros Kusmu, and Shawn Moorhead for their able assistance in preparing the manuscript.

I would also like to thank my editor, Emily Carleton, for her enthusiasm and deep commitment to the project, as well as for her many editorial suggestions that helped shape the final book. Thanks also to my agent, Larry Kirshbaum, for his editorial suggestions in preparing the initial book proposal and for positioning the book for the global market.

A special thanks to Angelo Consoli, who has directed our European operations for the past nine years. Mr. Consoli's political acumen and tireless dedication has been instrumental in making the Third Industrial Revolution vision a reality across Europe.

Finally, I would like to thank my wife, Carol Grunewald, for her trusted advice and consul over the past twenty-two years. Our shared dream of creating a more sustainable world for every human being, as well as for all of our fellow creatures, has been the inspiration that has guided our journey.

INTRODUCTION

WASHINGTON, DC

Our industrial civilization is at a crossroads. Oil and the other fossil fuel energies that make up the industrial way of life are sunsetting, and the technologies made from and propelled by these energies are antiquated. The entire industrial infrastructure built on the back of fossil fuels is aging and in disrepair. The result is that unemployment is rising to dangerous levels all over the world. Governments, businesses and consumers are awash in debt, and living standards are plummeting. A record one billion human beings—nearly one-seventh of the human race—face hunger and starvation.

Worse, climate change from fossil fuel–based industrial activity looms on the horizon. Our scientists warn that we face a potentially cataclysmic change in the temperature and chemistry of the planet, which threatens to destabilize ecosystems around the world. Scientists worry that we may be on the brink of a mass extinction of plant and animal life by the end of the century, imperiling our own species' ability to survive. It is becoming increasingly clear that we need a new economic narrative that can take us into a more equitable and sustainable future.

By the 1980s the evidence was mounting that the fossil fuel–driven Industrial Revolution was peaking and that human-induced climate change was forcing a planetary crisis of untold proportions. For the past 30 years I have been searching for a new paradigm that could usher in a post-carbon era. In my explorations, I came to realize that the great economic revolutions in history occur when new communication technologies converge with new energy systems. New energy regimes make possible the creation of more interdependent economic activity and expanded commercial exchange as well as facilitate more dense and inclusive social relationships. The accompanying communication revolutions become the means to organize and manage the new temporal and spatial dynamics that arise from new energy systems.

In the mid-1990s, it dawned on me that a new convergence of communication and energy was in the offing. Internet technology and renewable energies were about to merge to create a powerful new infrastructure for a Third Industrial Revolution (TIR) that would change the world. In the coming era, hundreds of millions of people will produce their own green energy in their homes, offices, and factories and share it with each other in an "energy Internet," just like we now create and share information online. The democratization of energy will bring with it a fundamental reordering of human relationships, impacting the very way we conduct business, govern society, educate our children, and engage in civic life.

I introduced the Third Industrial Revolution vision at the Wharton School's Advanced Management Program (AMP) at the University of Pennsylvania, where I have been a senior lecturer for the past sixteen years on new trends in science, technology, the economy, and society. The five-week program exposes CEOs and business executives from around the world to the emerging issues and challenges they will face in the twenty-first century. The idea soon found its way into corporate suites and became part of the political lexicon among heads of state in the European Union.

By the year 2000, the European Union was aggressively pursuing policies to significantly reduce its carbon footprint and transition into a sustainable economic era. Europeans were readying targets and benchmarks, resetting research and development priorities, and putting into place codes, regulations, and standards for a new economic journey. By contrast, America was preoccupied with the newest gizmos and "killer apps" coming out of Silicon Valley, and homeowners were flush with excitement over a bullish real estate market pumped up by subprime mortgages.

Few Americans were interested in sobering peak oil forecasts, dire climate change warnings, and the growing signs that beneath the surface, our economy was not well. There was an air of contentment, even complacency, across the country, confirming once again the belief that our good fortune demonstrated our superiority over other nations.

Feeling a little like an outsider in my own country, I chose to ignore Horace Greeley's sage advice to every malcontent in 1850 to "Go West, young man, go West," and decided to travel in the opposite direction, across the ocean to old Europe, where new ideas about the future prospects of the human race were being seriously entertained.

I know at this point, many of my American readers are rolling their eyes and saying, "Give me a break! Europe is falling apart and living in the past. The whole place is one big museum. It may be a nice destination for a holiday but is no longer a serious contender on the world scene."

I'm not naïve to Europe's many problems, failings, and contradictions. But pejorative slurs could just as easily be leveled at the United States and other governments for their many limitations. And before we Americans become too puffed up about our own importance, we should take note that the European Union, not the United States or China, is the biggest economy in the world. The gross domestic product (GDP) of its twenty-seven member states exceeds the GDP of our fifty states. While the European Union doesn't field much of a global military presence, it is a formidable force on the international stage. More to the point, the European Union is virtually alone among the governments of the world in asking the big questions about our future viability as a species on Earth.

So I went east. For the past ten years, I have spent more than 40 percent of my time in the European Union, sometimes commuting weekly back and forth across the Atlantic, working with governments, the business community, and civil society organizations to advance the Third Industrial Revolution.

In 2006, I began working with the leadership of the European Parliament in drafting a Third Industrial Revolution economic development plan. Then, in May 2007, the European Parliament issued a formal written declaration endorsing the Third Industrial Revolution as the long-term economic vision and road map for the European Union. The Third Industrial Revolution is now being implemented by the various agencies within the European Commission as well as in the member states.

A year later, in October 2008, just weeks after the global economic collapse, my office hurriedly assembled a meeting in Washington, DC, of eighty CEOs and senior executives from the world's leading companies in renewable energy, construction, architecture, real estate, IT, power and utilities, and transport and logistics to discuss how we might turn the crisis into an opportunity. Business leaders and trade associations attending the gathering agreed that they could no longer go it alone and committed to creating a Third Industrial Revolution network that could work with governments, local businesses, and civil society organizations toward the goal of transitioning the global economy into a distributed post-carbon era. The economic development group—which includes Philips, Schneider Electric, IBM, Cisco Systems, Acciona, CH2M Hill, Arup, Adrian Smith + Gordon Gill Architecture, and Q-Cells, among others—is the largest of its kind in the world and is currently working with cities, regions, and national governments to develop master plans to transform their economies into Third Industrial Revolution infrastructures.

The Third Industrial Revolution vision is quickly spreading to countries in Asia, Africa, and the Americas. On May 24, 2011, I presented the five-pillar TIR economic plan in a keynote address at the fiftieth anniversary conference of the Organization for Economic Cooperation and Development (OECD) in Paris, attended by heads of state and ministers from the thirty-four participating member nations. The presentation accompanied the rollout of an OECD green growth economic plan that will serve as a template to begin preparing the nations of the world for a post-carbon industrial future.

This book is an insider's account of the unfolding Third Industrial Revolution vision and economic development model, including a look into the personalities and players—heads of state, global CEOs, social entrepreneurs, and NGOs—who are pioneering its implementation.

In designing the EU blueprint for the Third Industrial Revolution, I have been privileged to work with many of Europe's leading heads of state, including Chancellor Angela Merkel of Germany; Prime Minister Romano Prodi of Italy; Prime Minister José Luis Rodríguez Zapatero of Spain; Manuel Barroso, the president of the European Commission; and five of the presidents of the European Council.

Is there anything we Americans can learn from what's happening in Europe? I believe so. We need to begin by taking a careful look at what our European friends are saying and attempting to do. However falteringly, Europeans are at least coming to grips with the reality that the fossil fuel era is dying, and they are beginning to chart a course into a green future. Unfortunately, Americans, for the most part, continue to be in a state of denial, not wishing to acknowledge that the economic system that served us so well in the past is now on life support. Like Europe, we need to own up and pony up.

But what can we bring to the party? While Europe has come up with a compelling narrative, no one can tell a story better than America. Madison Avenue, Hollywood, and Silicon Valley excel at this. What has distinguished America is not so much our manufacturing acumen or military prowess, but our uncanny ability to envision the future with such vividness and clarity that people feel as if they've arrived even before they've left the station. If and when Americans truly "get" the new Third Industrial Revolution narrative, we have the unequalled ability to move quickly to make that dream a reality.

The Third Industrial Revolution is the last of the great Industrial Revolutions and will lay the foundational infrastructure for an emerging collaborative age. The forty-year build-out of the TIR infrastructure will create hundreds of thousands of new businesses and hundreds of millions of new jobs. Its completion will signal the end of a two-hundred-year commercial saga characterized by industrious thinking, entrepreneurial markets, and mass labor workforces and the beginning of a new era marked by collaborative behavior, social networks, and boutique professional and technical workforces. In the coming half century, the conventional, centralized business operations of the First and Second Industrial Revolutions will increasingly be subsumed by the distributed business practices of the Third Industrial Revolution; and the traditional, hierarchical organization of economic and political power will give way to lateral power organized nodally across society.

At first blush, the very notion of lateral power seems so contradictory to how we have experienced power relations through much of history. Power, after all, has traditionally been organized pyramidically from top to bottom. Today, however, the collaborative power unleashed by the merging of Internet technology and renewable energies is fundamentally restructuring human relationships, from top to bottom to side to side, with profound implications for the future of society.

As we approach the middle of the century, more and more commerce will be overseen by intelligent technological surrogates, freeing up much of the human race to create social capital in the not-for-profit civil society, making it the dominant sector in the second half of the century. While commerce will remain essential to human survival, it will no longer be sufficient to define human aspirations. If we succeed in meeting the physical needs of our species in the next half century—a big if—transcendent concerns are likely to become an ever more important driver of the next period of human history.

In the pages that follow, we will explore the underlying features and operating principles of the Third Industrial Revolution infrastructure and economy, track its likely trajectory over the next four decades, and explore the obstacles and opportunities that exist along the way to its implementation in communities and countries around the world.

The Third Industrial Revolution offers the hope that we can arrive at a sustainable post-carbon era by mid-century and avert catastrophic climate change. We have the science, the technology, and the game plan to make it happen. Now it is a question of whether we will recognize the economic possibilities that lie ahead and muster the will to get there in time.

PART I
THE THIRD INDUSTRIAL REVOLUTION

CHAPTER ONE

THE REAL ECONOMIC CRISIS EVERYONE MISSED

t was 5 a.m. and I was running on my treadmill, only half listening to the early news on cable TV when I heard a reporter talking excitedly about a new political movement calling itself the "Tea Party." I stepped off the machine, not sure if I had heard correctly. The screen was full of angry middle-aged Americans hoisting yellow "Don't Tread on Me" flags, complete with the coiled snake insignia. Others were thrusting signs at the camera declaring "No taxation without representation," "Close the borders," and "Climate change is a hoax." The reporter, barely audible above the chants, was saying something about a spontaneous grassroots movement that was spreading like wildfire across the heartland, protesting big government in Washington, DC, and liberal career politicians who cared only about enriching themselves at the expense of their constituents. I couldn't believe what I was seeing and hearing. It was like witnessing a perverse inversion of something I had organized nearly forty years ago. Was this some kind of cruel cosmic joke?

THE BOSTON OIL PARTY OF 1973

December 16, 1973. Snow began falling just after sunrise. I felt a chilling wind against my face as I approached Faneuil Hall in downtown Boston, once the meeting place where firebrands and radicals like Sam Adams and Joseph Warren railed against the colonial policies of King George III and his corporate emissaries—the most notorious and hated being the British East India Company.

The city had been bunkered down for weeks. Traffic, which is generally heavy and often gridlocked in town, had been sparse for several days, largely because many gas stations had run out of fuel. At the few stations still pumping gas, motorists lined up for blocks, waiting an hour or more to fill up their tanks. Those lucky enough to find fuel were shocked at the prices being charged at the pump. Gas prices had doubled in just a few weeks, creating near hysteria in a country that, up to that time, was the largest oil producer in the world.

The public reaction was understandable given that it was America's abundant oil reserves and its wily ability to mass-produce affordable cars for a restless, nomadic people that catapulted the United States to commanding heights, making it the world's leading superpower in the twentieth century.

The jolt to our national pride came without warning. Just two months earlier, the Organization of Petroleum Exporting Countries (OPEC) slapped an oil embargo against the United States in retaliation to Washington's decision to resupply the Israeli government with military equipment during the Yom Kippur War. The "oil shock" reverberated quickly across the world. By December, the price of oil on the world market had shot up from $3 per barrel to $11.65.[1] Panic ensued on Wall Street and on Main Street.

The first and most obvious sign of the new reality was at neighborhood gas stations. Many Americans believed that the giant oil companies were taking advantage of the situation by arbitrarily spiking prices to secure windfall profits. The mood among motorists in Boston and around the country quickly turned sour. This was the backdrop for the tumultuous event that would unfold on the Boston wharf on December 16, 1973.

The day marked the two hundredth anniversary of the famed Boston Tea Party, the seminal event that galvanized popular sentiment against the British crown. Angered over a new tax imposed on tea and other products being exported to the American colonies by the mother country, Sam Adams spurred on a band of discontents, some of whom dumped tea cargo in the Boston Harbor. "No taxation without representation" quickly became the banner cry of the radicals. This first act of open defiance of British rule set off a series of reactions and counterreactions by the monarchy and its upstart thirteen colonies that would end in the Declaration of Independence in 1776 and the Revolutionary War.

In the weeks leading up to the anniversary, a groundswell of anger was building up against the giant oil companies. Many Americans were furious over what they considered to be unjustified price gouging by callous global companies threatening to undermine what Americans had come to regard as a basic right as revered as free speech, free press, and free assembly—the right to cheap oil and auto mobility.

I was twenty-eight years old at the time—a young activist weaned on the anti–Vietnam War and civil rights movement of the 1960s. A year earlier, I had launched a national organization, the People's Bicentennial Commission, which I hoped would serve as a radical alternative to the official American Bicentennial Commission established by the Nixon administration to commemorate the various historical events leading up to the two hundredth anniversary of the signing of the Declaration of Independence in 1776.

I conceived of the idea of an alternative celebration in part because of my growing alienation from my colleagues in the New Left movement. Having grown up in a working-class neighborhood on the deep south side of Chicago—a community of tradesmen and mechanics, policemen and firemen, and families who worked in the Chicago stockyards, rail yards, and nearby steel plants—patriotism was in my blood. On any given day, a visitor could not help noticing the flutter of American flags on front porches scattered across my neighborhood. Every day was Flag Day.

I was raised on the American dream and developed a deep appreciation for the radical sentiments of our founding fathers—Thomas Jefferson, Benjamin Franklin, Thomas Paine, George Washington—the small group of revolutionary thinkers who put their lives on the line in pursuit of the inalienable human rights to life, liberty, and the pursuit of happiness.

Many of my friends in the New Left hailed from a more privileged background, having grown up in America's elite suburban enclaves. Although deeply committed to the pursuit of social justice, equality, and peace, they increasingly drew their inspiration from other revolutionary struggles abroad, especially the anticolonial struggles of the post–World War II era. I recall countless political gatherings in which the thoughts of Mao, Ho Chi Minh, and Che Guevara were called forth to provide guidance and spur selfless action. All of this was strange to me, having been raised to believe that our homegrown American revolutionaries were the inspiration for all other anticolonial struggles over the past two centuries.

The American Bicentennial Celebration offered a unique opportunity for a younger generation to reconnect with America's radical promise—especially when the official White House observance, overseen by President Nixon and a legion of commercial boosters, appeared to be more rooted in the monarchical trappings of aristocratic privilege than in a sense of economic and social justice more befitting those early American heroes we were supposed to be celebrating.

Our plan was to turn the Tea Party anniversary into a protest against the oil companies. We were unsure whether anyone would come out onto the streets and join us. After all, there had never been a protest against big oil, so there was no way to predict what people might do. My fear of an embarrassingly low turnout grew as the snow began to fall. During the 1960s, we always scheduled antiwar protests in the spring because we were more likely to draw a crowd. In fact, none of the seasoned activists organizing the event could recall a single mass protest ever held in the dead of winter.

As I turned the corner onto Faneuil Hall, I looked in amazement. Thousands of people were lining the streets leading to the building. They were hoisting signs and banners reading "Make the oil companies pay," "Down with big oil," and "Long live the American Revolution." People were packed into the hall chanting, "Impeach Exxon."

After I delivered a short speech calling on the protestors to remember this day as the beginning of a second American Revolution for "energy independence," we took to the streets, following the exact route that the "tea partiers" from two hundred years ago took to Griffin's Wharf. Along the way, thousands more Bostonians joined our ranks—students, blue-collar workers, middle-class professionals, and entire families. By the time we reached the docks where the official Salada Tea Company ship (a recreation of the original ship) was anchored, upwards of twenty thousand protesters lined the waterfront, chanting, "Down with big oil." The protest overwhelmed the carefully orchestrated ceremony. An armada of local fishing boats from towns as far north as Gloucester broke through the police blockades and headed toward the Salada Tea ship, where federal and local dignitaries awaited the official ceremonies. Fishermen came aboard, seized the ship, climbed the masthead, and began throwing empty oil barrels, rather than tea crates, into the river, to the cheers of thousands of protestors. The next day the *New York Times* and other newspapers around the county recounted what had happened in Boston, dubbing the event "The Boston Oil Party of 1973."[2]

THE ENDGAME FOR THE SECOND INDUSTRIAL REVOLUTION

Thirty-five years later in July 2008, the price of oil on the world market peaked at a record $147 per barrel.[3] Just seven years earlier, oil was selling at under $24 per barrel.[4] In 2001, I suggested that an oil crisis was in the making and that the price of oil might tip over $50 per barrel within a few short years. My comments were greeted with widespread skepticism and even derision. "Not in our lifetime" came the retort from the oil industry, as well as most geologists and economists. Shortly thereafter, the price of oil dramatically rose. When the price went over $70 per barrel in mid-2007, the price of products and services across the entire global supply chain began to rise as well, for the simple reason that virtually every commercial activity in our global economy is dependent on oil and other fossil fuel energies.[5] We grow our food in petrochemical fertilizers and pesticides. Most of our construction materials—cement, plastics, and so on—are made of fossil fuels, as are most of our pharmaceutical products. Our clothes, for the most part, are made from petrochemical synthetic fibers. Our transport, power, heat, and light are all reliant on fossil fuels as well. We have built an entire civilization on the exhumed carbon deposits of the Carboniferous Period.

Assuming our species somehow manages to survive, I often wonder how future generations living fifty thousand years from now will regard this particular moment in the human saga. They will likely characterize us as the fossil fuels people and this period as the Carbon Era, just as we have referred to past periods as the Bronze and Iron Ages.

When the price of oil passed the $100-per-barrel mark, something unthinkable just a few years earlier, spontaneous protests and riots broke out in twenty-two countries because of the steep rise in the price of cereal grains—tortilla protests in Mexico and rice riots in Asia.[6] The fear of widespread political unrest sparked a global discussion around the oil-food connection.

With 40 percent of the human race living on $2 per day or less, even a marginal shift in the price of staples could mean widespread peril. By 2008, the price of soybeans and barley had doubled, wheat had almost tripled, and rice had quintupled.[7] The United Nations Food and Agricultural Organization (FAO) reported that a record one billion human beings were going to bed hungry.

The fear spread as middle-class consumers in the developed countries began to be affected by the steep oil price rise. The price of basic items in the stores shot up. Gasoline and electricity prices soared. So did the price of construction materials, pharmaceutical products, and packaging materials—the list was endless. By late spring, prices were becoming prohibitive and purchasing power began plummeting around the world. In July of 2008, the global economy shut down. That was the great economic earthquake that signaled the beginning of the end of the fossil fuel era. The collapse of the financial market sixty days later was the aftershock.

Most heads of state, business leaders, and economists have yet to fathom the real cause of the economic meltdown that has shaken the world. They continue to believe that the credit bubble and government debt are unrelated to the price of oil, not understanding that they are intimately tied to the waning of the oil age. The longer the conventional wisdom remains mired in the belief that somehow the credit and debt crisis are merely the fault of failing to properly oversee deregulated markets, world leaders will be unable to get to the root of the crisis and fix it. We will revisit this point shortly.

What occurred in July of 2008 is what I call peak globalization. Although much of the world is still unaware, it is clear that we have reached the outer limits of how far we can extend global economic growth within an economic system deeply dependent on oil and other fossil fuels.

I am suggesting that we are currently in the endgame of the Second Industrial Revolution and the oil era upon which it is based. This is a hard reality to accept because it would force the human family to quickly transition to a wholly new energy regime and a new industrial model, or risk the collapse of civilization.

The reason we have hit the wall in terms of globalization is "global peak oil per capita," which is not to be confused with "global peak oil production." The latter is a term used among petro-geologists to denote the point when global oil production reaches its zenith on what is called the Hubbert bell curve. Peak oil production occurs when half of the ultimately recoverable oil reserves are used up. The top of the curve represents the midpoint in oil recovery. After that, production drops as fast as it climbed.

M. King Hubbert was a geophysicist who worked for the Shell Oil Company back in 1956. Hubbert published what has subsequently become a famous paper forecasting the peak of oil production in the lower forty-eight states sometime between 1965 and 1970. His projection was ridiculed by colleagues at the time who noted that America was the leading producer of oil in the world. The very idea that we might lose our preeminence was unthinkable and dismissed. His prediction, however, turned out to be correct. US oil production peaked in 1970 and began its long decline.[8]

For the past four decades, geologists have been arguing about when global peak oil production will most likely occur. The optimists believed, based on their modeling, that it would probably happen sometime between 2025 and 2035. The pessimists, which included some of the leading geologists in the world, projected global peak oil to occur between 2010 and 2020.

The International Energy Agency (IEA), a Paris-based organization that governments rely on for their energy information and forecasts, may have put the issue of global peak oil production to rest in its 2010 World Energy Outlook report. According to the IEA, global peak production of crude oil probably occurred in 2006 at seventy million barrels per day.[9] The admission stunned the international oil community and sent shudders down the spine of global businesses whose life line is crude oil.

According to the IEA, to even keep oil production flat at slightly below seventy million barrels per day—to avoid a precipitous plunge in the global economy—would require a staggering investment of $8 trillion over the next twenty-five years to pump the difficult-to-capture remaining oil from existing fields, to open up less promising fields already discovered, and to search for new fields that are increasingly harder to find.[10]

But here we're primarily concerned with global peak oil per capita, which occurred way back in 1979 at the height of the Second Industrial Revolution. BP conducted a study, which has since been confirmed by other studies, concluding that the available oil, if equally distributed, peaked in that year.[11] While we've found more oil since then, the world population has grown much more quickly. If we were to equally distribute all of the known oil reserves today to the 6.8 billion human beings living on Earth, there would be less available per person.

When China's and India's economies took off at a blistering growth rate in the 1990s and the early 2000s—in 2007 India grew at a rate of 9.6

percent and China at 14.2 percent—bringing one-third of the human race into the oil era, the demand pressure on existing oil reserves inevitably pushed the price of oil up, leading to the aforementioned peak of $147 per barrel, soaring prices, a free fall in consumption, and a global economic shutdown.[12]

In 2010, the economy began a tepid recovery, mostly to replenish exhausted inventories. But as soon as growth began, the price of oil rose concomitantly to $90 a barrel by the end of 2010, again forcing up prices across the entire supply chain.[13]

In January 2011, Fatih Birol, the chief economist for the International Energy Agency, pointed to the inseparable relationship between increased economic output and the rise in oil prices. He warned that as the economic recovery gains momentum, "oil prices are entering a dangerous zone for the global economy." In 2010, according to the IEA, oil imports for the mostly rich thirty-four countries in the Organization for Economic Co-operation and Development (OECD), rose from $200 billion at the beginning of the year to $790 billion at year's end. The European Union's oil import bill alone rose by $70 billion in 2010. That equals the combined budget deficits of Greece and Portugal. The US oil bill went up by $72 billion. The high cost of oil represents a loss of 0.5 percent of OECD gross domestic product.[14]

Developing countries were even harder hit in 2010, with oil imports rising by $20 billion, equal to a loss of income of nearly 1 percent of the GDP. The ratio of countries' oil import bills to GDP is nearing the levels seen in 2008, just before the collapse of the global economy, leading the IEA to publicly worry that "the oil import bills are becoming a threat to the economic recovery."[15]

On the same day that the IEA made its 2010 report public, Martin Wolf, the economic columnist for the *Financial Times,* wrote an essay on the historic convergence taking place in "output per head" in China, India, and the Western powers. According to data published by the US Conference Board, between the 1970s and 2009, the ratio of Chinese output per head to that of the United States rose from 3 percent to 19 percent. In India, the ratio rose from 3 percent to 7 percent.[16]

Wolf notes that China's output per head, relative to that of the United States, is approximately the same as Japan's when it began its economic recovery after World War II. Japan shot up to 70 percent of US levels by the 1970s and 90 percent by 1990. If China followed a similar trajectory, it would approach 70 percent of US output per head by 2030. But here is the difference. By 2030, China's economy would be nearly three times the size of the US economy, and larger than the United States and Western Europe put together.[17]

Ben Bernanke, Chairman of the US Federal Reserve Board, pointed out in a November 2010 speech that in the second quarter alone, the aggregate real output in the emerging economies was 41 percent higher than in the beginning of 2005. China's aggregate output was 70 percent higher and India's was 55 percent higher.[18]

What does all this mean? If aggregate economic output throttles up again at the same rate as it did in the first eight years of the twenty-first century—which is exactly what is happening—the price of oil will quickly rebound to $150 per barrel or more, forcing a steep rise in prices for all other goods and services, and will lead to another plunge in purchasing power and the collapse of the global economy. In other words, each new effort to regain the economic momentum of the past decade will stall out at around $150 per barrel. This wild gyration between regrowth and collapse is the endgame.

Naysayers argue that the rise in the price of oil had little to do with demand pressure against supply and more to do with speculators gaming the oil market to make a killing. While speculators may have added fuel to the fire, the incontrovertible fact is for the past several decades we have been consuming three and a half barrels of oil for every new barrel we find.[19] This reality is what determines our present condition and future prospects.

Now, the pressure of rising aggregate demand against dwindling reserves of crude oil is compounded by the growing political unrest in the Middle East. Millions of young people across the region—in Tunisia, Egypt, Libya, Iran, Yemen, Jordan, Bahrain, and other countries—took to the streets in early 2011 in opposition to corrupt autocratic regimes that have ruled for decades and, in some cases, for generations. The youth rebellion, which is reminiscent of the youth revolt in the 1960s in the West, represents a generational shift of immense historical significance.

For a younger, educated generation that is becoming part of a global community and is as likely to identify with Facebook as with traditional tribal loyalties, the old ways are an anathema. The patriarchal thinking, rigid social norms, and xenophobic behavior of their elders is so utterly alien to the generation that has grown up in social media networks, with an emphasis on transparency, collaborative behavior, and peer-to-peer relations, that it marks a historic divide in consciousness itself.

Tired of being ruled by arbitrary and brutal leaders and living in a society rank with corruption, where patronage rather than merit is the custom and those in power enrich themselves at the expense of the growing poverty of the masses, young people are demanding changes. In just a few weeks, they forced the fall of the governments of Tunisia and Egypt, brought Libya to civil war, and threatened the collapse of regimes from Jordan to Bahrain.

To a great extent, it is oil that has played a pivotal role in the ruin of the region. The black gold has turned out to be more of a dark curse, transforming much of the Middle East into a one-resource society under the control of the ruling oligarchs. The flow of oil made sheikhs into billionaires, while their populations were kept docile with meager public welfare handouts and government employment. The result is that these countries never created the economic conditions for establishing a robust, multifaceted, entrepreneurial economy or a workforce to manage it. Generations of young people have languished, never fully developing their human potential.

Emboldened and empowered, young people are breaking away from the timidity of their elders and standing up to the powers that be with electrifying results that not even they could have imagined. The old order is beginning to waver, and while there is likely to be vacillating progress and wrenching retrenchment, it is unlikely that the old patriarchal rule over society, which has for so long determined the fate of generations of people living in the Arab world, will survive the next decade.

What we are seeing in the Middle East is a great transformation from hierarchical to lateral power. The Internet generation, which began by challenging the centralized media conglomerates in the West with peer sharing of music and information, is now beginning to flex its peer power in the Middle East by challenging the centralized political rule of autocratic governments.

The increasing political instability in the Middle East is going to wreak havoc on the price of oil on the world market for years to come. In early 2011, the political mayhem in Libya shut down oil fields across the country, taking 1.6 million barrels of crude oil a day out of production and forcing oil to spike to $120 a barrel.[20] Oil analysts worry that if Saudi Arabia or Iran were to experience similar disruptions in oil production, it could cause a 20–25 percent increase in oil prices overnight, seriously crippling any hope of an even weak global economic recovery.[21]

No international observer close to the political upheaval unfolding in the Middle East believes that the region will ever go back to business as usual. It is not coincidental that the end of the oil era is also signaling the end of the authoritarian governments that have long ruled atop the most elite and centralized energy regime in history.

While the awakening of the youth of the Middle East is to be applauded and supported, it comes with a realization that the years ahead are going to be fraught with oil crisis after oil crisis brought on by the tug of two related phenomena: the rise of aggregate demand, forcing oil prices up to $150 or even $200 a barrel or more, and disruptions caused by political instability in the oil-rich states of the region, leading to similar price hikes.

THE COLLAPSE OF WALL STREET

How does the credit bubble and financial crisis feed into this Second Industrial Revolution endgame? To understand the relationship between the two, one needs to go back, once again, to the last half of the twentieth century. The Second Industrial Revolution—the coming together of centralized electricity, the oil era, the automobile, and suburban construction—went through two stages of development. A juvenile Second Industrial Revolution infrastructure was laid down between 1900 and the beginning of the Great Depression in 1929. That infantile infrastructure remained in limbo until after World War II. The passage of the Interstate Highway Act of 1956 provided the impetus to mature the infrastructure for the auto age. The establishment of an intercontinental highway grid—which at the time was heralded as the most ambitious and expensive public works project in all of human history—created an unparalleled economic expansion, making the United States the most prosperous society on Earth. Similar highway construction projects commenced in Europe shortly thereafter, with a commensurate multiplier effect.

The interstate highway infrastructure hastened a construction boom as businesses and millions of Americans began to relocate in newly built suburban enclaves off the interstate highway exits. The commercial and residential real estate surge peaked in the 1980s with the completion of the interstate highways, as did the Second Industrial Revolution. Commercial and residential builders overshot demand, leading to a real estate slump in the late 1980s and early 1990s and a dip into a serious recession, which quickly spread to the far corners of the world. But with the Second Industrial Revolution beginning its long decline in the late 1980s, how was the United States able to extricate itself from recession and regrow its economy in the 1990s?

The US economic recovery was built largely on the savings amassed in the halcyon decades of the Second Industrial Revolution, combined with record credit and debt. We became a nation of runaway spenders. It turns out that the money we were spending, however, was not so much new money generated by new income. American wages had been slowly leveling off and declining as the Second Industrial Revolution passed into its mature stage in the 1980s.

There was a great deal of hype about the emerging IT and Internet revolutions. The new innovation corridors springing up in places like Silicon Valley in California, Route 128 in Boston, Interstate 495 in Washington, and the Research Triangle in North Carolina promised a high-tech cornucopia, and the media was more than willing to gush over the latest marvels to come out of companies like Microsoft, Apple, and AOL.

There is no denying that the communication revolution of the 1990s created new jobs and helped transform the economic and social landscapes. But for all the spin, the fact remains that the IT sector and the Internet did not in and of themselves constitute a new industrial revolution. For that to happen, the new communications technologies would have to converge with a new energy regime, as has been the case with every great economic revolution heretofore in history. New communications regimes never stand alone. Rather, as mentioned in the introduction, they are the mechanism that manages the flow of activity made possible by new energy systems. It is the laying down of a communication-energy infrastructure, over a period of decades, that establishes a long-term growth curve for a new economic era.

The problem was one of timing. The new communications technologies differed fundamentally from first-generation electricity communication technology. The telephone, radio, and television were centralized forms of communications designed to manage and market an economy organized around centralized fossil fuel energies and the myriad centralized business practices that flowed from that particular energy regime. The new, second-generation electricity communication, by contrast, is distributed in nature and ideally suited to manage distributed forms of energy—that is, renewable energy—and the lateral kinds of business activity that accompany such an energy regime. The new distributed communications technologies would have to wait another two decades to hook up with distributed energies and create the basis for a new infrastructure and a new economy.

In the 1990s and the first decade of the twenty-first century, the Information and Communication Technology (ICT) revolution was grafted on to the older, centralized Second Industrial Revolution. It was, from the start, an unnatural fit. While ICT enhanced productivity, streamlined practices, and created some new business opportunities and jobs—which probably extended the useful life of an aging industrial model—it could never achieve its full distributed communication potential because of the inherent constraints that come with being attached to a centralized energy regime and commercial infrastructure.

In lieu of a powerful new communication-energy mix, we began to grow the economy by living off the accumulated wealth generated in the four decades following World War II. The easy extension of credit, brought on by the credit card culture, acted like an intoxicant. Buying became addictive and consumption became something akin to a mass collective potlatch. It was as if we were unconsciously on a death spiral, speeding down the backside of the Second Industrial Revolution bell curve to our ruin, determined to devour the vast wealth we had generated over a lifetime.

We succeeded. The average family savings rate in the early 1990s was around 8 percent. By the year 2000, family savings had shrunk to around 1 percent.[22] By 2007, many Americans were spending more than they made.

We lifted the global economy on the back of American purchasing power. What we weren't willing to admit to ourselves, however, was that the whole thing was paid for by depleting the savings of American households.

By the mid-1990s Americans were awash in debt. Bankruptcies were at a record high. In 1994, a whopping 832,829 Americans filed for bankruptcy.[23] Incredibly, by 2002, bankruptcies had soared to 1,577,651.[24] Yet credit card debt continued to climb.

It was around this time that the mortgage banking industry began to push a second credit instrument—subprime mortgages requiring little or no money down. Millions of Americans took the bait, buying houses they could not afford. The housing construction boom created the biggest bubble in US history. Home values doubled and tripled in some areas of the country in just a few years. Homeowners began to see their houses as lucrative investments. Many used their new investments as cash cows, refinancing mortgages two and three times to secure needed cash to pay down credit card accounts and continue their buying sprees.

The real estate bubble burst in 2007.[25] Housing prices plummeted. Millions of Americans, who thought they were rich, now suddenly found themselves unable to pay the interest on mortgages that had been deferred but were now coming due. Foreclosures skyrocketed. Banks and other lending institutions in America—that had willingly bought into what amounted to a sophisticated global Ponzi scheme—went into paralysis. In September 2008 Lehman Brothers went under. Then AIG—a company that held subprime mortgage bonds and loans totaling billions—was threatened with a meltdown; if this had occurred, it would have taken the rest of the American economy and much of the world economy down with it. Banks stopped lending. An economic collapse on the scale of the Great Depression loomed, forcing the United States to come to the rescue, bailing out Wall Street financial institutions to the tune of $700 billion. The rationale for the bailout was that these institutions were simply "too big to fail."

The so-called Great Recession began and real unemployment contin- ued to rise month after month, reaching 10 percent of the workforce by the end of 2009 (17.6 percent of the workforce if we count the discour- aged workers, who gave up looking for work and were no longer counted, and marginally attached workers, who were working only part time, but desired full-time employment). This represents nearly twenty-seven mil- lion Americans, the highest percentage of unemployed and underemployed workers in the United States since the Great Depression in the 1930s.[26]

President Obama's bailout package saved the banking system but did little for American families. By 2008, the accumulated household debt in the United States was closing in on $14 trillion.[27] To get an idea of how deeply in debt American households are, consider that twenty years ago, the average family's debt equaled about 83 percent of its income. Ten years ago, household debt had risen to 92 percent of family income, and by 2007, household debt had risen to 130 percent of income, leading economists to use a new term, "negative savings," to reflect the deep change in the spend- ing and savings patterns of American families.[28] Unemployed, underem- ployed, and saddled with debt, a record 2.9 million homeowners received foreclosure notices on their houses in 2010.[29]

Even more ominous, the ratio of household debt to GDP, which was 65 percent in the mid-1990s, reached 100 percent in 2010, a sure sign that American consumers would no longer be propping up globalization with their purchasing power.[30]

The credit bubble and the financial crisis did not occur in a vacuum. They grew out of the deceleration of the Second Industrial Revolution. That slowdown began in the late 1980s, when the suburban construction boom—brought on by the laying down of the interstate highway system—peaked, signaling the high-water mark of the auto age and the oil era.

It was the marriage of abundant, cheap oil and the automobile that drove America to the top of the world economy by the 1980s. Unfortunately, we used up that accumulated wealth in less than half the time it took to create it, in an extraordinary buying binge designed to keep the economic engine artificially revved up while the real economy was winding down. When our savings dried up, we borrowed trillions more, living off the myth of our still-unrivaled economic prowess, and continued to spend money we didn't have—all of which fueled the globalization process. Millions of people all over the world were more than happy to provide the goods and produce the services in return for our dollars.

The global buying spree and the dramatic rise in aggregate output that accompanied it pushed up the demand for an ever-dwindling oil supply, resulting in a steep increase in prices on world markets. The sharp acceleration in the price of oil triggered price hikes across the global supply chain for everything from grain to gasoline, finally leading to a worldwide collapse of purchasing power when oil hit a record $147 per barrel in July 2008. Sixty days later, the banking community, awash in unpaid loans, shut off credit; the stock market crashed, and globalization came to a standstill.

The upshot of eighteen years of living off extended credit is that the United States is now a failed economy. The gross liabilities of the US financial sector, which were 21 percent of GDP in 1980, have risen steadily over the past twenty-seven years to an incredible 116 percent of GDP by 2007.[31] Because the US, European, and Asian banking and financial communities are intimately intertwined, the credit crisis swept out of America and engulfed the entire global economy. Even more troubling, the International Monetary Fund forecasts that the federal government debt could equal the GDP by 2015, throwing in doubt the future prospects of the United States of America.[32]

THE ENTROPY BILL FOR THE INDUSTRIAL AGE

If this weren't enough to contend with, there is a second debt building up—one far bigger and more difficult to pay back. The entropy bill for the

First and Second Industrial Revolutions is coming due. Two hundred years of burning coal, oil, and natural gas to propel an industrial way of life has resulted in the release of massive amounts of carbon dioxide into the Earth's atmosphere. That spent energy—the entropy bill—blocks the sun's radiant heat from escaping the planet and threatens a catastrophic shift in the temperature of the Earth, with potentially devastating consequences for the future of life.

In December 2009, government leaders representing 192 nations assembled in Copenhagen to address the greatest challenge to ever face the human race—industrial-induced climate change. A report issued in Paris by the UN Intergovernmental Panel on Climate Change in March 2007 presented a stark account of the scope of the problem. More than 2,500 scientists from more than 100 nations contributed to the findings. This was the fourth in a series of reports that extended over fifteen years, in what is regarded as the largest scientific study ever undertaken.[33]

The first thing that grabbed my attention upon reading the UN report was that for twenty-seven years I had gotten it wrong. I first wrote about climate change in my 1980 book, *Entropy,* one of the first books to raise public awareness around the issue. I went on to spend a significant amount of my time during the 1980s building public awareness of the long-term threat posed by global warming.

In 1981, The Congressional Clearinghouse on the Future, a legislative service organization of Congress made up of more than one hundred congressmen and senators, invited me to present two informal, off-the-record, lectures for members of Congress on the thermodynamic consequences of industrially induced CO_2 emissions. To my knowledge, these sessions were among the earliest discussions on climate change in the US Congress.

In 1988, my office hosted the first gathering of scientists and environmental NGOs from around the world to discuss ways to work together to create a global movement to address climate change. We founded the Global Greenhouse Network, a coalition of climate researchers, environmental organizations, and economic development experts, and launched a decade-long effort that helped move the climate change debate from academia into the public policy arena.

Although I had long understood the urgency of global warming, like many of my colleagues, I continued to underestimate the speed at which the temperature of the Earth was rising. I didn't properly appreciate the powerful synergistic effects that could result from unanticipated positive feedback events. For example, when the ice in the Arctic melts from a rise in the Earth's temperature because of increased CO_2 in the atmosphere, it prevents heat from escaping the Earth. The diminished snow cover means a loss of reflective capacity—white reflects heat and black absorbs heat—and less heat escaping the planet. This, in turn, heats up the Earth even more and melts the snow faster in an accelerating positive feedback cycle. Now take this one feedback loop and multiply the possibilities almost endlessly, as other abrupt changes in the Earth's biosphere trigger their own feedback loops, and the immensity of what we are facing becomes utterly terrifying.

The fourth UN Climate Report was an urgent reminder that the chemistry of the planet is changing. The news is not good. Our scientists tell us to expect at least a three degree Celsius rise in the temperature on Earth by the end of the century.[34] It could go significantly higher. While three degrees doesn't sound all that bad, we need to understand that a temperature rise in this range puts us back to the temperature on Earth three million years ago in the Pliocene epoch. The world was a very different place back then.

A mere 1.5 to 3.5 degrees Celsius shift in temperature, according to our scientists, could lead to a mass extinction of plant and animal life in less than one hundred years. The models indicate an extinction rate of 20 percent on the low end and more than 70 percent on the high end.[35] We need to grasp the enormity of what the scientists are saying. The Earth has experienced five waves of biological extinction in the last 450 million years.[36] Each time there was a wipeout, it took about ten million years to recover the biodiversity that was lost.[37] How does the rise in temperature affect the survival rate or extinction of life?

Let's look at a simple example. The loss of trees in stressed ecosystems worries scientists. Imagine the Northeast region of the United States having the climate of Miami by the second half of the twenty-first century. While human beings can migrate quickly in response, trees cannot. Tree varieties have adapted to relatively stable temperature zones over thousands of years. Moreover, they are slow to reproduce. Therefore, when the temperature changes radically in just a few decades, the trees cannot migrate quickly enough to catch up to their temperature zone. This has tremendous implications for the viability of the Earth's creatures. Twenty-five percent of the planet's land surface is forested and serves as the habitat for many of the remaining species of life.[38] A sudden loss of trees would wreak havoc on animal life.

Scientists working in Costa Rica have noticed that as temperatures have risen over the past sixteen years, there has been a steady decline in the growth rate of trees.[39] Researchers cite similar recordings all over the world, adding to the growing concern that we may be already in the early stages of a mass extinction event.

The most important impact of a global rise in temperature is on the water cycle. Every increase in temperature of one degree Celsius leads to a 7 percent increase in the moisture-holding capacity of the atmosphere.[40] This causes a radical change in the way water is distributed, with more intense precipitation, but a reduction in duration or frequency. The consequence is more floods and longer periods of drought. Ecosystems that have adapted to a specific weather regime over a long period cannot adjust quickly enough to these abrupt changes in precipitation, and instead become unstable and die off.

We are already experiencing the hydrological impacts of a half degree rise in the Earth's temperature on hurricane intensity.[41] A 2005 study published in the journal *Science* states that the number of 4 and 5 category storms has doubled since the 1970s.[42] Katrina, Rita, Gustav, and Ike are a sober reminder of what's in store for the human race as we move deeper into the current century.

Scientists also project a rise in sea water levels and the loss of coastlines around the world. Small island chains like the Maldives in the Indian Ocean and the Marshall Islands in the Pacific might entirely disappear under the ocean. Snow atop many of the world's great mountain ranges is melting. Some glaciers are expected to lose over 60 percent of their ice volume by 2050.[43] More than one-sixth of the human race lives in mountain valleys and relies on the snow for irrigation, sanitation, and drinking water.[44] Relocating nearly a billion people in less than forty years seems unfathomable.

Scientists are particularly worried about the Arctic. New studies forecast 75 percent less summer ice cover by 2050.[45] In August 2008, there were open waters stretching around the Arctic. This is the first time this has occurred in at least 125,000 years.[46]

What most concerns the climatologists are the feedback loops that are difficult to anticipate but have the ability to trigger vast changes in the biosphere and spike the Earth's temperature to far higher levels than the models now project. For example, consider the permafrost that has cloaked the Siberian subarctic region since the onset of the last ice age. Before that time, this region, which is roughly the size of France and Germany combined, was a lush grassland teaming with wildlife. Permafrost trapped the organic matter underneath the ground in a kind of time capsule. Scientists say there is more organic matter under the permafrost in Siberia than in all of the tropical rainforests in the world.

The UN Intergovernmental Panel on Climate Change mentioned the permafrost problem, in passing, in its fourth assessment report, noting that if the permafrost coat melts, it could trigger a potentially catastrophic release of carbon dioxide into the atmosphere and lead to a dramatic rise in the Earth's temperature, far above the levels now being projected. But there was no data available to ascertain the situation.

Recent field studies reported in the journal *Nature,* however, have shaken researchers. The rising temperature on Earth is already beginning to melt the permafrost at an alarming rate. Scientists at the Institute of Arctic Biology at the University of Alaska in Fairbanks warn we may cross a threshold sometime in this century, with a significant loss of ice cover, releasing vast amounts of carbon dioxide and methane into the atmosphere in just a few short decades.[47] If this happened, there is nothing our species could do to prevent a wholesale destruction of our ecosystems and catastrophic extinction of life on the planet.

The European Union went to the Copenhagen climate talks with a proposal that the nations of the world limit global carbon dioxide emissions to 450 parts per million by 2050, with the hope that if we were to do so, the increasing temperature on Earth could be held to two degrees Celsius. Although a rise in temperature of two degrees would have a devastating impact on the ecosystems of the planet, we might still be able to survive. Unfortunately, the other nations of the world were unwilling to take even this minimum measure to avert the ravages of climate change.

The Brussels proposal came into question, however, from an unexpected quarter. The US government's own chief climatologist James Hansen, the head of the NASA Goddard Institute for Space Studies, suggested on the basis of his team's research that the EU had miscalculated the projection of how much the temperature would rise if carbon emissions were limited to 450 parts per million. Hansen's team pointed out that preindustrial levels of carbon dioxide in the atmosphere had not exceeded 300 parts per million for the past 650,000 years, as determined by ice core samples. The current industrial levels are already well above that, at 385 parts per million and quickly rising. Based on his team's findings, human-induced climate change could lead to a staggering six-degree rise in the Earth's temperature by the end of the century or shortly thereafter, and the literal demise of human civilization. Hansen concluded that

> if humanity wishes to preserve a planet similar to that on which civilization developed and to which life on Earth is adapted, paleoclimate evidence and ongoing climate change suggest that CO_2 will need to be reduced from its current 385 ppm to at most 350 ppm, but likely less than that.[48]

Not a single government in the world is suggesting a radical change in the structuring of economic life that would bring us anywhere near the 350 parts per million level that Hansen says is necessary to save human civilization.

Pandemonium broke out at the Copenhagen climate talks. Governments accused each other of playing geopolitics with the future of the planet and of putting short-term economic interest before the survival of the human race. In the final hours, President Obama barged in, unannounced, demanding to sit in on a closed meeting of the Chinese, Indian, Brazilian, and South African heads of state—something unheard of in international diplomatic meetings. In the end, world leaders went home without cutting a deal to limit carbon emissions. All in all, it was a disgraceful performance. Despite the fact that human-induced climate change is the single greatest threat to human survival since our species first appeared on Earth, our leaders were unable to agree on a formula to save the world.

We are sleepwalking. Even with the mounting evidence that the Industrial Age, based on fossil fuels, is dying and that the Earth now faces potentially destabilizing climate change, the human race, by and large, refuses to recognize the reality of the situation. Instead, we continue to pin our hopes on finding a dwindling supply of oil and natural gas to keep the addiction alive, in an effort to ward off the unthinkable proposition of what we would need to do if we are truly in an endgame.

Nowhere is the shortsightedness more apparent than in the public's reaction to the oil spill in the Gulf of Mexico in April 2010. A BP-leased oil rig blew up in the deep waters, killing eleven workers and rupturing a pipeline a mile below the surface, unleashing nearly five million barrels of oil into one of the world's most treasured ecosystems.[49] A stunned public watched week after week as oil gushed out of the deep crevasse in the ocean floor, spreading a black plume in every direction, killing wildlife, destroying delicate habitats, and threatening to turn the Gulf of Mexico into a dead sea. The environmental disaster became a painful reminder that in our desperation to keep the economic engine running, we are willing to undertake ever more risky ventures to find scarce fossil fuels, even if it means the destruction of our ecosystems.

One would think that the largest oil spill in history and subsequent widespread devastation would turn the national debate to our oil dependency and the impact it's having on our environment. While it's true that millions of Americans would like to have just such a discussion, even more Americans, according to opinion polls, have turned their anger to the more narrow question of BP's culpability and the government's inability to ensure that appropriate safety procedures were in place to avoid such mishaps. In fact, more Americans than not favor continuing offshore oil drilling in the Gulf of Mexico and elsewhere, having bought the idea that it's the best way to secure energy independence.[50]

Former Republican vice presidential candidate Sarah Palin's now famous exhortation, "Drill, baby, drill," though ridiculed by environmentalists, is echoed by a majority of Americans. Even President Obama, the so-called green president, called for a lifting of the long-standing moratorium against deep-water offshore oil drilling along the Southeast Atlantic Coast just weeks before the calamity.

Palin and Obama should know better. These potentially dangerous oil drilling expeditions in remote terrains yield an insignificant amount of oil at best. Consider, for example, the hotly contested question of whether the US government should open part of the Alaska National Wildlife Refuge, the East and West Coasts, the eastern Gulf of Mexico, and the Rocky Mountains to oil drilling. According to a 2011 study commissioned by the American Petroleum Institute, which represents all of the leading oil and gas companies, drilling in every possible place in the United States where there are still remaining oil reserves would add only two million barrels per day by 2030, or less than 10 percent of current US consumption—all in all, a marginal increase in production with little appreciable impact on forestalling the end of the oil era.[51]

Many people have simply not come to grips with the fact that the fossil fuel–driven industrial age is ending. This doesn't mean that the oil spigot will suddenly run dry tomorrow. Oil will continue to flow but at dwindling rates and higher costs. And because oil is aggregated and priced in a single world market, there is no magic formula by which any particular country can isolate itself under the banner of "energy independence." As for conventional natural gas, the global production curve roughly shadows that of oil.

What about coal in China, tar sands in Canada, heavy oil in Venezuela, and shale gas in the United States? While still relatively abundant, these energy sources are costly to extract and emit far more carbon dioxide than either crude oil or conventional natural gas. Were we to make a significant shift into these more polluting fuels to stave off the closure of the fossil fuel era, the dramatic rise in global temperatures might inevitably be the final arbiter of our fate.

What about nuclear power? Most of the world stopped building nuclear power plants in the 1980s after the 1979 accident at the Three Mile Island nuclear plant in Pennsylvania and, later, in 1986, with the meltdown at the Chernobyl facility in Russia. Unfortunately, public memory is often short. The nuclear industry has reinvented itself in recent years, riding back in on the coattails of the climate change debate, arguing that it is a "clean" alternative to fossil fuels because it doesn't emit CO_2, and therefore, is part of the solution to addressing global warming.

Nuclear power was never a clean energy source. The radioactive materials and waste have always posed a serious threat to human health, our fellow creatures, and the environment. The partial meltdown of the Fukushima nuclear power plant in the wake of the earthquake and tsunami in Japan in 2011 touched off a political earthquake around the world, resulting in most governments putting on hold all plans to build new nuclear power plants, diminishing the long-term prospects of a resurrection of this twentieth century technology.

To quote a now famous cliché uttered by a former Clinton advisor James Carville, "It's the economy, stupid." True. But we continue to believe, erroneously, that our economic woes stem from being overly dependent on oil imports from the Middle East—actually, Canada is the largest supplier of oil to the United States—and from overly restrictive environmental restraints on the economy, which only cripple economic growth.[52] In fact, the problem lies much deeper.

THE TEA PARTY MOVEMENT

Americans sense that something is going terribly wrong in our country, that our economy is eroding and our way of life is being upended. This feeling of foreboding took on a very public face in 2009 with the rise of the Tea Party movement, a grassroots rebellion against big government, pork barrel politics, and exorbitant taxes.

Nearly half a million Tea Partiers cast their votes online for a so-called Contract from America, a list of ten agenda items they considered to be of the highest priority to their movement. Number two on the list, right after measures to protect the United States Constitution, is the rejection of cap and trade legislation to limit carbon dioxide emissions. Also of high priority is authorizing "the exploration of proven energy reserves to reduce our dependence on foreign energy sources from unstable countries . . . ."[53]

When I first heard of the Tea Party movement and its agenda, it struck me as the dark nemesis of what unfolded on the streets of Boston more than thirty-seven years ago at the Boston Oil Party. Instead of throwing empty oil barrels into the Boston Bay to protest the policies of the oil companies while chanting, "Down with big oil," the new mantra of "Drill, baby, drill" is growing louder with every passing day.

The Tea Party activists and millions of other Americans are justifiably frightened and angry about what is happening in America. They are not alone. Families all over the world are scared as well. Drilling for more oil, however, won't get us out of the crisis because oil *is* the crisis. The reality is that the oil-based Second Industrial Revolution is aging and will never rebound to its former glory. And everywhere people are asking, "What do we do?" If we are to put people back to work, curtail climate change, and save civilization from ruin, we will need a compelling new economic vision for the world and a pragmatic game plan to implement it.

CHAPTER TWO
A NEW NARRATIVE

The economy is always a confidence game. While we used to think of commerce and trade as being backed up by gold or silver, in reality, it has always been backed up by a more important reserve—public trust. When that trust is robust, the economy flourishes, and the future beckons us forward. When the public trust is shattered, economies fail and the future dims.

Has America lost its mojo? It seems that everywhere we turn, we are at each other's throat, carping and whining, playing the blame game, replaying old slights and hurts, boorishly reminiscing about the good old days, eulogizing the greatest generation, romanticizing the 1960s generation of peace and love, and disparaging every generation since—the selfish, over-empowered generation X, and the facile, hyperactive, distracted millennial generation. A nation that obsessively relives the past, complains incessantly about the present, and laments a future that is not yet here needs to "get a life," as the kids might say.

President Barack Obama was swept into the White House, in part because, for just the briefest moment of time, he was able to lift the spirit of the American people out of the doldrums of despair and rally the collective consciousness of a nation to the idea that we can do better. He gave Americans, especially the young, a feeling of hope, crystallized in three spiffy words: "Yes we can."

Unfortunately, no sooner had the young president settled into the White House than he squandered the most delicate and precious asset any leader possesses—the ability to unite people behind a common vision of a better future. To be fair, I have seen this phenomenon over and over in my dealings with heads of state. They come into office on fire with ambitious visions of the future, only to succumb to the daily slog of putting out little fires.

On his first day in office, President Obama turned immediately to the issue of resuscitating the economy. His administration latched on to the idea of bundling economic recovery with the two other critical challenges facing the country—energy security and climate change. The president began to talk up the prospect of a green economy and how it would create thousands of new businesses and millions of new jobs.

The message resonated with many members of Congress. But the reason an overarching new economic game plan has never been rolled out is not just because we need to cut back public spending and reduce government deficits, but because the administration is missing, to quote former president George W. Bush, the "vision thing."

Whenever President Obama mentions his green economic recovery, he rattles off a laundry list of programs and initiatives his administration is either doing or proposing. And there are real dollars behind these initiatives. The federal government has already committed $11.6 billion for energy efficiency, $6.5 billion for renewable energy generation (primarily wind and solar), $4.4 billion for grid modernization to develop a smart grid, and $2 billion to advance battery technology for electric plug-in and fuel cell vehicles.[1] The president also takes every opportunity to visit a solar or wind turbine park, a factory manufacturing solar panels, or a car company testing electric vehicles to demonstrate his sincere commitment to a green economic future.

What Obama is lacking is a narrative. We are left with a collection of pilot projects and siloed programs, none of which connects with the others to tell a compelling story of a new economic vision for the world. We're strapped with a lot of dead-end initiatives—wasting billions of dollars of taxpayer money with nothing to show for it.

The man who inspired a nation to greatness during his election campaign, suddenly morphed into a caricature of the Washington policy wonk, droning on about the latest technology breakthroughs without any sense whatsoever of how they might fit together as part of a larger story. If President Obama clearly understood the underlying dynamics of the next great Industrial Revolution, he might have been able to sell the American public on a comprehensive economic plan for the country's future.

When Brussels began to take a serious look at a new sustainable economic vision for the European Union back in 2002, it faced the same problem of being awash in sentences but lacking a story line.

The story line begins with an understanding that the great economic transformations in history occur when new communication technology converges with new energy systems. The new forms of communication become the medium for organizing and managing the more complex civilizations made possible by the new sources of energy. The infrastructure that emerges annihilates time and shrinks space, connecting people and markets in more diverse economic relations. When those systems are put in place, economic activity advances, moving along a classic bell-shaped curve that ascends, peaks, plateaus, and descends in tandem with the strength of the multiplier effect established by the communications-energy matrix.

Infrastructure, at the deepest level, is not a static set of building blocks that serves as a kind of fixed foundation for economic activity as we've come to regard it in popular economic lore. Rather, infrastructure is an organic relationship between communications technologies and energy sources that, together, create a living economy. Communication technology is the nervous system that oversees, coordinates, and manages the economic organism, and energy is the blood that circulates through the body politic, providing the nourishment to convert nature's endowment into goods and services to keep the economy alive and growing. Infrastructure is akin to a living system that brings increasing numbers of people together in more complex economic and social relationships.

The introduction of steam-powered technology into printing transformed the medium into the primary communications tool to manage the First Industrial Revolution. The steam printing machine with rollers, and later the rotary press and linotype, greatly increased the speed of printing and significantly reduced the cost. Print material, in the form of newspapers, magazines, and books, proliferated in America and Europe, encouraging mass literacy for the first time in history. The advent of public schooling on both continents between the 1830s and 1890s created a print-literate workforce to organize the complex operations of a coal-powered, steam-driven rail and factory economy.

In the first decade of the twentieth century, electrical communication converged with the oil-powered internal combustion engine, giving rise to the Second Industrial Revolution. The electrification of factories ushered in the era of mass-produced goods, the most important being the automobile. Henry Ford began to manufacture his gasoline-powered Model T car, altering the spatial and temporal orientation of society. Virtually overnight, millions of people began to trade in their horses and buggies for automobiles.

To meet the increased demand for fuel, the nascent oil industry revved up exploration and drilling, making the United States the leading oil producer in the world. Within two decades, cement highways were laid out across vast stretches of the American landscape and American families began relocating in new suburban communities that only a few years earlier were isolated rural hamlets. Thousands of miles of telephone lines were installed, and later radio and television were introduced, recasting social life and creating a communication grid to manage and market the far-flung activities of the oil economy and auto age.

Today, we are on the cusp of another convergence of communication technology and energy regimes. The conjoining of Internet communication technology and renewable energies is giving rise to a Third Industrial Revolution (TIR). In the twenty-first century, hundreds of millions of human beings will be generating their own green energy in their homes, offices, and factories and sharing it with one another across intelligent distributed electricity networks—an intergrid—just like people now create their own information and share it on the Internet.

The music companies didn't understand distributed power until millions of young people began sharing music online, and corporate revenues tumbled in less than a decade. Encyclopedia Britannica did not appreciate the distributed and collaborative power that made Wikipedia the leading reference source in the world. Nor did the newspapers take seriously the distributed power of the blogosphere; now many publications are either going out of business or transferring much of their activities online. The implications of people sharing distributed energy in an open commons are even more far-reaching.

THE FIVE PILLARS OF THE THIRD INDUSTRIAL REVOLUTION

The Third Industrial Revolution will have as significant an impact in the twenty-first century as the First Industrial Revolution had in the nineteenth century and the Second Industrial Revolution in the twentieth century. And just as in the two former industrial revolutions, it will fundamentally change every aspect of the way we work and live. The conventional top-down organization of society that characterized much of the economic, social, and political life of the fossil fuel–based industrial revolutions is giving way to distributed and collaborative relationships in the emerging green industrial era. We are in the midst of a profound shift in the very way society is structured, away from hierarchical power and toward lateral power.

Like every other communication and energy infrastructure in history, the various pillars of a Third Industrial Revolution must be laid down simultaneously or the foundation will not hold. That's because each pillar can only function in relationship to the others. The five pillars of the Third Industrial Revolution are (1) shifting to renewable energy; (2) transforming the building stock of every continent into micro–power plants to collect renewable energies on site; (3) deploying hydrogen and other storage technologies in every building and throughout the infrastructure to store intermittent energies; (4) using Internet technology to transform the power grid of every continent into an energy-sharing intergrid that acts just like the Internet (when millions of buildings are generating a small amount of energy locally, on site, they can sell surplus back to the grid and share electricity with their continental neighbors); and (5) transitioning the transport fleet to electric plug-in and fuel cell vehicles that can buy and sell electricity on a smart, continental, interactive power grid.

The critical need to integrate and harmonize these five pillars at every level and stage of development became clear to the European Union in the fall of 2010. A leaked European Commission document warned that the European Union would need to spend €1 trillion between 2010 and 2020 on updating its electricity grid to accommodate an influx of renewable energy. The internal document noted that "Europe is still lacking the infrastructure to enable renewables to develop and compete on an equal footing with traditional sources."[2]

The European Union is expected to draw one-third of its electricity from green sources by 2020. This means that the power grid must be digitized and made intelligent to handle the intermittent renewable energies being fed to the grid from tens of thousands of local producers of energy.

Of course, it will also be essential to quickly develop and deploy hydrogen and other storage technologies across the European Union's infrastructure when the amount of intermittent renewable energy exceeds 15 percent of the electricity generation, or much of that electricity will be lost. Similarly, it is important to incentivize the construction and real estate sectors to encourage the conversion of millions of buildings in the European Union to mini power plants that can harness renewable energies on site and send surpluses back to the smart grid. And unless these other considerations are met, the European Union won't be able to provide enough green electricity to power millions of electric plug-in and hydrogen fuel cell vehicles being readied for the market. If any of the five pillars fall behind the rest in their development, the others will be stymied and the infrastructure itself will be compromised.

The European Union set out with two goals in mind at the beginning of the current century—transforming itself into a sustainable, low-carbon emission society and making Europe the world's most vibrant economy. Becoming a low-carbon emission economy means shifting from a Second Industrial Revolution run on fossil fuel energies to a Third Industrial Revolution run by renewable energies. While a considerable task, we should keep in mind that the transformation of the European and American economies from wood-based fuels to coal-powered steam technologies took place over a half century, as did the shift from coal and steam-powered rail technology to an oil, electricity, and auto economy. These historical trends should give us some confidence that the transition to a renewable energy era should be possible in a comparable time frame.

Finding the new Third Industrial Revolution narrative wasn't easy. As every author knows, having a story line is just the beginning. It's then necessary to develop the narrative. A good narrative is an organic process that builds on itself and begins to take on a life of its own, often leading an author in directions he hadn't anticipated. In this case, the story line—the convergence of Internet communication technology and renewable energies—led us to each of the five pillars that together make up the interactive narrative of a Third Industrial Revolution. The search for the story took us on a remarkable journey, with a number of surprising twists and turns along the way.

GOING FOR GREEN ENERGY

In 2000 and 2001 there was already serious discussion in Europe about setting a target of 20 percent renewable energy generation by 2020. This would mean that 30 percent of the electricity would be coming from green energy sources by the end of the second decade of the twenty-first century. Pillar 1—the shift to 20 percent renewable energies—became a benchmark.

The transition to a new renewable energy system is coming much quicker than anyone had anticipated just a few years ago. The price of conventional fossil fuels and uranium continue to rise on world markets as they become increasingly scarce. The costs are compounded by the rising externalities brought on by CO_2 emissions, which is having a dramatic negative effect on the climate of the planet and the stability of the Earth's ecosystems.

Meanwhile, the price of the new green energies is falling rapidly due to new technology breakthroughs, early adoption, and economies of scale. The cost of photovoltaic (PV) electricity is expected to decline at a rate of 8 percent a year, halving the cost of generation every eight years.[3] With electricity rates expected to rise by a moderate 5 percent, it is estimated that PV will reach grid parity across all European markets by 2012 (grid parity means that the cost of generating electricity from alternative sources will be the same or less than the cost of generating conventional power from fossil fuels or nuclear sources).[4]

The growing differential between the rising costs of the old fossil fuel energies and the declining cost of renewable energies is setting the stage for an upheaval of the global economy and the emergence of a new economic paradigm for the twenty-first century. The commercial growth in solar and wind technology is reminiscent of the dramatic growth in personal computers and Internet use. The first personal computers were introduced into the mass market in the late 1970s. By 2008, there were more than one billion.[5] Similarly, the number of Internet users more than doubled in the first decade of the twenty-first century, reaching two billion in 2010.[6] Now, solar and wind installations are doubling every two years and are poised to follow the same trajectory as personal computers and Internet use over the next two decades.[7]

However, the old energy industries continue to be a powerful force, primarily because of deep pockets that help them influence the shaping of government energy policies. Government subsidies and other forms of favoritism artificially prop up the aging energy sector, giving it an unfair advantage over the new green energy industries. While the oil, coal, gas, and nuclear industries begrudgingly concede that green energies are ascending, they argue that they are too soft and insufficient to ever run a global economy, and will at best serve as supplements to fossil fuels and nuclear power. Their argument, however, doesn't hold up under scrutiny.

Scientists point out that one hour of sunlight provides enough power to run a global economy for a full year.[8] In the European Union alone, 40 percent of the roofs and 15 percent of all the building facades are suitable for photovoltaic applications. The European Photovoltaic Industry Association (EPIA) estimates that the installation of PVs on all existing viable building surfaces could generate 1,500 gigawatts of power, covering 40 percent of the total electricity demand in the European Union.[9]

In a 2007 study reported in *Scientific American*, researchers calculated that if only 2.5 percent of the solar irradiation found in the southwest region of the United States were converted to electricity, it would equal the nation's total electricity consumption in 2006. The study concluded that the same region could provide 69 percent of US electricity and 35 percent of the country's total energy by 2050.[10]

Europe is currently far ahead of the rest of the world in solar energy, accounting for 78 percent of all the installed photovoltaic power in 2009, with Japan, the United States, and China significantly further behind.[11]

In 2009, more wind power was installed in the European Union than any other power source—making up 38 percent of the total deployment of new energy. The industry, which currently employs nearly 200,000 workers across the European Union and generates 4.8 percent of the electricity, is forecasted to provide nearly 17 percent of the electricity for the European market by 2020 and 35 percent of all the electricity in Europe by 2030, when it will have a workforce of nearly half a million people.[12]

The United States has enough wind resources to power the entire nation several times over.[13] In October 2010, Google and the financial firm Good Energies announced plans to lay down a $5 billion underwater electricity transmission line for offshore wind farms along a 350-mile stretch from Norfolk, Virginia, to northern New Jersey.[14] The new transmission backbone would allow eastern states to ramp up offshore wind generation and greatly increase the amount of green electricity in their energy mix.

A Stanford University study of global wind capacity estimates that harnessing 20 percent of the available wind on the planet would provide seven times more electricity than the world now uses.[15] In urban and suburban areas, stand-alone wind turbines near building sites will likely become a fast-growing part of the green wind market by the end of the decade as millions of homes, offices, and industrial sites add generation capacity. Companies like Southwest Windpower in the United States provide small wind turbines that can generate 25–30 percent of the electricity needed to power an average home. The wind turbine costs between $15,000 and $18,000 and has a payback in as few as fourteen years.

Hydropower currently makes up the largest portion of green generated electricity in the world. In the European Union, hydropower generates 180,000 megawatts of electricity, much of which is concentrated in mature large-scale operations. The untapped potential, say industry experts, is in small distributed hydropower installations. The economically viable sites scattered across Europe could generate 147 terawatt hours (TWH) annually. In the United Kingdom, according to the federal government's Environment Agency, small hydropower could provide power for 850,000 homes in the future.

In the United States, hydropower composes 75 percent of the current renewable electricity generation. The Electric Power Research Institute (EPRI) estimates an increase of 23,000 megawatts of hydropower by 2025 from a combination of large damns, micro–hydropower generation, and ocean wave energy.[16]

Geothermal energy beneath the Earth's surface represents a vast reservoir of virtually untapped green power. Temperatures in the interior regions of the Earth reach 4,000 degrees Celsius or more, and that energy is continuously flowing to the surface. Europe's hot spots for geothermal energy are Italy and France. Other countries rich in geothermal energy include Germany, Austria, Hungary, Poland, and Slovakia.

In the United States, the geothermal energy within two miles of the Earth's surface is approximately three million quads, or enough energy to provide for America's needs for 30,000 years.[17]

Installed geothermal energy around the world increased by 20 percent between 2005 and 2010. Still, in the thirty-nine countries that have the potential to meet 100 percent of their electricity needs with geothermal energy, only nine have developed any significant installed power.[18]

While the United States leads in the amount of installed geothermal power, with power plants producing 3,086 megawatts, there is still huge untapped potential. An MIT study estimates that a modest investment of $300 to $400 million over fifteen years would make geothermal power generation competitive in the US electricity market. With a public and/or private investment of $800 million to $1 billion over the same fifteen-year time period, the MIT panel estimates that geothermal power could produce more than 100,000 megawatts of commercially available power by 2050.[19]

Biomass is the final slice of the growing green energy mix and includes fuel crops, forestry waste, and municipal garbage. Biomass is the most contentious of the green energy options. The World Bioenergy Association claims that "the world's bioenergy potential is large enough to meet the global energy demand in 2050."[20] Bryan Hannegan of the Electric Power Research Institute (EPRI) agrees that bioenergy could play a significant role in green energy production but suggests, on the basis of current economic analysis, that it will likely provide only 20 percent of global energy demand by 2050.[21] Still, that's a considerable amount. The Natural Resources Defense Council (NRDC) reports that thirty-nine million tons of crop residue go unused in the United States alone each year—sufficient waste to produce enough electricity to power every home in New England.[22]

Several constraints must be factored into the production of bioenergy. For example, growing corn to produce bioethanol is actually counterproductive. The amount of energy input required to grow the crop and process and transport the ethanol makes the energy value of the final product a near wash.[23]

The major considerations in producing energy from agricultural crops and forest residue are the amount of land and water taken up that could be used more productively for producing food and fiber, and the increase in global warming gasses from growing biomass and processing and transporting energy.

The conversion of municipal waste to energy for the production of electricity and heat is probably the most promising application of biomass. In 2010, the world population produced approximately 1.7 billion tons of municipal solid waste (MSW). More than a billion tons ended up in landfills, while only 0.2 billion tons were converted from waste to energy—indicating the significant untapped potential of this green energy resource. Nearly 98 percent of the energy is generated from mass-burn and refuse-derived fuel (RDF) combustion, which have deleterious impacts on the environment, including the emission of harmful gases. The remaining 2 percent of waste to energy is produced using more benign thermal and biological treatment technologies.

A study conducted by Pike Research estimates that the global market for thermal and biological waste technologies, which reached $3.7 billion in 2010, will grow to $13.6 billion in 2016 as municipal authorities and commercial operations switch over to the new, cleaner conversion technologies.[24]

The ability to bring all of these green energies online will depend on commercial scalability. To expedite the process, governments are putting in place various incentives to encourage the shift to green energies. Currently, more than fifty countries, states, and provinces have "feed-in tariffs," which offer producers of renewable energy a premium price above market value for green electricity they sell back to the grid.[25] Feed-in tariffs have opened the commercial floodgates for solar and wind-generated power by giving early adopters lucrative incentives to enter the market.

Feed-in tariffs have also generated hundreds of thousands of jobs in the past few years. For example, in Germany in 2003, conventional energy employment (coal, oil, gas, and uranium) accounted for 260,000 jobs. By 2007, renewable energy accounted for 249,300 jobs. More impressive, however, is that renewable energy used for primary energy consumption remains below 10 percent. In other words, less than 10 percent of the energy produced by renewable sources created nearly as many jobs as all other energy sources combined.[26]

Spain is another example of an explosive shift toward a renewable energy regime. The Spanish economy, which supports over 188,000 renewable energy jobs and 1,027 renewable energy companies, has produced five times the employment of the conventional energy industry.[27]

Even without feed-in tariffs, jobs in the US renewable energy industry are surging, while employment in the conventional energy sector is declining. In the wind industry alone, over 80,000 jobs have been created over the past decade—the same number of jobs that exist in the entire US coal mining industry. And wind still makes up only 1.9 percent of the US energy mix, while coal accounts for over 44.5 percent of US energy production.[28]

190 MILLION POWER PLANTS

Europe's future has been staked to green power. The question is how to collect the solar, wind, hydro, geothermal heat, and biomass energies. The first inclination was to go to places where the sun always shines, like southern Europe and the Mediterranean, and create giant solar parks to collect the energy. Similarly, grab the wind where it is most abundant, such as off the Irish Coast and other wind corridors. Get the hydro from Norway and Sweden, and so on.

For power and utility companies, not to mention banks and governments, which were used to gathering fossil fuels that were concentrated at limited sites, doing the same with renewable energies seemed to make sense. And big centralized solar parks and wind farms began popping up in scattered parts of Europe where those energies are abundant.

Around 2006, however, some energy entrepreneurs, policy analysts, nongovernmental organizations, and politicians made a simple observation that inevitably led to a profound change in the discussion around a sustainable economic model. The sun shines on every part of the Earth every day, even if the intensity varies. The wind blows all over the world, even if the frequency is intermittent. Wherever we tread, there is a hot geothermal core under the ground. We all generate garbage. In agricultural areas, there is crop and forestry waste. On the coasts, where a large portion of our population lives, the waves and tides come in every day. People living in valleys rely on the steady stream of water coming from mountain glaciers for their hydroelectricity. In other words, unlike fossil fuels and uranium, which are elite energies and only found in certain regions of the world, renewable energies are everywhere. This realization fundamentally changed the thinking of my colleagues. If renewable energies are distributed and found in various proportions and frequencies everywhere in the world, why would we want to collect them in only a few central points?

We realized we were using outmoded twentieth-century ways of thinking about energy based on our previous experiences with fossil fuels. While none of us oppose giant wind farms and solar parks—I even think they are essential to making a transition to a post-carbon Third Industrial Revolution economy—we began to believe these alone would not be sufficient.

If renewable energy is found everywhere, how do we collect it? In early 2007, the European Parliament Energy and Climate Change committees were preparing reports on next steps in energy security and global warming. I received a call from Claude Turmes, the European Parliament's leading authority on renewable energy. He urged me to enlist the construction industry in our efforts. Claude knew that I was in touch with some of Europe's and America's leading construction companies working in sustainable design and that I was beginning to give talks about the need to convert building stock into mini power plants. He reminded me that the construction industry is the "elephant in the room" when it comes to the day-to-day economy and one of the largest industrial employers in the European Union, representing 10 percent of the GDP.[29] Claude suggested that the construction industry might be a key ally and a counterweight to the big energy companies, who were continually thwarting green legislation and sustainable development policies at the Commission and in the member states.

If "It's the economy, stupid," then it's construction that generates business activity and creates new jobs. There are an estimated 190 million buildings in the twenty-seven member states of the European Union.[30] Each of these buildings is a potential mini power plant that could suck up the renewable energies on site—the sun on the roof, the wind coming up the external walls, the sewage flowing out of the house, the geothermal heat underneath the buildings, and so on.

If the First Industrial Revolution gave rise to dense urban cores, tenements, row housing, skyscrapers, and multilevel factories, and the Second Industrial Revolution spawned flat suburban tracts and industrial parks, the Third Industrial Revolution transforms every existing building into a dual-purpose dwelling—a habitat and a micro–power plant. We had found pillar 2.

The construction industry and the real estate sector are now teaming up with renewable energy companies to convert buildings into mini power plants to collect green energies on site to power the buildings. Frito-Lay's Casa Grande Arizona plant is among this new generation of micro-power plants. The concept is called "net-zero." The factory will generate all of its own energy by placing solar concentrators on site to cook potato chips in the factory.[31] In Aragon, Spain, GM's production facility has installed a 10-megawatt solar plant on its roof, which produces enough electricity to power 4,600 homes. The initial investment of $78 million will be paid back in less than ten years, after which electricity generation will be virtually free.[32] In France, the construction giant Bouygues is taking the process a step further, putting up a state-of-the-art "positive power" commercial office complex in the Paris suburbs that collects sufficient solar energy to provide for all of its own needs and even generates surplus energy.[33] Even homeowners can now turn their houses into mini power plants. For an upfront cost of around $60,000, a homeowner can install solar panels on his or her roof and generate enough electricity to power much or all of the home. Any surplus can be sold back to the grid, and payback can run anywhere from four to ten years.

Twenty-five years from now, millions of buildings—homes, offices, shopping malls, industrial and technology parks—will have been converted or constructed to serve as both power plants and habitats. The wholesale reconversion of each nation's commercial and residential building stock into mini power plants over the next three decades will touch off a building boom—creating thousands of new businesses and millions of new jobs—with an economic multiplier effect that will impact every other industry.

How does this translate at the local level? In the United Kingdom alone, the Cameron government estimates that simply insulating the country's twenty-six million homes to make them more energy efficient and prepare them to more effectively utilize subsequent green energy production could create as many as 250,000 jobs.[34]

Converting buildings to micro–power plants will spawn even more diverse business opportunities and tens of millions of jobs. Let me give you a single example of the commercial possibilities that lie ahead in the construction and real estate sectors. In 2008, my global policy team entered into a conversation with Raffaele Lombardo, the president of the region of Sicily, on how to remake the island into a TIR economy. Sicily's five million inhabitants are relatively poor by Western European standards but enjoy an abundance of solar irradiation. A study commissioned by the region found that if just 6 percent of the rooftop surface area was equipped with solar panels over the next two decades, the island could produce a thousand megawatts of electricity—enough to provide the electricity needs for one-third of the Sicilian population. The same study identified more than 36,000 local small- and medium-sized construction companies, architectural firms, and engineering companies that could carry out the installation process. The partial conversion to a TIR economy would create a €4 to €5 billion market and generate an additional €35 billion in revenue for small- and medium-sized businesses and Sicilian families over a twenty-year period.[35]

Italy's feed-in tariff provides the important commercial impetus to jump-start the process. The tariff is paid for by the citizenry in the form of a 5 percent increase in electricity rates. To date, the vast majority of applications for installing solar electricity have been for large PV plants, with far fewer applications going to distributed power generation projects. That ratio could be reversed, however, if the government were to underwrite loans to small- and medium-sized enterprises (SMEs) and homeowners to help pay for the solar installations.

Green mortgages could also help facilitate the building conversions. Banks and other lending companies could provide lower interest rates for businesses and homeowners that install solar panels. Assuming an average of eight to nine years for payback on the energy savings from the installation, businesses and homeowners holding a twenty-year mortgage would be generating all of their own electricity off grid for the last eleven to twelve years of their loan. The monthly savings on the electricity bills could be leveraged against the monthly mortgage payment and be the basis for a reduced interest rate. The reconfiguration of the building as a power plant, in turn, appreciates the assessed value of the real estate holding. Some banks are already beginning to offer special green mortgages. In the years ahead, green mortgages are likely to restructure the mortgage lending business and help create a building boom in countries around the world.

Now, let's zoom up to thirty thousand feet to see the macro employment impacts of increasing the energy efficiency of buildings and installing renewable energies. Researchers at the Energy and Resources Group and the Haas School of Business at the University of California at Berkeley developed an analytical jobs creation model for the power sector between 2009 and 2030, based on synthesized data from fifteen separate studies on increasing energy efficiency and installing and servicing renewable energy in US buildings. The model takes into account a wide range of variables including jobs lost in other parts of the power sector from the shift to energy efficiency and renewables, indirect job creation because of increased spending by workers, and the multiplier effects of the initial economic activity on other commercial enterprise. The study forecasts that "cutting the annual rate of increase in electricity generation in half and targeting a 30% RPS (Renewable Portfolio Standard) generates about four million cumulative job-years through 2030."[36] If the RPS standards were to be raised to 40 percent—several regions of the world have already reached as high as 60 percent RPS, and many more are targeting even higher RPS standards by 2030—the net number of new jobs in the United States would exceed 5.5 million.

As we discuss in a later section, these job numbers take into consideration only pillars 1 and 2—renewable energy and converting buildings to micro–power plants—as stand-alone initiatives unconnected to energy storage, the establishment of an intelligent utility network for distributing energy, and the transformation of the transport fleet to electric plug-in and hydrogen fuel cell vehicles. By way of an analogy, the above jobs model forecast is akin to projecting employment twenty years into the information technology (IT) revolution, but before the creation of the Internet. When all five pillars of the TIR are interconnected, they create a new nervous system for the economy, spurring a leap in energy efficiency and untold new business opportunities and jobs.

After a century of big energy companies dominating the economy, not to mention wielding influence over government policies and the geopolitics of international relations, a new plan was being proposed that would democratize the production and distribution of energy by creating millions of mini energy entrepreneurs. As one observer remarked, this is all about "power to the people."

THE SUN ISN'T ALWAYS SHINING,
THE WIND ISN'T ALWAYS BLOWING

Although renewable energies are abundant and clean and allow us to seriously entertain the idea of living in a sustainable world, they come with their own unique problems. The sun isn't always shining and the wind isn't always blowing, or when it is blowing, it may not be needed. Renewable energies are, for the most part, intermittent; whereas the hard energies, while finite and polluting, are nonetheless a fixed stock.

In May 2002, I sat down for a little chat with Romano Prodi, then president of the European Commission, at the EU embassy in Washington, DC. I confided in Romano that I was deeply concerned about achieving 20 percent renewable energy by 2020, which would mean that nearly one-third of Europe's electricity would be dependent on wind, sun, and other intermittent sources of energy. I said, "Romano, let me paint a picture for you. It's 2020, and the EU has achieved its target of 20 percent renewable energy. It's a very hot summer. In the middle of July, cloud cover blocks the sun's rays for several weeks across much of Europe. Equally bad luck, the wind stops blowing over much of Europe at the same time. And if that weren't enough, the water tables are down at hydroelectric sites because of climate change–induced draught, and the electricity goes out across Europe. What do we do?"

Romano, a professor and highly regarded economist by background, twice prime minister of Italy and one of Europe's most revered senior politicians is, in fact, rather modest and quiet. He put his chin in his hand, as if to ponder the full meaning of what he had just been told, and then threw the ball back in my court. "Any ideas?" he asked. "Yes," I said. "We need to quickly invest in research to bring technologies online that can store renewable energies. If we don't, we won't be able to employ renewable energy on a scale that will get us to a post-carbon era. Without storage we're sunk." (Eight years later, Bill Gates would echo the sentiment that cost effective, reliable storage technology is the key to a sustainable future.)

Power and utility companies were already grumbling that when 15 to 20 percent or more of the electricity on the grid comes from renewable energy, the grid would be at the mercy of the weather, and we'd be faced with the prospect of periodic brownouts and blackouts across the continent. There are a number of promising storage technologies, including flow batteries, flywheels, capacitors, and pumped water. I had been researching the various possibilities and had recently come to the conclusion that while we should advance all of these storage options, hydrogen probably offered the best long-term hope as a storage medium because of its flexibility.

Hydrogen had long been sought after by scientists and engineers as the Holy Grail for a post-carbon era. It is the lightest and most abundant element in the universe—the stuff of the stars—and contains not a single carbon atom. Hydrogen is found everywhere on Earth, but it rarely exists free-floating in nature. Rather, it is embedded in other energy sources. It can, for example, be extracted from coal, oil, and natural gas. In fact, most of the hydrogen used for various industrial and commercial activities is derived from natural gas. Hydrogen can also be extracted from water. Every student recalls the electrolysis experiment in high school chemistry class. Two electrodes, one positive and the other negative, are submerged in pure water that has been made more conductive by the addition of an electrolyte. When electricity—direct current—is applied, the hydrogen bubbles up at the negatively charged electrode (the cathode) and oxygen at the positively charged electrode (the anode). The key challenge is whether it's economically feasible to use renewable forms of energy that are carbon free, like photovoltaic, wind, hydro, and geothermal, to generate electricity that is then used in the electrolysis process to split water into hydrogen and oxygen.

I reminded Romano that for nearly fifty years our astronauts had been circling the Earth in spaceships powered by hydrogen fuel cells and said that it was time to bring the technology down to Earth to provide a storage carrier for renewable energies.

Here's how it works. When the sun is shining on the photovoltaic panels on the roof, electricity is generated, most of which is used instantly to power the building. If, however, there is a surplus of electricity that is not immediately needed, it can be used in the process of electrolysis to sequester hydrogen in a storage system. When the sun isn't shining, the hydrogen can be transformed back into electricity by a fuel cell to provide power.

Romano was intrigued. He already knew quite a bit about hydrogen. His older brother Vittorio, a world-class nuclear physicist, was a member of the European Parliament and an expert on the subject. Vittorio and I became good friends, and he took on the important task of educating legislators and the business community on the workings and benefits of hydrogen as a storage medium for renewable energy.

Within weeks of our meeting, I provided Romano with a strategic memorandum on the possibilities of using hydrogen as a storage carrier for renewable energies. President Prodi wasted no time. In June of 2003, at a Brussels conference, he announced a €2 billion hydrogen research initiative by the Commission to ready Europe for a hydrogen economy. In his opening remarks he explained the historic significance of employing hydrogen as a storage medium for a Third Industrial Revolution infrastructure: "But let us be clear about what makes the European hydrogen program truly visionary. It is our declared goal of achieving a step-by-step shift towards a fully integrated hydrogen economy, based on renewable energy sources, by the middle of the century."[37] Pillar 3 was now in place.

In 2006, I prepared a second memo on the subject for Chancellor Merkel, suggesting that Germany launch its own hydrogen research and development initiative. She did, committing significant funds to advancing the new storage technology. In 2007, the European Commission, under President Barroso, announced a €7.4 billion public-private partnership—a Joint Technology Initiative (JTI)—to move from hydrogen research and development to deployment across Europe.[38]

The first three pillars—the creation of a renewable energy regime, loaded by buildings and partially stored in the form of hydrogen—suggested the need for the fourth pillar: a way to distribute all the energy being generated and stored by millions of buildings to communities across Europe.

THE ENERGY INTERNET

The idea of creating a smart grid was gaining currency by the middle of the decade but still had not found its way into any formal EU or member state initiatives. IBM, Cisco Systems, Siemens, and GE were all gearing up to enter the field, hoping to make the smart grid the new superhighway for transporting electrons. The power grid would be transformed into an info-energy net, allowing millions of people who produce their own energy to share surpluses peer-to-peer.

This intelligent energy network will embrace virtually every facet of life. Homes, offices, factories, and vehicles will continuously communicate with one another, sharing information and energy on a 24/7 basis. Smart utility networks will be connected to weather changes, allowing them to continuously adjust electricity flow and internal temperatures to both weather conditions and consumer demand. The network will also be able to adjust the electricity used by appliances, and if the grid is experiencing peak energy use and possible overload, the software can direct, for example, a homeowner's washing machine to skip one rinse cycle per load to save electricity.

Since the true price of electricity on the grid varies during any twenty-four-hour period, real-time information displayed on digital meters in every building would allow for dynamic pricing, letting consumers increase or decrease their energy use automatically, depending on price. Consumers who agree to slight adjustments in their electricity use will receive credits on their bills. Dynamic pricing also will let local energy producers know the best time to sell electricity back to the grid, or to go off the grid altogether.

The US government recently allocated funds to develop the smart grid across the country. The funds will be used to install digital electric meters, transmission grid sensors, and energy storage technologies to enable high-tech electricity distribution; this will transform the existing power grid into an Internet of energy. CPS Energy in San Antonio, Texas; Xcel Utility in Boulder, Colorado; and PG&E, Sempra, and Southern ConEdison in California will be laying down parts of the smart grid over the next several years.

The smart grid is the backbone of the new economy. Just as the Internet created thousands of new businesses and millions of new jobs, so too will the intelligent electricity network—except "this network will be 100 or 1,000 times larger than the Internet," says Marie Hattar, vice president of marketing in Cisco's network systems solutions group. Hattar points out that while "some homes have Internet access, . . . some don't. Everyone has electricity access—all of those homes could potentially be connected."[39]

For twenty years, heads of state and global business leaders asked me, "How do you expect to manage the energy needs of a complex global economy with 'soft' renewable energies?" The old guard in government and in the power and utility industry are as unaware of the potential of distributed power to change the very nature of energy as the music moguls were when first confronted with file sharing.

The invention of second-generation grid IT has changed the economic equation, tipping the balance of power from the old, centralized fossil fuel and uranium energies to the new, distributed renewable energies. We now have advanced software that allows companies and industries to connect hundreds of thousands and even millions of small desktop computers. When connected, the lateral power exceeds, by a magnitude, the computing power of the world's largest centralized supercomputers.

Similarly, grid IT is now being used to transform the electricity power grid in several regions of the world. When millions of buildings collect renewable energies on site, store surplus energy in the form of hydrogen, and share electricity with millions of others across intelligent intergrids, the resulting lateral power dwarfs what could be generated by centralized nuclear, coal, and gas-fired power plants.

A study prepared by KEMA, a leading energy consulting firm, for the GridWise Alliance—the US smart grid coalition of IT companies, power and utility companies, academics, and venture capitalists—found that even a modest $16 billion in government incentives to smarten the nation's power grid would catalyze $64 billion worth of projects and create 280,000 direct jobs.[40] Because the smart grid is critical to the growth of the other four pillars, it will generate hundreds of thousands of additional jobs in the renewable energy sector, the construction and real estate markets, the hydrogen storage industry, and electric transportation, all of which rely on the smart grid as an enabling platform. These employment estimates are small, however, in comparison to the jobs that will be created with the €1 trillion the European Commission now projects is needed for public and private investment over the next ten years to bring the distributed smart grid network online across the world's largest economy.[41]

Today's idea of a *distributed* smart grid was not what most of the major ICT companies had in mind when they first began to talk about intelligent utility networks. Their early vision was for a *centralized* smart grid. The companies foresaw digitalizing the existing power grid, with the placement of smart meters and censors, to allow utility companies to collect information remotely, including keeping up-to-the-minute information on electricity flows. The goal was to improve the efficiency of moving electricity across the grid, reduce the costs of maintenance, and keep more accurate records on customer usage. Their plans were reformist but not revolutionary. As far as I knew, there was little discussion about using Internet technology to transform the power grid into an interactive info-energy network that would allow millions of people to generate their own renewable energy and share electrons with one another.

In 2005, IBM executives in Germany began corresponding with me on the possible future uses of the smart grid. I had been talking up the possibility of transforming the power grid into an intergrid for sharing energy in my Wharton School's Executive Education classes and in presentations with utility companies like Scottish Power, Cinergy, and the National Grid. The idea of an intelligent electricity grid was the central theme of my 2002 book, *The Hydrogen Economy*. I wasn't the only one talking about it. Amory Lovins, in particular, had been raising the prospect for a number of years, as had a number of other power and utility wonks.

As early as 2001, the Electric Power Research Institute (EPRI) observed in its report, "Perspectives for the Future," that distributed generation would likely evolve

> in much the same way the computer industry has evolved. Large mainframe computers have given way to small, geographically dispersed desktop and laptop machines that are interconnected into fully integrated, extremely flexible networks. In our industry, central-station plants will continue to play an important role, of course. But we're increasingly going to need smaller, cleaner, widely distributed generators . . . all supported by energy storage technologies. A basic requirement for such a system will be advanced electronic controls: these will be absolutely essential for handling the tremendous traffic of information and power that such a complicated interconnection will bring.[42]

The IBM guys in Germany put me in touch with Guido Bartels, a Dutch national who was doing a lot of work pushing IBM's intelligent utility network concept around the world. Guido was also chairman of GridWise, the consortium of IT and power and utility companies working with the Department of Energy in the United States to move the smart grid forward. Guido and I began a series of discussions on IBM's future. Still, it was pretty clear that the company's primary thrust was reforming the grid using a traditional, central-management style. The idea of microgrids connecting and selling energy back to the grid, while acknowledged as a potential function of the company's intelligent utility network, had not yet reached prime time to become the centerpiece of a new economic vision—although IBM was clearly interested in taking the next steps into a TIR future. Bartels and Allan Schurr, in particular, grasped the potential of a truly distributed smart grid and worked to advance a TIR infrastructure with clients around the world.

Pier Nabuurs, another Dutch national, and the CEO of KEMA, was also beginning to talk of the merits of a bidirectional info-energy network. Nabuurs was Bartels's counterpart in the European Union, heading up the SmartGrids European Technology Platform. Like GridWise in the United States, SmartGrids was composed of IT and power and utility companies working with the European Union to advance smart grid implementation across the European continent. Nabuurs pushed for an internet for energy that would aggregate and route electricity generated from thousands of micro-grids.

Nabuurs sensed a change taking place in European power and utility companies—something not yet shared by their American counterparts. Intense discussions were taking place inside the corporate suites. These companies had been, for more than a century, attached at the hips to giant energy companies whom they relied on for the fossil fuels to generate electricity. A younger generation of executives, noticing a heightened interest from local municipalities, regions, small- and medium-sized enterprises, cooperatives, and homeowners, in producing their own renewable electricity on micro-grids, saw an opportunity to recast the role of their companies. They envisioned power and utility companies adding a new function and, with it, a new business model to accompany their traditional role as suppliers of energy and managers of transmission and distribution. Why not use intelligent utility networks to better manage the existing flow of electrons coming from centralized fossil fuels and uranium fuel, while also using the distributed capability of the new smart grids to collect and transmit electrons coming in from thousands of on-site micro-grids? In other words, go from a unidirectional to a bidirectional management of electricity.

In the new scenario, the companies would give up some of their traditional top-down control over both supply and transmission of electricity to become, at least partially, an integral part of an electricity network involving thousands of small energy producers. In the new scheme, the utility part of the power and utility companies becomes far more important. The company becomes the manager of an info-energy network. It moves increasingly away from selling its own energy to becoming a service provider, using its expertise to manage other people's energy. By this new reasoning, utilities in the future will co-manage companies' use of energy across their entire value chain, just as IT companies like IBM help businesses manage their information. The potential new business opportunities would eventually exceed their conventional business of simply selling electrons.

The young upstarts got a boost for their vision from an unlikely source. Neelie Kroes, the EU commissioner responsible for competition policy, dropped a bombshell on the power and utility sector in early 2006. Deregulation of the electricity market had allowed a handful of national power and utility giants to spread their wires across borders and buy smaller players. The European Commission was becoming increasingly concerned over the ability of a few mega power and utility companies to control access to markets by monopolizing both the supply and distribution of power. Kroes declared war on the power and utility companies. From that point on, the companies would be required to unbundle networks from supply activities—or, put more simply, they would not be allowed to own both the supply of power and the transmission lines to distribute that power. Kroes made very clear the European Commission's intention, saying that

> one of the issues of real concern is, indeed, a market structure with bundled infrastructure and supply activities. This is a concern for all network industries where the underlying infrastructure is very costly to duplicate. Owners and operators of critical networks often compete with companies that need to have access to those same networks. Can we expect such integrated companies to treat competitors in a fully fair manner? Their own self-interest would suggest not. . . . [T]he sector inquiry has shown that new entrants often lack effective access to networks, the operators of which are alleged to favour their own affiliates.[43]

Speaking on a very personal note, Kroes said, "I very much welcome the moves towards full structural unbundling (i.e., separation of the supply and retail business from monopoly infrastructures)."[44]

The action by the competition commissioner was not taken in a vacuum. It was part of a larger concerted effort to open the door to the new green distributed energies of the Third Industrial Revolution. Anecdotal evidence was mounting all over Europe that the power and utility companies were making it difficult for local producers of renewable energy to sell their electricity to the grid. This obstructionist policy by the power and utility companies flew in the face of EU directives supporting the increasing generation of electricity from local renewable energy sources.

As far as the European Commission is concerned, Kroes said, "it is the clear objective of the liberalization process to ensure that new companies can enter and prosper on the market, in order to increase competition and to provide a greater choice for consumers, e.g., for 'green' electricity."[45]

The German and French governments were quick to register their displeasure with Kroes. Both countries were headquarters for some of the giants in the European power and utility business—E.ON and RWE in Germany and EDF in France. What the media and public didn't know is that behind the scenes all hell was breaking loose, at least inside the offices of some of the sector's major players.

In March of 2006, around the same time Kroes was out on the hustings talking up "unbundling," Utz Claassen, the tough CEO of EnBW, the fourth largest power and utility company in Germany, invited me to Berlin to speak to his company and clients on climate change, energy security, and the transformation of the power and utility sector. Even though 45 percent of EnBW was owned by EDF of France, a company that produces 78 percent of French electricity from nuclear power, Claassen picked up on the theme of distributed generation of renewable energy.[46] Three months later, he invited me to Heilbronn, Germany, to address his entire company. Some five hundred employees filled the hall. After I laid out the vision of a Third Industrial Revolution, Claassen took the podium. To the surprise of many of his employees, who had cut their teeth on conventional fossil fuels and nuclear energy and were used to a centralized, top-down flow of power, Claassen said the energy market was changing and so was EnBW. He pledged that EnBW would be at the front of the pack, leading the charge to a new distributed energy era. He was quick to assert that while the old energies and business models were not being retired, the company had to make room for the new energies and the new business models that would accompany them.

By early 2008, power and utility companies across Europe were taking baby steps into the new energy era, including NTR of Ireland and Scottish Power. Even staunch bulwarks of the old order like E.ON, the gargantuan German power and utility company, were having second thoughts about their future.

I had been asked by E.ON to engage in a marathon two-hour debate with its chairman and CEO, Dr. Johannes Teyssen, in March 2008 in Rotterdam. When I met him, he seemed like the very epitome of the traditional German business leader, sporting a severe expression and a traditional black three-piece suit. In fact, he turned out to be very cordial and engaging. Teyssen argued that every conceivable source of energy would be needed to meet the energy demands of Europe in the coming decades, including fossil fuels, nuclear, and even renewable energy. He was mute, however, on the question of distributed power.

I couldn't help but notice that throughout the debate a British gentleman, whom I suspected was in his forties, was continuously whispering in Teyssen's ear when I was talking. After the debate, he came up and introduced himself. His name was Kenton Bradbury, and he was the senior vice president responsible for infrastructure management and future strategies at E.ON. He said that the company was starting to look at the whole issue of smart grids, micro-generation, and distributed power, and was keen to know more, especially about how some power and utility companies were beginning to work with construction companies to develop smart buildings that could serve as mini power plants and feed electricity back to the grid.

In the ensuing months we corresponded by email and talked by phone. I also connected him with some of the members of our policy group, including Guido Bartels at IBM; Pier Nabuurs at KEMA; and Rudy Provoost, the CEO at Philips Lighting. Kenton presented some of the new business opportunities that would arise out of a Third Industrial Revolution infrastructure at an E.ON board meeting a few months later.

Recall that I mentioned that a younger generation of execs were anxious to take their companies into a new business model—without abandoning the conventional business plan—in which their utilities would become advisors and consultants, working with clients to help manage their energy, like IBM and other IT companies do with information management. Interestingly, I heard that E.ON had gone into a deep retreat in the fall of 2008, and using the IBM disruptive change model as a case study, examined various scenarios by which they might overhaul the mission and strategic agenda of the company toward the Third Industrial Revolution paradigm.

The IBM case study, which has now become famous to the point of being a cliché in MBA programs, refers to the company's decision in the mid-1990s to shift its focus from selling computers—its core business—to selling services. IBM had come to the realization by then that there was very little value left in simply selling computers. With dozens of companies selling the "boxes," and with Asian competitors able to produce the machines with the same degree of quality but at lower prices, IBM saw diminishing margins in continuing to emphasize the product side of their business.

Louis Gerstner, IBM's CEO, saw the writing on the wall and began to envision a new business model. First, he asked, "What is IBM's core competency?" The answer was "managing the flow of information." With the new image of itself in hand, this technology titan of the twentieth century turned its giant ship into new waters, selling its consulting expertise to companies looking to better manage their information. Soon, companies everywhere were introducing a chief information officer (CIO) to their executive suite.

For the power and utility companies, "managing energy" is their core competence. But what their clients really want from them is advice on how to implement energy systems that are more efficient and use less energy. In a highly competitive world where energy costs are now eclipsing labor costs in some industries, the name of the game is energy savings—it's one of the few areas in which substantial gains can keep margins from shrinking and even collapsing altogether.

So how do E.ON and other power and utility companies go from trying to sell more and more electrons to a new business model in which their mission is to advise clients and create programs designed to use fewer electrons? The most difficult aspect, from a management perspective, is the delicate process of phasing out of the old business model over a period of time—without killing it off prematurely—while also aggressively pursuing the new business model. This will test the management skills of the best and brightest among the younger generation of executives in the power and utility sector.

As for IBM, it appears that they are envisioning two very different kinds of smart grids, a reformist model for the United States and a revolutionary one for Europe. As mentioned previously, IBM's initial vision of the super grid was narrow and reform-minded: digitalize the grid, improve its performance, and provide up-to-the-moment information to the power and utility companies to help them better manage their operations. At least, that's what everyone was hearing.

The IBM game plan began to change in early 2007 as the European Union and a growing number of its member states, regions, and municipalities, as well as various players in the business community, began to gravitate toward a Third Industrial Revolution model. IBM began talking about a distributed intelligent utility network for the European Union. One industry analyst confided in me that the distributed model better fits the architecture of the European Union, which is, after all, a network of localities, regions, and member states whose governance pattern is far less hierarchical and flatter than elsewhere. What about IBM's plans for the United States and North America? The same source was unequivocal on the matter. A centralized super grid would likely make more sense.

Thus far, American power and utility companies, for the most part, have been reticent about introducing a TIR business model. Ed Legge, of the Edison Electric Institute, the lobbying arm for America's power and utility industry, is blunt on the matter: "We're probably not going to be in favor of anything that shrinks our business. All investor-owned utilities are built on the central-generation model that Thomas Edison came up with: You have a big power plant. . . . [D]istributed generation is taking that out of the picture—it's local."[47]

There's a lot involved in the weighty decision to build two different smart grids—a centralized, top-down system in the United States and a distributed and collaborative system in the European Union. Industry observers estimate that it will cost approximately $1.5 trillion between 2010 and 2030 to transform the existing US power grid into an intelligent utility network.[48] If the smart grid is unidirectional rather than bidirectional in design, the United States will have lost the opportunity to join with Europe in the Third Industrial Revolution and, with it, the prospect of retaining its leadership in the global economy.

PLUG-IN TRANSPORT

One last pillar must be integrated into the network to make a Third Industrial Revolution: transport. Converting buildings into mini power plants and creating an energy internet will provide the infrastructure to power electric plug-in and hydrogen fuel cell vehicles—the first of which rolled off the assembly lines in 2011. The US government has invested $2.4 billion to bring the new generation of electric automobiles to the market and is even offering a $7,500 tax incentive to assist with the purchase of a new electric vehicle.[49]

Plug-in electric vehicles are causing a sea change in the energy and transport sectors. For a hundred years, the auto industry engaged in an intimate relationship with the oil companies, just like power and utility companies did in the past. That relationship is now beginning to fray. Over the past twelve months, the major car companies have signed agreements with the leading electric power and utility companies to prepare a new infrastructure for the smart electric plug-in transport of the twenty-first century.

Electric utilities are hurriedly installing electric power charging stations along motorways, in parking lots, garages, and commercial spaces to provide the electricity for the new plug-in vehicles. General Motors is partnering with utility companies—including ConEdison, New York Power Authority, and Northeast Utilities—in its 2011 rollout of the Chevrolet Volt. In Berlin, Daimler and RWE, Germany's second largest power company, have launched a project to establish charging points for electric Smart and Mercedes cars around the German capital. Toyota has joined with EDF, France's largest utility, to build charging points in France and other countries for its plug-in electric cars.

Small companies like AeroVironment, Coulomb Technologies, and ECOtality have already entered the market with electric vehicle charger stations; and now GE, Siemens, and Eaton are preparing to join the competition with their own electric vehicle chargers. Most of the charging stations, which run between $3,000 and $5,000 per unit, are currently being marketed to municipalities to build public charging docks. The companies are beginning, however, to eye the potentially lucrative residential market, hoping that millions of prospective electric cars buyers will pay $1,000 for their own home charging units. The electric power charging market is expected to climb quickly from the current $69 million to $1.3 billion by 2013, as electric vehicles begin to roll out in larger numbers.[50]

A 2010 study by the global management consulting firm PRTM projects that by 2020, the electric vehicle value chain is likely to be approximately $300 billion and create more than a million jobs in the global economy. An aggressive effort by US car makers could account for more than 275,000 of those jobs.[51]

By 2030, charging points for plug-in electric vehicles and hydrogen fuel cell vehicles will be installed virtually everywhere, providing a distributed infrastructure for sending electricity both from and to the main electricity grid. And by 2040, it is estimated that 75 percent of light-duty vehicle miles traveled will be electrically powered.[52]

The enormous distributed power embedded in the TIR infrastructure becomes apparent when we consider the potential of electric plug-in and hydrogen-powered fuel cell vehicles as power plants on wheels. Since the typical car is parked about 96 percent of the time, it can be plugged back into the interactive electricity network to provide premium power back to the grid. An all-electric and hydrogen fuel cell fleet powered by green energy has four times the electricity storage capacity of the existing national power grid in the United States. If just 25 percent of the vehicles were to sell energy back to the grid—when the price of electricity is right—it would replace every conventional, centralized power plant in the country.[53]

The automobile companies are locked into a fierce competition to get electric plug-in and hydrogen-powered fuel cell vehicles to market. Inside the automotive industry, however, there is a heated discussion going on among those who favor electric vehicles and others who believe that electric vehicles are a transitional strategy toward fully operable hydrogen transport. Most automotive companies are readying both electric and hydrogen vehicles for market, Daimler among them. Its management is particularly bullish about the prospects of fuel cell vehicles. Let me share the story of how I first heard of Daimler's plan.

I had asked Jens Weidmann, Chancellor Merkel's economic advisor, whether the chancellor might be willing to host a small dinner of a dozen or so of Germany's key business leaders to discuss the future prospects for a green German economy, particularly Germany's role in transitioning the world into a Third Industrial Revolution. As circumstances would have it, the global financial system had shut down just weeks earlier. The mood at the dinner was somber and introspective. Halfway into the evening, a messenger hurried into the room and whispered into the chancellor's ear. She halted the table discussion to announce that the US House of Representatives had just voted "no" on President Bush's bailout package. Her announcement was met with incredulity around the room. I could see that each of the participants were mulling over what this vote in Congress would mean for their companies in Germany.

Anxious to lighten up the mood and rekindle a more optimistic discussion about the future, the chancellor turned to Dr. Dieter Zetsche, the chairman of Daimler, and asked him what his company's plans were for the future. He told the chancellor that Daimler is set on a course to revolutionize the car industry and is moving aggressively to mass-produce hydrogen-powered fuel cell cars, trucks, and buses in 2015. The shift from the internal combustion engine to the fuel cell, according to Zetsche, would be a critical watershed in transforming the German economy.

Merkel was taken aback, as was everyone else in the room. While we were all aware that Daimler and other companies were working on electric and fuel cell vehicles, this was the first time Daimler's chairman slipped with the news that his company had decided to "go for it," as we say in America, and bring the future into the present.

The chancellor scanned the table to see the reaction of others and stopped for a brief extra moment when passing by me. Recall that I had asked her to commit the German government to a hydrogen research program back in 2006, which she did. Zetsche's decision to commit the world's oldest automotive company to a hydrogen future seemed to herald the beginning of a new economic era for the country that had launched the Second Industrial Revolution, with the introduction of the internal combustion engine.

In September 2009, Daimler joined with seven industrial partners—EnBW, Linde, OMV, Shell, Total, Vattenfall, and the National Organization of Hydrogen and Fuel Cell Technology—to establish a network of fuel cell stations across Germany to ready the market for the mass introduction of fuel cell vehicles in 2015.[54]

It's still anyone's guess if Daimler's gamble will pay off. Whether we settle on electric batteries or fuel cells or some combination of both, what's clear is that the oil-powered internal combustion engine—the central technology of the Second Industrial Revolution—is on the way out. Our children will be driving vehicles that are silent, clean, smart, and plugged into an interactive network that is flat, distributed, and collaborative. This fact alone is a sign that we are at the end of one economic era and at the beginning of another.

The creation of a renewable energy regime, loaded by buildings, partially stored in the form of hydrogen, distributed via smart intergrids, and connected to plug-in, zero-emission transport, opens the door to a Third Industrial Revolution. The entire system is interactive, integrated, and seamless. This interconnectedness is creating new opportunities for cross-industry relationships and, in the process, severing many traditional Second Industrial Revolution business partnerships.

To appreciate how disruptive the Third Industrial Revolution is to the existing way we organize economic life, consider the profound changes that have taken place in just the past twenty years with the introduction of the Internet revolution. The democratization of information and communication has altered the very nature of global commerce and social relations as significantly as the print revolution in the early modern era. Now, imagine the impact that the democratization of energy across all of society is likely to have when managed by Internet technology.

The Third Industrial Revolution build-out is particularly relevant for the poorer countries in the developing world. We need to keep in mind that 40 percent of the human race still lives on two dollars a day or less, in dire poverty, and the vast majority have no electricity. Without access to electricity they remain "powerless," literally and figuratively. The single most important factor in raising hundreds of millions of people out of poverty is having reliable and affordable access to green electricity. All other economic development is impossible in its absence. The democratization of energy and universal access to electricity is the indispensible starting point for improving the lives of the poorest populations of the world. The extension of micro credit to generate micro power is already beginning to transform life across the developing nations, potentially giving millions of people hope of improving their economic situation.

But can we make the jump? Although there was the beginning of an understanding in Brussels that the five pillars that make up the Third Industrial Revolution needed to be integrated as a single system, there was an equally strong counterweight that threatened to derail the process.

NO MORE PILOTS

"No more pilot buses" came from the far side of the giant conference table. Ten pairs of eyes nervously turned in unison to gaze on Herbert Kohler, a Daimler vice president in charge of group research and advanced engineering. Pier Nabuurs, the CEO of KEMA, who was sitting next to Kohler, delivered the punch line, blurting out, "we're piloted out." Our eyes darted over to Jose Manuel Barroso, the powerful president of the European Commission, who was hosting the meeting, to see his reaction. He paused, and then a slight smile curled up on his lips, which was followed by a similar relieved reaction across the table.

Kohler was venting a frustration shared by everyone in the room. Around the table were representatives from some of the leading businesses in the world. What they had in common was that each of their companies was beginning to break away from the Second Industrial Revolution architecture and journey into a new commercial era, and each was just becoming aware of how its individual pursuits might fit into a larger economic picture. They all wanted scale-up, realizing it was key to assuring speedy market penetration.

It was December 6, 2006. I had asked President Barroso for the meeting, suggesting that it would be helpful for some of Europe's and America's leading companies to share their thoughts on how to make the European

Union both the most sustainable economy in the world and, at the same time, the most commercially successful.

President Barroso's agenda was a complicated one. Under his stewardship, the European Union was readying a 20–20–20 by 2020 formula, which would put the world's leading economy far ahead of other nations in addressing the threat of climate change. The proposal called for a 20 percent reduction in greenhouse gas emissions by 2020, based on 1990 emission levels; a 20 percent increase in energy efficiency by the same year; and a 20 percent increase in the deployment of renewable energies, again by 2020. The targets would require compliance across the twenty-seven member states. Chancellor Merkel of Germany would later rally the other EU states to the ambitious agenda during her rotating presidency of the EU Council in the spring of 2007.

The European Union was equally committed, however, to reaching the Lisbon Agenda goal—which European heads of state had agreed to back in March 2002—to make Europe the world's most competitive economy. The European Union was already the leading economy in the world. As mentioned previously, the GDP of its twenty-seven member states exceeded— and still does—the GDP of our fifty United States.[55] Still, there was concern that the European Union might begin to lag behind the United States, as well as China and India, Asia's awakening giants, in the years ahead.

The European Union had staked out its claim to be the "most sustainable" economy on the planet. But could it reach its climate change targets and still achieve economic growth? This seemingly contradictory agenda was a source of continuing tension, both among the member states and even within President Barroso's own commission.

Our companies were in the room to tell the president, "Yes, we can!" All of this brings us back to the retort, "no more pilots," that changed the tenor of the meeting.

Daimler, whose founders, Gottlieb Daimler and Karl Benz, were the first inventors to successfully put an internal combustion engine on wheels, was determined to lead the automotive world again by putting the first mass-produced hydrogen fuel cell cars on the market. The company was well advanced in its research and development, having effectively tested fuel cell vehicles on the roads for several years. In fact, Daimler's hydrogen-powered buses (as well as other companies') were already carrying passengers in Hamburg, Amsterdam, London, Berlin, Madrid, and other cities as part of the CUTE (Clean Urban Transport for Europe) project, an EU initiative to replace the gas-powered internal combustion engine with a zero-emission vehicle whose only exhaust is pure water and heat.

The problem for Daimler, like the other companies sitting across the table, was one of scale-up. The entire CUTE bus order was only forty-seven buses, an order so miniscule that the cost of producing each bus was more than €1 million. CUTE, like so many programs being offered in Europe and other countries, including the United States, Japan, and China, was a pilot. Governments like pilots because they introduce sexy, green technologies that don't require spending significant public funds to ensure scale-up and a commercial market. What Kohler was saying, in effect, is that it's time to "fish or cut bait." He realized that the only way to effectively move this new revolution in transport to the consumer market was to first get government buy-in on a large scale, with a sizable expenditure of public funds committed to purchasing large numbers of vehicles for public fleets—early mass adoption by governments would bring the costs of production down and create the scale-up necessary to move into the broader commercial market. Forty buses wouldn't cut it.

Everyone else in the room had a similar story to tell. They were fed up with pilots and anxious to create an economic revolution, but felt stymied in their efforts—even despairing that their breakthrough technologies and products might sit on the shelf for decades, if not forever.

THE SILO EFFECT

There was a second, related problem that needed to be addressed if the European Union was going to tackle climate change, secure energy independence, and grow a sustainable world-class twenty-first-century economy all at the same time. The way the European Commission's departments and agencies were set up encouraged siloed initiatives—that is, programs and projects that were autonomous, self-contained, and unconnected to efforts going on in other departments and agencies. This phenomenon is not unique to Brussels. In fact, it's endemic in governments around the world. By failing to connect initiatives across departments and agencies, governments diminish the prospects of finding synergies and creating a more holistic approach to advancing the general well-being of society. Siloed thinking inevitably leads to isolated pilot projects.

President Barroso and his commissioners were aware of the problem and making efforts to work on joint initiatives across agencies. I was particularly impressed by the "big picture" thinking of some of the key commissioners who would come to play a critical role in fashioning the various elements of a TIR economic plan—Günter Verheugen and Margot Wallström, vice presidents of the European Commission; Andris Piebalgs, the commissioner for energy; Janez Potočnik, the commissioner for science and research; Stavros Dimas, the commissioner for environment; Neelie Kroes, the commissioner for competition; and Joaquín Almunia, the commissioner for economic and monetary affairs. Still, systemic thinking is a difficult task in a bureaucratic environment where there is a strong drive to hold on to turf and protect domains. This is what leads to what I call the DG (director general) abyss—the process by which big-picture ideas, agreed to at the ministerial level and even higher at the head-of-state level, lose their heft and become increasingly smaller and more narrow in vision and scope as they descend down into the departments and agencies, finally ending up as a shadow of their former selves, languishing in the minutia of countless reports, studies, and evaluations, whose purposes become increasingly obtuse, even to those tasked with managing them.

To her great credit, Catherine Day, the secretary-general of the European Commission—who is responsible for coordinating the various initiatives of the commission's departments and agencies—was relentless in her efforts to keep the various sustainable development efforts on track, mindful of the need to find synergies and coherency between all of the many projects being pursued. Despite her best efforts and those of the commissioners, there was an almost endemic bureaucratic drive to disassociate initiatives into autonomous enclaves.

We came into the meeting with President Barroso prepared to discuss how we might begin to address the issues of perpetual pilots and the silo effect. Several members of the group were actively involved in some of the European Union's technology platforms—formal EU public/private research initiatives made up of representatives of key industries and sectors whose mission is to recommend new EU-wide programs to advance the European economy.

Claude Lenglet, an engineer representing Bouygues, the giant French construction company, was a lead player in the European Construction Platform. As mentioned previously, another member of our group, Pier Nabuurs, the CEO of KEMA, was serving as president of SmartGrids Europe, the EU technology platform made up of IT and power and utility companies. Both gentlemen pointed out to President Barroso that few of the thirty-six European technology platforms talked to each other or exchanged any kind of information, despite the many potential synergies that existed among them. We ran down a list of thirteen technology platforms, among the thirty-six, whose missions were critical to each other's success and needed to be integrated if we were to establish a comprehensive approach to usher in a Third Industrial Revolution in the European Union. They included the Construction Technology Platform, the SmartGrids Platform, the various renewable energy platforms, the hydrogen and fuel cell technology platform, the European Road and Rail Transport Platforms, and the Sustainable Chemistry Platform, among others. Together, these platforms represented the technologies, industries, and sectors of an emerging TIR infrastructure. President Barroso's response was, "Let's put this together, get them talking, and see what emerges." With the help of Maria da Graça Carvalho, principal adviser to the Bureau of European Policy Advisers (BEPA), we began immediately and held several meetings with the thirteen platforms in the spring of 2007 to explore potential collaboration.

Barroso was at least trying to connect some of the dots. There was a deeper reason, however, for why the European Union and governments everywhere were toying with green pilot projects and becoming bogged down in siloed initiatives, seemingly unable to move beyond them: they didn't know what "beyond" meant. What was missing was a compelling narrative that could tell the story of a new economic revolution and explain how all of these seemingly random technological and commercial initiatives fit into a bigger game plan. The business leaders attending the Barroso meeting were there to lay out that larger vision and hoped to persuade the president that the European Union needed to seize the moment and commit the world's largest economy to a new Third Industrial Revolution.

The groundwork had already been laid earlier that year. Getting the European Union behind a change of this magnitude—transforming the industrial infrastructure of the continental economy and creating a new economic era—required the backing of Germany, Europe's economic engine. As fortune would have it, just months after arriving in office, the new chancellor of Germany, Angela Merkel, had asked me to come to Berlin to debate one of Germany's leading economists, on how to create new jobs and grow the German economy in the twenty-first century. I began my remarks by asking the chancellor, "How do you grow the German economy, the EU economy, or, for that matter, the global economy, in the last stages of a great energy era and an industrial revolution built on it?" (The price of oil was already rising in world markets but wouldn't peak at $147 per barrel until July 2008.) I went on to outline a Third Industrial Revolution vision and expressed my belief that Germany would lead the way into the new economic era.

After the debate, we shared a glass of wine and settled into a more informal discussion. I was aware that the chancellor had previously been the environmental minister in Chancellor Helmut Kohl's government and that she was a physicist by training. She thoroughly understood the technological aspects of creating a distributed and collaborative Third Industrial Revolution and the vast commercial opportunities that could flow from it, and told me she particularly liked the idea for Germany. I asked why Germany, thinking she would discuss the economic reasons why her country—at the time, the number-one exporting nation in the world—might want to lead the charge and continue to hold its commanding edge in the global economy. Instead, she shifted focus from commerce to politics and said, "Jeremy, you need to be more knowledgeable about the history and politics of Germany. We are a federation of regions. All politics here are locally driven. The federal government is the mediator. Our role is to find consensus and promote collaboration among the regions and lead the country forward. The Third Industrial Revolution, because of its distributed and collaborative nature, fits German politics."

The chancellor's enthusiasm was critical, especially since, as mentioned, her government would take over the six-month rotating presidency of the European Council in January of 2007. During her presidency, the EU heads of state would have to decide on a binding deal to address energy security and climate change.

I would be remiss if I didn't point out that Merkel's governing coalition partner at the time, the Social Democrats, were equally enthusiastic about the Third Industrial Revolution and would come to play an important role in ensuring that the 20–20–20 benchmarks being proposed by the European Commission would be supported by the European Council. Sigmar Gabriel, Germany's Social Democrat environmental minister, was particularly active in making sure that the environmental ministers of the other twenty-six member countries were on the same page when it came to forging an agreement on climate change targets. Germany's Socialist foreign minister, Frank-Walter Steinmeier, made sure that the foreign ministers of the EU member states were also on board with the proposed climate change benchmarks. Although the Green Party was not part of the governing coalition, it had played a prophetic role in German politics for more than two decades, warning of the dangers of climate change and the need to transition into post-carbon renewable energies. As far as German politics goes, the stars were all perfectly aligned for Germany to make its mark during Merkel's presidency of the European Council by gaining passage of the 20–20–20 by 2020 formula, and thus propelling the European Union to the forefront of a new, sustainable economic and environmental agenda for the world.

THE EUROPEAN PARLIAMENT ENDORSES THE THIRD INDUSTRIAL REVOLUTION

Merkel's presidency of the European Council heightened interest around climate change and energy independence and what kind of economic initiatives would be needed to realize the 20–20–20 by 2020 benchmarks. The prospect of a green economic model for Europe in the twenty-first century was circulating in the political corridors in Brussels and in the member states.

A group of us began holding a series of strategy meetings in Brussels and by teleconference, with an eye toward winning over the European Parliament to a Third Industrial Revolution vision and game plan for the European Union. Joe Leinen, a leader in the European Socialist Party and one of the Parliament's most respected senior members, was chairman of the Constitutional Affairs Committee at the time and the man responsible for drafting the declaration. He was joined by Claude Turmes of the Greens, the Parliament's passionate point man on climate change, and Angelo Consoli, a seasoned political operative who represented my office in Brussels. The formal written declaration, if passed by the Parliament, would commit the EU legislative body to a long-term Third Industrial Revolution economic sustainability plan for Europe.

Written declarations are difficult to achieve in the European Parliament. Few ever pass. Knowing we only had three months, according to the European Parliament rules and procedures, to secure the needed support to gain a majority (written declarations must be passed within ninety days), our group decided to concentrate on securing the support of party leaders and the chairpersons of key Parliamentary committees—never an easy task in a legislative body encompassing so many diverse interests and fractious political affiliations. To ensure the needed votes for passage, Leinen teamed up with five highly regarded parliamentarians, each representing the major political groupings in Parliament—Anders Wijkman of the European Peoples Party (EPP), Vittorio Prodi of the Liberal Party, Zita Gurmai of the Socialists, Claude Turmes of the Greens, and Umberto Guidoni of the Parties of the Left. Thanks to the tireless efforts of the group, and especially Mr. Consoli, we were able to secure the endorsement of Hans-Gert Pöttering, the president of the European Parliament, the titular leaders of all of Europe's leading political parties from right to left as well as the support of important committee chairpersons including Angelika Niebler of the powerful Industry, Research and Energy Committee, Karl-Heinz Florenz, chairperson of the Environment Committee, and Guido Sacconi of the Climate Change Committee.

In May 2007, the European Parliament passed a formal declaration, committing the legislative body of the twenty-seven member states of the European Union to a Third Industrial Revolution. The Parliament's strong support of the new economic vision sent a clear signal to the rest of the world that Europe was embarking on a new economic journey.[56]

In the closing weeks of the German presidency of the European Council, the German government asked me to present a keynote address to the twenty-seven environmental ministers of the EU member states in Essen, Germany, laying out the new Third Industrial Revolution economic game plan that would accompany the 20–20–20 by 2020 mandate brokered by the chancellor. I told the ministers that what the European Union needed was not a climate change plan or energy plan but, rather, a sustainable economic development plan that would bring Europe, and hopefully the world, to a zero-emissions post-carbon era by 2050 and, by so doing, address the fundamental challenge of both global warming and energy security. Many of the environmental ministers had already come to that realization, while a few others were still siloed in strict environmental policies that were only marginally attached to broader economic initiatives.

THE CHECKLIST

All five of the pillars described above make up the infrastructure for a new economic system—one that can take us into a green future.

Making the change from a carbon-based fossil fuel energy regime to a renewable energy regime: check! Reconfiguring the building stock of the world, transforming every dwelling into a mini power plant that can collect renewable energies on site: check! Installing hydrogen and other storage technology in every building, and across the entire infrastructure of society, to store intermittent renewable energy and ensure a continuous, reliable supply of green electricity to meet demand: check! Using Internet communication technology to convert the electricity grid into an intelligent utility network so that millions of people can send green electricity generated near and on their buildings back to the grid to share with others in open-source commons, not unlike the way information is generated and shared on the Internet: check! Transitioning the global transportation fleet—cars, buses, trucks, trains—to electric plug-in and fuel cell vehicles powered by renewable energies generated at millions of building sites and creating charging stations across countries and continents where people can buy and sell electricity on the distributed electricity grid: check!

When these five pillars come together, they make up an indivisible technological platform—an emergent system whose properties and functions are qualitatively different from the sum of its parts. In other words, the synergies between the pillars create a new economic paradigm that can transform the world.

Europe is further along than the United States, Japan, China, and other nations in the transition to a Third Industrial Revolution. Still, I don't want to leave the impression that the European Union is at a full gallop. Quite the contrary is true. It's just finding its legs. There is a growing awareness within the business community, in the civil society, and in the political corridors of governments of the nature of the journey Europe has set out for itself. Yet, not everyone is prepared or even ready to take the trip. But, at least there is intent and a sense of mission in the air—although there is no guarantee that the European Union will even stay on course. It could conceivably run out of steam or even backtrack. If that were to happen, I'm not sure which other nations might step to the gate and take the world into the next era.

THERE IS NO INEVITABILITY to the human sojourn. History is riddled with examples of great societies that collapsed, promising social experiments that withered, and visions of the future that never saw the light of day. This time, however, the situation is different. The stakes are higher. The possibility of utter extinction is not something the human race ever had to consider before the past half century. The prospect of proliferation of weapons of mass destruction, coupled now with the looming climate crisis, has tipped the odds dangerously in favor of an endgame, not only for civilization as we know it, but for our very species.

The Third Industrial Revolution is not a panacea that will instantly cure the ills of society or a utopia that will bring us to the Promised Land. It is, however, a no-frills, pragmatic economic plan that might carry us through to a sustainable post-carbon era. If there is a plan B, I have yet to hear it.

CHAPTER THREE
TURNING THEORY
TO PRACTICE

September 2008. It was a very hot summer—the twelfth hottest on record.[1] Climatologists took note of the heat and warned that it was another sign that the planet was entering a new phase. Real-time climate change was here, more than a century earlier than scientists had previously predicted.

The weather wasn't the only thing heating up. In July, the price of oil had hit a peak of $147 per barrel, spreading fear around the world. Purchasing power plummeted. Sixty days later, the US banking community, already hemorrhaging from bad loans in the subprime mortgage market, froze lending, bringing Wall Street to a standstill.

There was uncertainty everywhere about the future of the global economy—did we even have a future? A sense was bubbling up in the collective consciousness that this time it was different. Pundits and political leaders began using the "D" word; and although no business tycoons were jumping out of windows, the stock market was plunging, conjuring memories of unemployed people in the 1930s selling apples on street corners.

But what did they mean when they said, "This time it's different?" Bankers and politicians would spend more than two years in endless peripheral discussions about the nature of the crisis, never seeming willing or quite able to peel open the sheath and see what was underneath. Had they done so, they would have seen a Second Industrial Revolution on life support. While it was becoming acceptable, even fashionable, to talk about giant financial institutions that were simply "too big to fail," the idea of an economic era failing was too big to imagine—and so any such discussion was shelved indefinitely.

Many of the global companies and policy people I was regularly in touch with were not yet ready to admit that the Second Industrial Revolution was on its deathbed, preferring instead to go with the conventional wisdom that the bad times were a result of failed regulatory, monetary, or fiscal policies. Nonetheless, they sensed that the industrial way of life we grew up with in the twentieth century had passed its prime and was showing signs of senescence and decline. What's more important, each of them was pushing new, even radical business ideas that, if put together in the proper mix, were revolutionary.

TIR BUSINESS LEADERS LAUNCH A MOVEMENT

I made a call to Mark Casso, a Washington insider and president of the Construction Industry Round Table, a small, elite trade association made up of one hundred of the leading CEOs of American construction companies. Earlier, in October 2007, Mark had invited me to Grand Cayman Island to address the annual meeting of his group. Word was spreading in the United States about the Third Industrial Revolution model rolling out in the European Union and Mark thought his members would be particularly interested in pillar 2, the reconfiguration of the global building stock, transforming millions of buildings into micro–power plants to collect renewable energy on site. There was genuine interest among the group in green construction. A number of US companies were thinking along the same lines as their European counterparts and experimenting on their own. Mark and I promised to stay in touch.

To my surprise, I was invited back the following year to talk to the group again. After the second meeting, we discussed the possibility of hooking up the construction companies with some of the other companies my office had been working with in related fields. It wasn't until the summer of 2008, however, with the housing market tanking, the price of energy careening into the stratosphere, and the financial market in jitters, that it occurred to me that perhaps the time was right to bring the many disparate companies involved in one or more of the five pillars of the Third Industrial Revolution together for a face-to-face discussion about what, if anything, we might do together as a group to advance a TIR vision and game plan for

Europe, America, and the world. Mark agreed to have his trade association cohost the gathering.

On October 24, CEOs and senior executives from eighty global companies and trade associations crammed into a small conference room at the City Club in downtown Washington, DC, for a daylong conference. We did the quick preliminaries—going around the room so people could introduce themselves and talk about why their company or trade association was there and what they hoped would come out of the meeting. By the time we finished introductions, we had come to an informal consensus.

The economic crisis offered a moment of opportunity to advance a Third Industrial Revolution. Our individual efforts were not scaling quickly enough because they were being grafted onto a Second Industrial Revolution infrastructure, which didn't allow them to optimize their full potential. Instead, we were left with dangling appendages, alien pilot projects laid down in an inhospitable terrain. We could no longer go it alone. The five-pillar infrastructure of a Third Industrial Revolution provided us with a new economic vision. The key was to pull together as a group, but to what end? We weren't quite sure. We agreed to call ourselves the Third Industrial Revolution Global CEO Business Roundtable and pursue conversations with governments to push forward the new economic model.

In December, a delegation from our CEO roundtable met with Günter Verheugen, the vice president of the European Commission and the commissioner for enterprise and industry. Our delegation was made up of some heavy hitters—including Anton Milner, the CEO of Q-Cells, the largest photovoltaic company in the world; Ralph Peterson, the president of CH2M Hill, one of the world's premier construction companies; and Carmen Becerril, the president of Acciona Energía, one of the world's leading renewable energy companies.

Verheugen had long been the skeptic in the Barroso commission when it came to climate-change initiatives. It wasn't that he didn't believe that global warming was a real and ominous threat to the planet; he did. But he cautioned that the European Union needed to develop an approach to climate change that would advance commerce and mitigate global warming without compromising either objective. Verheugen and I had shared the podium at several public forums over the years and had the occasion to see each other privately as well. He became sold on the five-pillar Third Industrial Revolution infrastructure strategy as a way forward to ensure both a robust internal economy within the European Union and competitiveness in the global economy, all while advancing the European Union targets of 20–20–20 by 2020. He publicly announced his support of the Third Industrial Revolution at a formal luncheon and press conference held with representatives from our global CEO roundtable. We agreed that our group would be available to advise and consult with the European Commission on Third Industrial Revolution strategies. Our first foray in the international arena was a success and helped solidify the group.

But we still didn't have a clear mission in mind, other than to draw public attention to the merits of a Third Industrial Revolution vision. What was missing was a game plan. We found our groove, strangely enough, not in Europe but in San Antonio, Texas, America's seventh-largest city.

I had just finished delivering a talk before the American Mortgage Bankers Association at a meeting in Dallas, Texas. It was March 2008 and the residential and commercial real estate markets were in shambles. My audience consisted of the men and women who run mortgage banking operations in America. The mood was grim as I delivered the bad news about the deteriorating state of the Second Industrial Revolution. I was hoping that spirits might pick up when I outlined a vision of transforming the housing and commercial real estate market into a dual-purpose sector— dwellings would become energy producers. I told those assembled that converting the nation's building stock into mini power plants would resurrect the industry, spur a construction surge, and appreciate the real estate stock over the next two decades.

Most of the people in the room, however, were likely thinking more about just keeping their jobs and hoping their institutions wouldn't go under as the financial crisis spread across the mortgage industry. Although I came off the stage with the slim hope—it may have been more of a rationalization—that I may have at least planted a few seeds that would take root after the impending foreclosure wave had run its course, the truth is that the folks attending my talk that morning might have simply felt overloaded by the time I finished.

I was chatting with a few dignitaries immediately after the presentation, when a woman came over to me and introduced herself. Her name was Aurora Geis and she was the chairperson of CPS energy, the municipal power and utility company for the city of San Antonio. She said she was inspired about the vision of a Third Industrial Revolution and what was going on in Europe and asked whether I would speak to her company at their annual board meeting in June. I agreed to do so.

The meeting was attended by top brass at CPS, members of the city council, representatives from the business community, and leaders of civil society organizations. The city was already well primed for a Third Industrial Revolution initiative. The mayor of San Antonio, Phil Hardberger, had set an ambitious goal of becoming the greenest city in Texas and positioning San Antonio as a national leader in the race to a sustainable, low-carbon future. Geis hoped that my visit with city leaders would galvanize support for a green agenda.

The talk was well received. But I could still sense some reluctance. After all, laying out a vision was one thing; transforming CPS and the entire city of San Antonio into a Third Industrial Revolution was quite another—especially since it had never been attempted before in the United States. Aurora and I sat down over a margarita, some salsa, and guacamole at her favorite Tex-Mex restaurant. I said, "Aurora, I've got an idea. Let me show you the future. The Third Industrial Revolution already exists. Tell your board of directors to get their passports in order, pack their bags, and make arrangements to fly to Spain where my European director, Angelo Consoli, will escort you around the country. You will meet executives of the leading Third Industrial Revolution companies, visit state-of-the-art solar and wind facilities, tour zero-emission buildings and Third Industrial Revolution technology parks." After thinking over my proposal for a few days and conferring with her board of directors, Aurora gave the green light.

The visit, which took place in November 2008, was anything but a vacation. Consoli kept the CPS board busy with fourteen-hour workdays, during which they visited with scientists, engineers, entrepreneurs, city officials, and community groups. By the end of the trip the board members were exhausted. More important, they were converts. The trip was a transformational moment. They were able to see and touch the future.

Within weeks, my office had signed a consulting contract with CPS and the city to prepare a master plan to convert San Antonio into the first post-carbon city on the North American continent.

PREPARING MASTER PLANS FOR THE WORLD

The following April, we held our first master plan workshop in San Antonio. Our team was made up of twenty-five high-level experts from some of the leading Third Industrial Revolution companies in the world—IBM, Philips, Schneider, GE, CH2M Hill, Siemens, Q-Cells, Hydrogenics, KEMA, and others. Our global policy team included Alan Lloyd, the former secretary of the California Environmental Protection Agency (EPA) and current president of the International Council on Clean Transportation; Byron McCormick, former executive director for hydrogen car development at GM; and world-renowned green architects and urban planning companies, such as Boeri Studio of Italy, Acciona, and Cloud9 of Spain. Seated on the other side of the table was an equally esteemed group of experts: engineers, department heads of city agencies, representatives from the mayor's office, and the management team of CPS energy.

Our Third Industrial Revolution Global CEO Business Roundtable had found its mission. In the next twelve months, our policy team would create master plans for Prince Albert II and the principality of Monaco, Mayor Gianni Alemanno and the city of Rome, and Vice Governor Wouter de Jong and the Province of Utrecht in the Netherlands. Three of those master plans can be reviewed on our website.

I'd like to walk you through what we've done and what we've learned, but there is a caveat. These master plans are works in progress and have a steep learning curve. With four master plans under our belt, we are picking up ideas every day, making new connections, revising past calculations, and rethinking projected targets. Nicholas Easley, our head of master plan operations, likes to say that taking hold of master plans is like being strapped into a roller coaster for a wild ride. The journey is exhilarating and full of surprises that require continuous mental repositioning along the way. The goal is to create infrastructure and an operable system for a new economic era, while keeping in mind the financials, including forecasting dependable return-on-investment schedules. Easley has spent many sixteen-hour days poring over reams of data and reports with our global team and representatives from the political jurisdictions we've contracted with to find workable formulas for delivering on the master plan's objectives. The truth of the matter is that we're all in one giant classroom, learning from each other as we go.

The TIR master plans are based on a revolutionary new conception of living space. Recall, I mentioned earlier that when new energy regimes converge with new communications mediums, the spatial orientation is fundamentally altered—what German psychologists call a "gestalt change." The First Industrial Revolution favored dense vertical cities that rose upward into the sky. The Second Industrial Revolution, by contrast, favored more decentralized suburban developments that stretched outward, in a linear fashion, to the horizon.

The Third Industrial Revolution brings with it a completely different configuration. Our development team is creating master plans that embed the existing urban and suburban spaces inside a biosphere envelope. We envision thousands of biosphere regions, each a node connected by Third Industrial Revolution energy, communications, and transport systems, in a network that spans continents.

We have little choice. We are stuck with an urban and suburban complex that will still be here well into the second half of the twenty-first century. But that same infrastructure, the inheritance of the First and Second Industrial Revolutions, is devouring vast amounts of fossil fuel energy and spewing carbon dioxide into the atmosphere. In the United States, approximately 50.1 percent of total energy and 74.5 percent of electricity is consumed by buildings, which constitutes 49.1 percent of all US carbon-dioxide emissions.[2]

The extent of the habitat problem came home to us in 2007. The year marked a great milestone in the human journey. According to the UN *State of the World's Cities Report 2008/2009,* for the first time in history, a majority of human beings were living in urban areas, many in megacities and suburban extensions with populations of 10 million or more.[3] We have become *Homo urbanus.*

Millions of people huddled together, stacked on top of each other in gigantic urban/suburban centers is a new phenomenon. Five hundred years ago, the average person on Earth might have met a thousand people in an entire lifetime. Today, a resident of New York City can live and work among 220,000 people within a ten-minute radius of their home or office in midtown Manhattan.

Only one city in all of history—ancient Rome—claimed a population of more than a million inhabitants before the nineteenth century. London became the first modern city with a population of more than one million people in the year 1820. By 1900, there were eleven cities with populations of more than one million people; by 1950, there were seventy-five such cities; and by 1976, 191 urban areas exceeded one million people. Currently, more than 483 cities contain populations of a million or more people and there's no end in sight because our population is growing at an alarming rate.[4] Currently, 364,000 babies are born every day on Earth.[5]

When the human race had to rely on solar flow, the winds and currents, and animal and human power to sustain life, the human population remained relatively small. The tipping point was the exhuming of large amounts of stored sun from beneath the surface of the Earth, first in the form of coal deposits, then as oil and natural gas. Fossil fuels harnessed by the steam engine and later the internal combustion engine, were converted to electricity and distributed across power lines, allowing humanity to create a host of other new technologies that dramatically increased food production and the manufacturing of goods and services. The increase in productivity led to an unprecedented growth in the human population and the urbanization of the world.

Still, no one is really sure whether this profound change in human living arrangements ought to be celebrated, lamented, or merely noted for the record. That's because our burgeoning population and urban way of life has been purchased at the expense of the demise of the Earth's ecosystems.

Incredibly, our species now consumes an estimated 31 percent of the net primary production on Earth—the net amount of solar energy converted to plant organic matter through photosynthesis—even though we only make up one-half of 1 percent of the total biomass of the planet.[6] With the human race expected to increase from nearly seven billion to more than nine billion people by midcentury, the strain on the Earth's ecosystems is likely to have devastating consequences for the future survival of all forms of life.[7]

The flip side of urbanization is what we are leaving behind on our way to a world of hundred-story office buildings, high-rise residences, and large swaths of land turned into suburban sprawl. It's no accident that as we celebrate the urbanization of the world, we are approaching another historic moment: the disappearance of the wild. Rising population, growing consumption of food, water, and building materials, expanding road and rail transport, and urban/suburban sprawl continue to encroach on the remaining wilderness, pushing its inhabitants to near extinction.

Our scientists tell us that within the lifetime of today's children, "the wild" will likely all but disappear from the face of the Earth. The Trans-Amazon Highway, which cuts across the entire expanse of the Amazon rainforest, is hastening the obliteration of the last great wild habitat. Other remaining wild regions from Borneo to the Congo Basin are fast diminishing with each passing day, making way for growing human populations in search of living spaces and resources.

Ancient Rome provides a sobering lesson on the consequences that flow from attempting to maintain unsustainable human populations in mega urban environments. Although it's difficult to imagine, Italy was a densely forested land at the beginning of Roman rule. Over a period of several centuries, however, the forest was stripped for lumber and the land was converted to crops and pasture for cattle. The destruction of forests left the land exposed to wind and flooding and led to the depletion of precious topsoil.

Over the same time period, Rome found itself increasingly relying on agricultural land across the Mediterranean to subsidize the luxurious lifestyles of the rich and to feed and clothe its slaves and armies. Agriculture made up over 90 percent of the government's revenue in the latter centuries of the empire as conquest of new lands gave way to colonization of rural land.[8] Already impoverished land continued to be overworked, in a desperate attempt to keep the revenue flowing to Rome—only further diminishing the soil base. By the third century, soil depletion in North Africa and across the Mediterranean led to mass depopulation of the countryside and the abandonment of agricultural lands.[9]

The loss of agricultural revenues weakened the central government and reduced services across the empire. Roads and infrastructure fell into disrepair. The once-powerful Roman armies, then ill-clad and poorly armed, found themselves spending more time scavenging for food than protecting the empire. Soldiers began deserting the ranks in droves, leaving Rome exposed to invading hordes from remote parts of the empire. By the sixth century, the invaders were at the Roman gates. The Roman Empire, which once ruled over most of the known world, collapsed. The city of Rome, which at its height claimed a population in excess of a million inhabitants, dwindled to less than a hundred thousand people living atop the rubble.[10] Mother Nature turned out to be a far more formidable foe than foreign armies in bringing the empire to its knees.

Now, try to imagine a thousand Romes forty years from now, each with one million or more inhabitants. It boggles the mind, and it is unsustainable. I don't want to spoil the party, but with the commemoration of the urbanization of the human race in 2007, we might have missed an opportunity to rethink the way we live on this planet. Certainly there is much to applaud in urban life; its rich cultural diversity, social intercourse, and dense commercial activity come readily to mind. But it's a question of scale. We need to consider how best to lower our population and develop sustainable urban environments that use energy and resources more efficiently, pollute less, and are better designed to foster human-scale living arrangements.

In the great era of urbanization and suburban extension, we increasingly distanced the human race from the natural world in the belief that we could conquer, colonize, and utilize the rich largesse of the planet without bringing ill consequences to future generations. In the next phase of human history, if we are to preserve our own species and conserve the planet for our fellow creatures, we will need to find a way to reintegrate ourselves with the rest of the living Earth.

With this in mind, our master plans introduce a five-pillar TIR infrastructure that reconnects existing living spaces, work spaces, and play spaces with the larger swath of the biosphere to which they belong.

THE ROMAN BIOSPHERE

What better city to showcase the new biosphere concept than Rome? When Mayor Gianni Alemanno asked us to create a forty-year master plan to transition the first great city of Western civilization into a Third Industrial Revolution city, we jumped at the opportunity.

What does it mean to extend the idea of Rome beyond its ancient walls to encompass the biosphere? The biosphere is the ecological zone that extends roughly forty miles from the ocean floor to the stratosphere and within which the Earth's geochemical processes interact with biological systems to maintain just the right conditions for the perpetuation of life on Earth. The complex feedback loops of the Earth's biosphere operate like an internal nervous system, assuring the well-being of the system as a whole.

Our growing awareness that the Earth's biosphere functions like an indivisible organism requires us to rethink our notions of the meaning of the human journey. If every human life, the species as a whole, and all other life forms are entwined with one another and with the geochemistry of the planet in a rich and complex symbiotic relationship, then we are all dependent on and responsible for the health of the whole organism. Carrying out that responsibility means living out our individual lives in our neighborhoods and communities in ways that promote the general well-being of the larger biosphere.

The Third Industrial Revolution economic development plan would transform the region of Rome into an integrated social, economic, and political space embedded in a shared biosphere community. The Roman biosphere is made up of three concentric circles. The inner circle comprises the historic core and residential neighborhoods. Beyond the city center is an industrial and commercial ring with many open spaces. And outside the industrial/commercial area, the land becomes even more open, forming the rural region that surrounds the metropolitan city. The biosphere model emphasizes zonal interconnectivity—bringing together the surrounding agricultural region with the commercial zone and the historic/residential core in a contiguous relationship connected by locally generated, renewable energies shared across a smart, distributed electricity power grid.

The city center will be renovated to assure accessible open space and traffic-free roads, allowing pedestrians to reclaim the streets and enjoy the historical surroundings. Improved public transport, cycling paths, and pedestrian routes will be phased in to facilitate this transition.

One of the primary concerns of the Roman government is how to increase inner-city population density and maintain a sense of community in the ancient heart of the city. Unfortunately, the current trend is toward depopulation of the city center and flight to suburban enclaves because of a lack of modern housing, severe traffic congestion, and air pollution. Although central Rome has a shortage of social housing, it has a surplus of office space. Therefore, our urban design group proposed that Rome convert now-defunct commercial buildings into new residential blocks— as both New York City and Chicago have done before—using innovative architectural techniques that echo some of the best elements of ancient Roman building design. The plan calls for leaving the historical facades intact to preserve the architectural heritage of central Rome, while excavating the central core of buildings to make room for communal gardens, like those of ancient Roman villas.

The greening of Rome will also include thousands of small public gardens scattered in neighborhoods across the historic/residential core. Carlo Petrini of the slow food movement has even initiated a project with Mayor Alemanno to lay out gardens in the city's schoolyards to be tended by Rome's students.

Surrounding a newly revitalized residential city center will be the green industrial/commercial circle—the hub of Rome's economy. We envision transforming the industrial/commercial ring into a laboratory for developing the technologies and services that will turn Rome into a model, low-carbon economy. Biosphere science and technology parks housing university extension centers, high-tech startup companies, and other businesses aimed at TIR industrial commerce and trade will be established across the industrial/commercial ring.

Similar TIR parks are already up and running in other countries. The Walqa Technology Park in Huesca, Spain, nestled in a valley in the Pyrenees, is among a new genre of technology parks that produce their own renewable energy on site to power virtually all of their operations. There are currently a dozen office buildings in operation at the Walqa Park, which are occupied by leading high-tech companies including Microsoft, Vodaphone, and other ICT and renewable energy companies.

The industrial/commercial ring will be designed as an attractive working environment with significant green space, and will be made up of zero-carbon-emission buildings and factories, powered by locally generated renewable energies and connected to combined heat, power, and distributed energy systems.

In the Roman biosphere, 80,000 of the 150,000 hectares of Roman land are designated as green space, a currently underused resource that could be more agriculturally productive. In the twentieth-century model of urban development, cities became increasingly divorced from the production of the food they consumed. The distant production and long-haul transportation of food has become a major source of greenhouse gas emissions. This problem is frequently underestimated, as urban carbon footprint calculations tend to focus only on emissions generated by processes within the city boundaries, rather than emissions embedded in the food consumed by city dwellers and produced elsewhere. A city's ecological footprint can be significantly impacted by its dietary choices. A beef-based diet, in particular, increases the emission of methane, nitrous oxide, and carbon dioxide, the critical greenhouse gases that have the most significant impact on climate change.

The Rome master plan calls for the resettlement of underutilized and abandoned rural land in the outer ring by introducing hundreds of organic farms growing native fruits, vegetables, and grains. The agricultural region will be a living exhibition of the Italian slow food movement, utilizing state-of-the-art ecological farming practices. Open-air country markets, country inns, and restaurants will feature local cuisine and promote the nutritional benefits of a Mediterranean diet. Agricultural research centers, animal sanctuaries, wildlife rehabilitation clinics, plant germplasm preservation banks, and arboretums will also be established in the rural circle to revitalize the Roman biosphere.

Rome's green outer circle also offers a tremendous opportunity as a site for large-scale renewable energy projects that utilize wind, solar, and biomass energies. Renewable energy parks will be situated throughout the agricultural ring and integrated unobtrusively into the rural landscape.

All of these innovations are designed to rejuvenate the Roman biosphere and transform the region into a relatively self-sufficient and sustainable ecosystem that can provide much of the basic energy, food, and fiber to maintain the Roman population. With imaginative planning and marketing, the rural ring could be turned into a magnificent biosphere park and become one of Rome's major tourist attractions for its millions of visitors.

The Rome master plan, which is being coordinated by Livio de Santoli, the Dean of the School of Architecture at La Sapienza University, on behalf of Mayor Alemanno, has been formally incorporated as the centerpiece of the long-term economic and social development plan of the city.

Reconceptualizing metropolitan areas and their surrounding regions as biospheres is a challenging task. But where do cities, regions, and countries get the money to finance changes on the scale we're proposing, especially in a period of slow growth and shrinking government revenues?

A GREEN BUSINESS PLAN FOR SAN ANTONIO

San Antonio, our first master plan city, offered a good test case. While it is the seventh largest US city, it's also relatively poor compared to many other major metropolitan regions. Compounding this difficulty is the fact that CPS, San Antonio's municipally owned power and utility company, is the city's cash cow, accounting for a fourth of its operating revenue. And because CPS is municipally owned, it has traditionally kept the price of electricity relatively low, compared to other metropolitan regions that rely on privately owned power and utility companies for their electricity.

How, then, do we accomplish San Antonio's goal of a 20 percent reduction in greenhouse gas emissions and a 20 percent increase in renewable energy generation by 2030? If CPS reduces the electricity sold in the city by a significant amount, it will reduce the city's revenue. If it attempts to increase the price of electricity to encourage efficiency and discourage waste, the population will be even poorer, which will negatively affect the local economy.

While one of America's major metropolitan areas, San Antonio is also the home of a large Latino minority that has benefited very little from the steady economic advances of the post–World War II era. When I first started meeting with city officials and business and civic leaders, I couldn't help noticing how much attention they focused on what they called the "two San Antonios." Hardly a single conversation passed without someone using the term. The nagging reality of a well-heeled, largely white middle class and a disenfranchised, underemployed Latino underclass is never far from anyone's mind in this city that claims to be the gateway between the Spanish-speaking world to the south and the English-speaking world to the north.

The intersection between the cultures, however, is sullied by history. At the very center of the city lies the Alamo, the famed Spanish mission where a major battle was fought in 1836 in the war between an incipient Republic of Texas and Mexico over territorial claims. Although the Texans were defeated at the Alamo, they went on to win the war, annexing much of the former Mexican territory into the new republic. The Alamo is now the most visited tourist destination in Texas, and a critical source of revenue for the city—making it a source of pride for some, and a constant reminder of loss for others.

CPS was hoping that the TIR master plan could generate a fresh new stream of economic activity for all of its residents, while transforming the region into the first near zero-carbon-emission, sustainable economy in North America. A tall order, by any account.

Fortunately, the city wasn't coming to the table empty handed. Unlike many northern, industrial cities that have been declining since the auto age peaked in the 1980s, Bexar County, which encompasses the larger San Antonio metropolitan region, has significantly outpaced the US economy between 1980 and 2008, with a 58 percent faster growth rate.[11] This is in part because of the strong financial and insurance sectors, which make up 20 percent of the employment.[12] The only declining sector in Bexar County is manufacturing. While US manufacturing employment grew by 25 percent, San Antonio experienced a net loss of 40,000 manufacturing jobs.[13]

The city was banking on the prospect that the creation of a five-pillar Third Industrial Revolution infrastructure over the next twenty years would put thousands of people back to work—especially in the manufacturing sector and building trades—and provide new vocational opportunities for a fast-growing younger population.

San Antonio's weak manufacturing sector turned out to be a plus. Because there was so little manufacturing activity in the county compared to other major metropolitan areas (the number of manufacturing jobs per capita in San Antonio is about half the number in other regions in the United States), San Antonio began with a smaller carbon footprint.

If San Antonio could narrow the socioeconomic gap between the Latino and Anglo communities and, at the same time, address the dual challenge of climate change and energy security, it would become a lighthouse for the rest of the country.

We created a detailed economic model of the city and projected growth trends, factoring in a wide range of economic and sociological variables, and then calculated what San Antonio's CO_2 gas emissions would be in a "business as usual" scenario—using a 2005 emissions inventory—between 2008 and 2030. We found that emissions would rise by 17 percent, from 27.2 million metric tons of CO_2 in 2008 to about 31.8 million metric tons by 2030.[14]

To achieve the global gas emission reduction targets we had set, however, the city and county would have to reduce their CO_2 emission from 27.2 million metric tons in 2008 to just over 16 million metric tons by 2030. The reductions would have to be even more dramatic between 2030 and 2050 if the metropolitan area was to reduce CO_2 by 80 percent of current levels by mid-century—the percentage scientists say is necessary throughout the developed world to mitigate global warming to a 2 degree Celsius rise or less.[15]

The master plan would require a complete rethinking of the San Antonio economy. When we ran the numbers, we found that reaching San Antonio's target would require an overall investment of between $15 and $20 billion between 2010 and 2030.[16] The key term here is *investment*. All of our master plans are economic development plans, not merely government expenditures. While governments are often deeply involved in the process, they expect a return on their investment.

At a time when governments are experiencing a decline in revenue and expenditures are being cut to balance budgets, the inevitable first question is, "How can we afford to make the transition?" But perhaps the better question is, "How can we afford not to?" With the Second Industrial Revolution in deep decline, the only way to stimulate growth in the economy is to transform it. And more important, the money is already there.

For one thing, every metropolitan region, county, and state invests a percentage of its GDP each year just to keep the economy afloat, whether it's for new roads, schools, transport, industrial equipment, new power plants, or transmission lines.

American companies are currently flush with reserves, holding a record $1.6 trillion in profits made over the past few years, despite the Great Recession.[17] San Antonio is projected to invest, on average, approximately $16 billion per year in the economy between 2010 and 2030. We calculated that if the city were to invest just 5 percent of its yearly economic commitment, or about $800 million a year, it could reach its targets and make the transition into a new economic era. In other words, if San Antonio's private and public sectors merely invested the equivalent of one year of its economic development money over the next twenty years—a total of $16 billion spread out over twenty years—it could become the nation's first low-carbon Third Industrial Revolution city.[18] That means that the city could still allocate 95 percent of its investment to shoring up the old Second Industrial Revolution infrastructure, ensuring it against a potential collapse during the period of transition.

Why is so little investment required? It is because the cost of maintaining an old infrastructure in steep decline, with mounting expenditures, is relatively high compared to that of creating a fresh, new infrastructure. Mending a worn-out infrastructure provides few new economic opportunities and adds little real value to the economy. New infrastructure, by contrast, spawns all kinds of symbiotic, synergistic, and ancillary business ventures and enterprises.

Again, this assumes that the city takes a systems approach in laying out a new infrastructure. The real multiplier effect occurs when the interaction between pillars gives rise to a new emergent paradigm. While each of the five pillars that make up the Third Industrial Revolution infrastructure, taken alone, would add only marginal value to the economy, when they are connected in an interactive system that acts like an evolving organism, the new economy takes off. And just like any organism, it passes through a juvenile, mature, and senescent stage.

I stress this because our team ran up against a miscommunication that threatened to undermine our efforts in the weeks just before CPS was to formally release the master plan to the public. CPS told news sources that our Third Industrial Revolution plan was going to cost a whopping $16 billion and significantly increase electricity bills. This figure was quoted out of context, without any accompanying information. The immediate reaction by a few media outlets, naturally, was that the master plan would drain the city coffers and rapidly increase the cost of electricity to city residents. We hurried to do damage control and explained that the $16 billion was to be spread out over twenty years and that it represented barely 5 percent of the annual economic investment that the private and public sector already spends. We further explained that the economic multiplier effect of creating a new infrastructure would regenerate the economy, creating all sorts of new businesses and jobs. When the report was finally published, and the business community, civic groups, and city council were able to place the $16 billion in context, the tempers abated, allowing the city to evaluate the plan in a thoughtful, reflective way.

A NUCLEAR MELTDOWN

The press misunderstanding was but a slight digression. Of far greater consequence was a serious error in judgment made by CPS executives in the weeks immediately before publication of the master plan, which would ignite a public scandal and force the resignation of key senior staff and the chairperson of the company's board of directors. The political fallout forced the master plan to the sidelines while the city sorted out the mess. Luckily, the scandal itself and the corrective actions taken by the mayor and city council eventually strengthened the case for a Third Industrial Revolution rollout for San Antonio.

From my earliest discussions with Aurora Geis, prioritizing the future energy sources for CPS and the city of San Antonio was an issue of great concern. CPS was headed down two energy paths, and each was being aggressively pursued. They had a stake in both nuclear power and wind, and were flirting with a significant ramp-up in solar power.

CPS is a major stakeholder in two nuclear power plants that provide a significant portion of the city's electricity. In 2006, with the US and San Antonio economies both experiencing blistering growth, CPS became concerned that if the existing growth curve continued upward, the city would face an energy shortfall by 2016. To fill the projected deficit, CPS management concluded that it would have to radically ratchet up its "base load" power—the minimum amount of power needed twenty-four hours a day—via either new coal power generation or nuclear power generation. They chose the latter, reasoning that nuclear power doesn't emit CO_2 and is therefore a clean-energy option that would allow the city to continue to pursue its sustainability goals.

CPS entered into a partnership with NRG Energy and together created a joint venture with Toshiba to develop two new nuclear reactors. Each company would own 40 percent of the project known as "Nuclear Innovation North America (NINA)" and a buyer would be found to take up the remaining 20 percent ownership share. In 2007, CPS and NRG submitted an application to the US Nuclear Regulatory Commission to build the nuclear reactors—this was the first new application to build nuclear power plants in the United States in twenty-eight years, since the near meltdown of the Three Mile Island nuclear power plant in Pennsylvania in 1979.[19] The city committed $276 million to preliminary site design work, but with the requirement that CPS reduce the 5 percent rate increase it wanted to impose on customers to help pay for the new power generation to 3.5 percent.[20]

At the same time, CPS was substantially increasing its wind generating capacity. With 910 megawatts of renewable energy already under contract—94 percent of which is Texas Wind—CPS could boast that it was producing more renewable wind power than any other municipally owned power company in the United States. Could CPS afford to expand both nuclear power and renewable energy?

There were three additional factors to consider. First, there was vocal public opposition to nuclear power expansion. Civic organizations were worried about environmental risks, as the specter of Three Mile Island had never fully receded. There was also concern over the nagging question, still unresolved sixty years into nuclear power generation, of how to transport and store deadly nuclear waste.

Second, the city council was anxious about cost overruns in building the two power plants, fearing that the city and taxpayers would be stuck with an ever-escalating bill, devastating the city's revenue stream and the local economy.

Third, there was the question of which of the two energy paths was more likely to spur new economic opportunities and create much-needed jobs.

These issues came up repeatedly in our private discussions with CPS Energy as well as in our public meetings. Aurora Geis had an epiphany of sorts after the field trip to Spain, but did she understand that the two energy paths CPS was pursuing were at philosophical loggerheads? The deeper issue was whether the city would continue relying on the traditional, centralized energies of the twentieth century or begin to make the long-term transition to the distributed energies of the twenty-first century. At stake were two very different approaches to providing energy—one top-down and the other peer-to-peer. Choosing the latter course would require a complete rethinking of what power and utility companies do to make money.

Interestingly, there was only a single mention of nuclear power in the entire 133-page master plan report. Our team had inserted a CPS graph detailing risk assumptions regarding the various energy sources CPS was considering. CPS's own analysis showed that the costs for building a nuclear facility could be 6 percent lower than projected on one end and as much as 50 percent higher than projected on the other end (CPS's first two nuclear reactors built in the 1980s ran a staggering 500 percent over the initial cost projection).[21] By contrast, the costs for installing wind could be 10 percent lower or 15 percent higher than projected. The spread risk for solar was approximately the same as for wind.[22] The graph was accompanied by the following text:

> Assumptions regarding the risks associated with projected costs for these options should be carefully considered. Any investment which ends up costing in the upper range of uncertainty could absorb the discretionary capital that might otherwise be available for investing in sustainable development initiatives that could contribute to the transition to the Third Industrial Revolution.[23]

This single reference to the potential cost risks associated with the installation of new nuclear power plants would come back to haunt CPS. As it turns out, just a month after our master plan was officially released, and three days before the San Antonio city council was to vote on investing an additional $400 million in the $8.5 billion nuclear project, the mayor's office was informed that Toshiba had increased its projected costs for the two nuclear reactors by an incredible $4 billion. Apparently some senior executives at CPS had known about this cost hike weeks earlier and had not informed the CPS board of directors or the city council.

When the news got out, heads rolled. Bartley was dismissed, and Aurora Geis, the CPS board chair, despite her innocence in the matter, was pressured by the new mayor, Julián Castro, to take responsibility for the concealment by tendering her resignation. Even before the disclosure of costs overruns, Geis had expressed concern that CPS was putting too much stock in nuclear at the expense of transitioning into the new renewable energies and distributed power. She had even been working quietly behind the scenes to reduce the city's commitment from 40 percent ownership to 20 percent—just enough investment to cover CPS's projected nuclear power needs. Mayor Castro had agreed to the new pared-down commitment in August.

With projected costs now hovering at $12 billion, and with new independent estimates putting the figure closer to $17 to $20 billion, the city decided to bail.[24] In an agreement between CPS, NRG, and Toshiba, brokered by Mayor Castro, CPS reduced its share in the Texas nuclear plants from its initial 40 percent to a final figure of 7.6 percent, or a total commitment of $1 billion.[25]

Incidentally, even though the city of San Antonio is off the hook, the American taxpayer is not. The joint venture with NRG, NINA, and Toshiba is still actively courting investors and seeking a loan guarantee from the US Department of Energy so it can green-light the project. If cost overruns were to occur, threatening the solvency of the venture, the American taxpayer would end up paying part of the bill.

The showdown over nuclear power highlighted another contentious issue for San Antonians: the question of jobs. When then-mayor Phil Hardberger hosted our global team at the three-day master plan workshop in April 2009, he made the point that the city's major interest was finding new ways to generate sustainable power while optimizing new employment opportunities, especially for the city's working class and poor. Our task was to examine new energy options that would both be clean and put people to work.

The nuclear industry likes to tout the fact that building large-scale nuclear reactors creates jobs. In a 2010 editorial, Christine Todd Whitman, the former New Jersey governor and EPA director under President George Bush, claimed that constructing a new generation of nuclear power plants could create "as many as 70,000 new jobs" across the country.[26] On closer inspection, however, the employment prospects look less attractive.

Building a single reactor produces only 2,400 construction jobs, and once the reactor is online, it requires only 800 full-time workers. To get to the 70,000 jobs the former governor projects, it would be necessary to build twenty-two nuclear power plants, at a cost of $200 billion or more, and it would take twenty years or more to construct them—a huge investment in time and money for such a small increment of growth in employment. In contrast, according to the Union of Concerned Scientists, one of the nation's most highly regarded scientific associations, if the federal government were to establish a requirement that utilities obtain 25 percent of their electricity from renewable energies, it would generate nearly 300,000 jobs. Moreover, the $12 to $18 billion or more price tag of putting up two new Texas nuclear reactors equals the approximate total economic investment that would be necessary over the next twenty years to lay down a five-pillar Third Industrial Revolution infrastructure and reach the city's carbon emission reduction targets.[27]

What about all the additional power that the nuclear power plants would have brought online? The energy growth projections CPS used were based on conventional models that may not be as relevant in the future. Utilities have long counted on load growth and annual sales growth between one and two percent.[28] This rule of thumb has remained constant for forty-five of the last fifty-eight years. But as consumers begin using less energy and producing more of their own power, there will be a noticeable decline in demand. Power demand in Texas was down 3.2 percent in 2009.[29] Similar declines in power use are occurring across America and Europe, forcing a reassessment of future power needs and growth predictions.

It's possible that an increase in electricity demand for Internet and other communications-related services and for plug-in electric vehicles could boost the growth of power in the years to come. The question is whether that demand is met primarily with conventional energies—fossil fuels and nuclear—or increasingly from renewable energy sources. CPS is clearly moving toward the latter.

The nuclear debacle put San Antonio's Third Industrial Revolution rollout on the back burner for the better part of a year. As of this writing, the city and the power company are just getting back in the saddle, as they like to say in Texas, in pursuit of their goals of leading the nation into a new post-carbon future. Their energy efficiency program is among the best in the country. CPS and the city have already saved 142 megawatts of electricity in the past two years and have set a target of a 771-megawatt reduction in electricity use by 2020. Building on their already significant achievement in renewable energy generation of 910 megawatts, San Antonio expects to generate 1,500 megawatts of renewable energy by 2020.[30] CPS is also beginning to assemble a smart grid, with a two-year initiative to install 40,000 smart meters in buildings across the metropolitan region. CPS has also entered into an agreement with GM to provide power charging stations for the Chevy Volt.[31] All in all, San Antonio is on its way toward a TIR economy.

COUNTERINTUITIVE COMMERCE

The most important challenge facing CPS is transforming its business model and management style to accommodate the requirements of a new distributed-energy era managed by Internet communication technology. European power and utility companies are facing a similar challenge, and soon, so will every other power and utility company in the world.

Like other power companies, CPS has traditionally produced its own power and then sold it to end users. Now, the new business model has CPS buying electricity from some of its own customers and distributing it back to others. Likewise, CPS's mission in the past had been to produce and sell more electricity. Now its goal is to improve energy efficiency, therefore paradoxically selling less and less electricity. Though CPS will continue in its traditional guise of generating power from fossil fuel and uranium in a centralized management and distribution system for some time to come, it's also going to need to move aggressively into the new business model of managing other people's energy and helping them optimize their energy uses while increasing their energy efficiency.

We suggested that CPS consider new business opportunities along the entire value chain of a Third Industrial Revolution infrastructure. For example, CPS Energy and the city could get into the business of financing, manufacturing, and servicing the various components and processes that make up the five-pillar infrastructure of a Third Industrial Revolution.

It's worth noting that neither CPS nor the city will be able to implement an economic game plan of this dimension alone. To achieve its objective of becoming America's leading Third Industrial Revolution region, the city and CPS will have to secure full customer participation. Small- and medium-sized enterprises (SMEs), cooperatives, Common Interest Developments (CIDs), neighborhood associations, and environmental and consumer groups are all potential players and partners in the implementation of a TIR game plan for San Antonio and South Texas.

Many of the challenges facing San Antonio are shared by the surrounding counties. We suggested that San Antonio position itself as the center of an energy network by bringing together utility companies, other energy providers, and users, with the aim of establishing a TIR infrastructure across the entire southern region of Texas.

During the time I spent with the folks at CPS Energy, I couldn't help but wonder what my mother would have thought about the radical experiment they were undertaking. My mom, who passed away in 2007 at the age of ninety-six, was born in El Paso, Texas, in 1911. Her side of the family had settled in Texas in the 1890s. On January 10, 1901, oil prospectors drilling at the Spindletop field in Beaumont, Texas, hit oil at 1,020 feet—letting loose a gusher that rose more than 150 feet into the air. That single well drew 100,000 barrels a day, more than all of the other oil wells in the United States at the time put together.

When my mother was growing up, thousands of wildcatters were drilling under the ground across Texas in the hopes of finding black gold. Many did, and Texas became synonymous in the public mind with big oil. America, in turn, became the preeminent world power of the Second Industrial Revolution.

How strange, or perhaps fitting, that a new generation of Texas wildcatters are harnessing the wind and sun, determined to make Texas the preeminent green power state. Their efforts could pave the way for the United States to grab hold of the reins of the next energy rush and regain its lead in the world by transitioning into the soft energies of the Third Industrial Revolution.

My mom, no doubt, would be tickled by the turnaround in Texas. She probably would remind me of the old Texas adage, "If you find yourself in a deep hole, stop digging"—a good piece of native wisdom at the end of the oil era.

FAST-TRACKING MONACO

Just three months after our global team conducted its three-day master plan workshop for San Antonio, I was invited by Prince Albert II of Monaco to bring the team to his tiny principality on the southern coast of France in the Côte d'Azur region.

I first met Prince Albert in February 2007 in Paris. I had been asked by French President Jacques Chirac to host a high-level workshop for government and business leaders from around the world on the day that the UN Intergovernmental Panel on Climate Change was to issue its long-anticipated *Fourth Assessment Synthesis Report* in Paris. The workshop was tasked with exploring the various economic initiatives that would be required to transition the global economy to a post-carbon era. Prince Albert was one of the panelists.

When most people think of Monaco, they picture the high life that attracts the rich and famous from around the world, the annual Formula

One Grand Prix race, and the gilded Belle Époque Casino. But there is another side of Monaco that is equally deserving of attention. Prince Albert's grandfather, Prince Albert I, was the first head of state to take up the cause of preserving the world's oceanic ecosystems. After a 1906 sailing trip around the world where he collected data and conducted studies on marine life, Prince Albert established the world-renowned Oceanographic Institute—the first scientific body to study the oceans in depth, with an eye toward conserving life under the sea. Prince Rainer III continued the work, becoming a respected international voice for marine protection. During his reign, Monaco became the first Mediterranean country to discharge only "clean, potable municipal wastewater and run off into the sea."[32]

What so impressed me at the Paris workshop was the Prince's in-depth knowledge of the science of climate change and the pragmatic approaches he was implementing in Monaco to address the crisis. Realizing the drastic impacts that climate change is already having on the world's oceans, Prince Albert II has turned his attention to the challenge of global warming and become a leading spokesman among world leaders on the issue. Under his guidance, the principality of Monaco has launched a series of environmental initiatives designed to make it a model for Europe and the world.

I caught up with the prince again in March 2009. I was in Monaco to address an annual conference on cutting-edge Third Industrial Revolution technologies that brings together some of the world's best minds in the tech sector with green entrepreneurs and financial institutions. The annual conference is the brainchild of Mungo Park, a savvy entrepreneur with a keen sense of the tech community and a talent for picking the likely winners among the thousands of green technologies competing for attention. Mungo enjoys a close relationship with the monarchy and suggested that the two of us meet with the prince to discuss issues of mutual interest.

We were ushered into a small room cluttered with books and ancient maps. It looked like the kind of early-twentieth-century study one might see in *Raiders of the Lost Ark*. Prince Albert is a quiet, self-effacing man who, I suspect, would have been just as comfortable devoting his lifetime to scientific pursuits, had he not been born into a royal family.

The prince was worried about the Copenhagen Climate Change talks scheduled for the end of the year and concerned that not enough attention was being given to developing a systematic, economic approach to addressing global warming. He was aware of the economic development model I had prepared for the European Union and asked how he could be helpful in advancing a Third Industrial Age. I suggested that what we needed were working models and that Monaco would be a good test site for some of the newest ideas—especially since it was already far along in its climate change initiatives. The prince agreed and we set a date to bring our team together with his ministers and technical experts to draft a Third Industrial Age master plan for the principality of Monaco. Our hope was that the master plan could be completed by October for Prince Albert to present it as a visionary game plan to other world leaders at the Copenhagen Climate Change talks. Given the short time, we rolled up our sleeves and got down to work.

Although Monaco, like San Antonio, brought our team in to help them reach the 20–20–20 by 2020 target, the two entities couldn't be more different. Monaco is an independent sovereign nation governed as a constitutional monarchy. While San Antonio is a sprawling city with a large underclass, Monaco is a dense, urban enclave, sandwiched between the Mediterranean Sea and the mountains, and home to some of the wealthiest people on Earth. The GDP per capita is €51,092 and it has zero percent unemployment. The government's operating budget is €744,209,751.[33] There is no income tax. Rather, government revenue is generated via a 20 percent value added tax and a 5 percent sales tax. The principality's landmass of less than two square kilometers is home to 35,000 inhabitants. The population doubles each day as a result of the commuter population and tourists.

Actually, I should probably clarify the notion of who resides in Monaco with an admission that was put on the table the first day our global team met with the principality's overseers. We were told that many of Monaco's wealthiest residents live there only infrequently, using their residences more as vacation homes. Because there is no income tax, however, they claim their homes as primary residences—all of which, we learned, creates an embarrassing, little-mentioned, environmental problem. In order to prove their primary-residence status, homeowners must provide monthly copies of their utility bills to show they are occupying the premises. The result is that appliances are often kept running, 24/7, even when the residences are not being occupied, wasting energy and adding to the tiny principality's CO_2 footprint. The government is trying to address the problem, in part, by offering a handsome subsidy to convert residences into green mini power plants that can send clean energy back to the grid (more about this later in the chapter).

The first question we asked was where does Monaco get its energy? Seventeen percent of its electricity comes from sea water pumping, while 25 percent of the heating and cooling demands are met through a waste-to-energy incineration plant.[34] Most of its electricity comes from France, which relies primarily on nuclear energy for power generation.

Monaco's building stock is crammed into such a small space that there is virtually no open land available for large-scale energy parks. What it does have, however, is six kilometers of coastline that could be harnessed to generate wave and wind energy and an unusually high solar irradiance rate, which could be harnessed via solar thermal or photovoltaic cells to generate energy.[35]

The big challenge in Monaco is how to collect the high solar irradiance on the buildings without compromising the architectural heritage. The principality made it very clear to us that it did not want to alter the look or feel of the buildings, including their color or form.

Twenty-four percent of Monaco is roof space, half of which is suitable for photovoltaics (that is, south-facing and not overshadowed). We estimated that more than 30 percent of Monaco's renewable energy target of fifty giga-watt hours by 2020 could be met by solar photovoltaic energy generation from rooftop panels.[36] We could double the solar energy generation using the facades of buildings as collection points. Much of the remaining solar potential could be harvested by leasing open land just over the border in France and erecting solar trackers. Our team also suggested testing a still-experimental offshore photovoltaic system that would allow the principality to collect the sun's energy over the Mediterranean Sea. A prototype offshore photovoltaic system, with a diameter of one hundred meters, is already being tested in Abu Dhabi in the Persian Gulf. Floating photovoltaic pods far off the shoreline and out of sight could provide an additional 15 percent of the renewable energy the principality needs to reach its 2020 target.[37]

The government is serious about turning its buildings into mini power plants and is offering a 30 percent subsidy—capped at a maximum of €30,000—to support the installation of solar photovoltaic systems.[38] But how do we do it without making the city look like a giant power generating system?

Our architectural group and urban planners consulted with our energy specialists and came up with some workable ways to get the energy without compromising the aesthetics of the urban landscape. Most photovoltaic cells are dark blue and attached to rather unattractive paneled scaffolding.

If Monaco's buildings were decked out in photovoltaic panels, the effect would be disastrous.

Fortunately, companies are now incorporating small photovoltaic cells directly into terracotta roof tiles, building canopies, walls, glass, shutters, and even blinds, concealing them in every available external surface.

Wind technology can also be incorporated on the buildings. This surprises many people, since when we think of wind generation, what comes to mind is giant wind turbines assembled in rows in large wind parks. Recently, however, new vertical axis wind turbines have been developed that do not need to rotate and can absorb the more turbulent air that exists in dense urban areas. These vertical axis wind turbines can be positioned on top of existing buildings in Monaco to expand its renewable power generation capability.

Green roofs and walls are also becoming vogue and we recommended them for Monaco. Incorporating plants onto the built infrastructure reduces storm water runoff, increases thermal mass (diminishing the urban heat island effect in summer and helping retain heat in winter), and expands urban biodiversity. In 1998 the city of Basel, Switzerland, launched a green-roof initiative and today 20 percent of the flat roof area of the city is green. Toronto, Canada, and Linz, Austria, now require all new flat-roof buildings to be green. All of these efforts—solar, wind, and green roofs—help reconnect Monaco to its own swath of the biosphere and encourage biosphere consciousness.

A final note on Monaco: Every world-class locale has its own unique cultural narrative. For Monaco, it's fast cars. Auto racing and Monaco are synonymous in the public mind. In our master plan, we proposed that the principality set an example for the world by changing over their small public bus fleet from gasoline-powered internal combustion engines to hydrogen-powered fuel cell vehicles. Because of Monaco's small size, it could make the transition quickly and at minimal cost, becoming the first country in the world to have a zero-emission public transport system.

After the wrap-up of our executive workshop in Monaco, Byron McCormick from our policy group and I sat down with Mungo Park at the hotel bar to brainstorm an idea Mungo had been playing with. What about having a second annual automobile race in Monaco with electric plug-in and hydrogen racing cars from around the world? The vehicles would be powered by the electricity garnered from solar cells, vertical wind, and other renewable energies collected by the buildings of Monaco. Could there be any better way to demonstrate the passing of the Second Industrial Revolution and the coming of the Third Industrial Revolution? I was curious to see Byron's reaction. Here was a man who had spent a lifetime at General Motors and was among a select few responsible for the company's future car development, including hydrogen fuel cell vehicles. His response was quick and earnest: "Where do I sign up?"

As our team finished its business in Monaco, packed up, and headed for the airport, my thoughts turned to whether the mecca that drew the rich and famous could be rebranded as the place where cutting-edge, high-tech sustainability became the new aesthetic standard for the world.

"DECARBONIZING" UTRECHT

If Monaco is all about play, Utrecht is all about work. Industrious by nature, entrepreneurial in spirit, and pragmatic to a fault, this small province, tucked into the hinterland of the Netherlands, is a no-nonsense place where business rules the day. The province is one of the fastest-growing regions in the European Union. Unemployment is low, the standard of living is relatively high, and the region boasts a world-class university, which makes it a critical hub in the European knowledge economy.

Unlike some of the other jurisdictions we worked with, Utrecht doesn't suffer from a lack of planning. They have plans up the wazoo—ten-year plans, twenty-year plans, which are worked out in the kind of detail one rarely sees at a provincial governing level. I suspect that people who have had to keep ahead of the flood waters for centuries have the planning instinct indelibly imprinted into their collective DNA.

The point is, the Dutch make a habit of preparing against dangers that lie ahead—even more so now, in a world facing evermore volatile energy prices and shortfalls and the potentially devastating ecological and social dislocations brought on by human-induced climate change.

With this in mind, the province has set an ambitious agenda: to lead the regions of the European Union into a Third Industrial Revolution with a target of 30 percent reduction (10 percent beyond the EU target) in global warming gases by the year 2020 and to become carbon neutral by 2040. Only a handful of regions are presently contemplating what Utrecht has in mind.

To help achieve its goal, the province and the Third Industrial Revolution Global CEO Business Roundtable began a collaborative partnership to rethink economic development in the twenty-first century. The mission was to prepare Utrecht to become the first province of the biosphere era. If Utrecht can move on a fast-track trajectory that can get it to zero emissions in thirty years, it would likely inspire thousands of other regions to follow its lead.

Like other densely populated regions, Utrecht needs to expand its metropolitan area and build out new suburban communities to meet its demographic needs over the next twenty years. Utrecht had already made plans for the development of two new communities: Rijnenburg and Soesterburg. Rijnenburg will be a community of about seven thousand homes, while Soesterburg is a planned community of around five hundred homes. The province also needs to upgrade the existing infrastructure in its older metropolitan area.

The jurisdiction faces the same difficult challenge that confronts other fast-growing cities and regions: how to expand into new developments while ensuring that older sectors of the city are not left behind. Our task was complicated by the need to maintain economic growth and keep pace with a booming population while reducing the region's carbon footprint.

Instead of entering into the typical dichotomy of economic progress vs. environmental sustainability, the province began exploring the possibility of using growth to finance green redevelopment. In other words, new buildings, which would normally require more energy and add to the existing CO_2 bill, would be required to maintain carbon neutrality, while assisting the older sectors of the city in upgrading their infrastructure.

The idea is similar to tax increment financing (TIF), which is used in redeveloping dilapidated areas in cities such as Chicago, Albuquerque, and Almeda. The basic idea is that the province would use the revenue generated from property taxes in the newly developed areas to finance urban renewal projects in the older sectors of the city. However, because the end goal of these initiatives is economic, the programs often receive criticism for being too much like a Robin Hood scheme—stealing from the rich and giving to the poor.

But if the notion of urban renewal also included energy savings and environmental protection for the whole region, "energy financing" would ultimately benefit both the rich and the poor. The property tax revenue from new developments could be put into a fund that would help subsidize building owners in blighted areas of the city to retrofit their buildings. Retrofitting buildings results in less energy used, more energy savings, and less

CO_2 released into the atmosphere, thereby conferring a positive benefit on homeowners, businesses, and society as a whole.

Even with such an innovative financing plan in place, however, retrofitting an entire city is much easier in theory than in real life. As with any economic problem, the question becomes one of prioritization. How does a jurisdiction decide which buildings to retrofit first? Weatherizing single homes is a great idea and can have a significant impact on energy use, but retrofitting the Willis Tower in Chicago, for example, will save enough electricity to power 2,500 homes.

It became clear that the province of Utrecht would need a plan that is inclusive and makes sense financially. Adrian Smith + Gordon Gill Architecture, an urban planning firm out of Chicago and a member of our global development team, proposed a software solution for Utrecht that would involve the entire community in reaching its zero-emissions goal.

The plan involves building a virtual 3-D model of the city. The first step would be to work with students and professors at the local university to conduct comprehensive energy audits of all buildings in Utrecht. Public buildings would be audited first, then residential and commercial buildings. Each building would then be classified based on its potential for energy savings (that is, the red buildings would have the most potential energy savings, the yellow buildings would have the second-greatest potential, and so on).

After the energy savings potential is quantified, the next step is to estimate the cost of retrofitting each of the structures. Once this information is available, it then becomes much clearer where the first investments should be made. With both the energy savings potential identified and the investment cost estimated, the only steps remaining are securing financing and vetting projects and proposals.

The virtual, 3-D decarbonization model creates an online marketplace for energy. One of the largest barriers to residential retrofits is profitability. For this reason, energy services companies (ESCOs) mostly focus on large, commercial projects because they are more profitable, while the margin on a single house, by comparison, is very small. Energy information freely available to the public via the Internet, however, creates the potential for solutions at scale. Instead of either a company creating a proposal for a single house or a resident trying to find a company to retrofit his or her building, all of the red buildings can be conjoined, or all of the yellow buildings in a neighborhood can be combined, so that an ESCO can pool a cluster of buildings together and offer a greatly reduced price for the retro-fitting—thus, creating a project that is comparable in size and profitability to a large, commercial contract. The clustering approach brings ESCOs and property owners together within and across neighborhoods in a very public conversation around sustainability. Because scale-up requires a sufficient number of homeowners in a cluster agreeing to come together and be part of a collective retrofit, the process of securing "buy in" begins to solidify residents' support of the TIR game plan across neighborhoods.

Anxious to encourage more of this kind of community participation, the province of Utrecht has put up a website that contains the TIR master plan's analysis and recommendations, including a list of priority projects, and has a begun a conversation with its citizenry, the local business community, university researchers, and even high schools—essentially inviting the entire region into the game. The master plan has gone lateral. It is now a platform for a province-wide discussion on how to achieve a transition into a TIR economy.

People are critiquing parts of the master plan platform, offering their own ideas, and even voting on their favorite projects. In the process, the new players are connecting up to share their expertise, pooling their mutual interests, and creating networks within and across the five-pillar skeleton vision. The TIR has become a community exercise, the Dutch version of the old American barn raising, where the whole community comes together to build the structure. This is democratization of energy, and what distributed capitalism is really all about.

And it's working. The population of the province is becoming intimately engaged in its own economic future. "Not in my backyard" is being replaced by a collaborative effort to steward the neighborhood biosphere.

If there is a single lesson to take away from the experience we've garnered in engaging in master plans, it is that the process itself is a community exercise. That is, it requires the active participation of all three sectors—government, the business community, and neighborhood civil society organizations. Revolutionizing the infrastructure of a city, region, or nation intimately affects the lives of everyone by changing the way they live, work, and play. Making sure that every interest is represented at every step of the deliberative process ensures community support. Without a broad consensus on goals and objectives, it is unlikely that any political jurisdiction will have sufficient social capital to rally its citizenry for such fundamental structural changes.

THE MASTER PLANS have been an eye-opening experience for both the development team and localities. Among other things, we're beginning to realize that the Third Industrial Revolution changes more than our energy regime. The new system that emerges from the harmonization of the five-pillar infrastructure is so utterly different from the existing system that it is creating completely new business models as well. The elite, fossil fuel energies of the First and Second Industrial Revolutions favored vertical economies of scale and the formation of giant, centralized enterprises across the supply chain, which were managed by rationalized hierarchical organizations competing in adversarial markets. The amply available renewable energies of the Third Industrial Revolution, in contrast, give rise to thousands of distributed firms coming together in collaborative business relationships embedded in networks that function more like ecosystems than markets.

In the new era, competitive markets are going to increasingly give way to collaborative networks, and top-down capitalism is going to be increasingly marginalized by the new forces of distributed capitalism.

PART II
LATERAL POWER

CHAPTER FOUR
DISTRIBUTED CAPITALISM

Energy regimes shape the nature of civilizations—how they are orga- nized, how the fruits of commerce and trade are distributed, how po- litical power is exercised, and how social relations are conducted. In the twenty-first century, the locus of control over energy production and distribution is going to tilt from giant fossil fuel–based centralized energy companies to millions of small producers who will generate their own re- newable energies in their dwellings and trade surpluses in info-energy com- mons. The democratization of energy has profound implications for how we orchestrate the entirety of human life in the coming century. We are entering the era of distributed capitalism.

To understand how the new Third Industrial Revolution infrastruc- ture is likely to dramatically change the distribution of economic, political, and social power in the twenty-first century, it is helpful to step back and examine how the fossil fuel–based First and Second Industrial Revolutions reordered power relations over the course of the nineteenth and twentieth centuries.

THE OLD POWER ELITE

Fossil fuels—coal, oil, and natural gas—are elite energies for the simple reason that they are found only in select places. They require a signifi- cant military investment to secure their access and continual geopolitical management to assure their availability. They also require centralized, top-down command and control systems and massive concentrations of capital to move them from underground to the end users. The ability to concentrate capital—the essence of modern capitalism—is critical to the effective performance of the system as a whole. The centralized energy infrastructure, in turn, sets the conditions for the rest of the economy, encouraging similar business models across every sector.

Consider the railroad, which arguably was the centerpiece of the coal-powered, steam-driven First Industrial Revolution. The railroad became the prototype of the centralized business enterprises that would come to dominate the First and Second Industrial Revolutions. To begin with, building a railroad required capital outlays far beyond the capital requirements of textile mills, ships, canals, or other big-ticket items of the period. Even the wealthiest families couldn't afford to single-handedly bankroll an entire railroad. Funds had to be raised externally and even from faraway sources. To raise needed capital, railroads began to sell securities. Initially, it was European investors—British, French, and German for the most part—who bankrolled much of the early US railroad expansion.[1] The need for large amounts of concentrated capital catapulted the tiny provincial New York Stock Exchange into a behemoth, and made Wall Street the epicenter of modern capitalism.[2]

With the coming of the railroads, ownership became separated from management. A new genre of professional administrators took to the helm of these giant new enterprises, while ownership was diffused to the far corners of the Earth. The new overseers bore little resemblance to the small family proprietors idolized by classical economic theorists like Adam Smith and Jean-Baptiste Say at the dawn of the market era in the late eighteenth century.

The organizational challenges in running a railroad were without precedent. Laying out tracks over hundreds of miles of often harrowing terrain was difficult enough. Maintaining rail beds, keeping engines and cars repaired, and preventing accidents added to the organizational woes. Routing cargo and keeping up-to-the-moment records on the location of thousands of rail cars in transit and guaranteeing reliable schedules and on-time delivery of passengers across an entire continent was a herculean task that required layers of management and a gargantuan workforce.

To get an idea of how big this new type of enterprise really was, ponder this: In 1891 the Pennsylvania Railroad employed 110,000 workers, while the US military had only 39,492 men in arms. Even more startling, the total expenditures of the Pennsylvania Railroad were $95.5 million in 1893, nearly 25 percent of the total public expenditures of the US government. Even more revealing, the Pennsylvania Railroad's revenues that year were $135.1 million, while the federal government's revenues were $385.8 million.[3] And the Pennsylvania Railroad was only one of seven railroad groups that controlled two-thirds of the rail traffic in the United States.[4]

Coordinating a massive commercial enterprise the size of continental railroads was a daunting task. Rationalizing business operations became an essential part of the process of optimizing commercial opportunities.

What exactly does the rationalization of the business model entail? Max Weber, the eminent sociologist of the early twentieth century, went to the heart of the matter by defining the criteria and operating assumptions that were first employed by the railroads and later picked up by businesses in other industries. The modern rational business bureaucracy is characterized by a number of essential elements. The structure itself is pyramidal, with authority flowing from the top down. There are preestablished rules that govern all operations and detailed instructions for how jobs are defined and how work is to be carried out at every level of the organization. To optimize output, tasks are broken down by division of labor and the work is organized in a fixed series of stages. Advancement is based on merit and objective criteria. These various rationalizing processes allow a business to aggregate and integrate multiple activities and, by so doing, achieve an accelerated production flow, while maintaining control of overall operations.

Business historian Alfred Chandler grasps the essence of the new railroad management structure and its significance in establishing the prototype business model for other industries. He notes that railroads

were the first to require a large number of salaried managers; the first to have a central office operated by middle managers and commanded by top managers who reported to a board of directors. They were the first American business enterprise to build a large internal organizational structure with carefully defined lines of responsibility, authority, and communication between the central office, departmental headquarters, and field units; and they were the first to develop financial and statistical flows to control and evaluate the work of many managers.[5]

It's worth reemphasizing that centralized, top-down bureaucratic organizations like those put in place by railroads required a literate workforce. How could a giant enterprise like the railroad manage a sophisticated logistics operation without the ability to issue written orders down the chain of command and receive written reports from its army of workers spread out over vast spaces? A literate workforce is equipped with the communication tool that makes possible a commercial contract culture. Without print, it would be impossible to coordinate complex market transactions and keep informed of commercial activity across the supply chain. Modern bookkeeping, bills of lading, invoices, checks, and schedules are critical management tools in the organization of the modern business enterprise. Print also facilitated a uniform pricing system that is so vital to the operations of an industrial economy.

Big, centralized railroads had an immediate impact on transforming the industries they did business with. The sheer scale of activity required to build the rail infrastructure favored the creation of giant contracting companies to oversee hundreds of subcontractors in the construction process. The railroads also developed their own ancillary businesses. The Pennsylvania Railroad, as well as other lines, bought mining properties to ensure a readily available supply of coal for its locomotives. The company even financed the Pennsylvania Steel Works Company to make sure it would have the steel it needed to make rails.[6]

The railroads also midwifed the telegraph industry. In the early decades, railroads relied on single tracks on which ran two-way traffic. Accidents were frequent and costly. Railroad management quickly seized on the telegraph as a communications medium to monitor and coordinate rail traffic along the tracks. Western Union soon eclipsed its competitors by running its wires alongside rail beds and setting up telegraph offices at rail depots. The company's success was due, in no small part, to its adapting the same centralized, top-down management style used by the railroads.

The kind of large, rationally structured, centralized bureaucracies adopted by railroads were ideally suited for coordinating the more complex commercial relationships made possible by coal and steam power. The shrinking of distances and the annihilation of time, resulting from the convergence of coal- and steam-powered technology with print communications, sped up commercial activity at every stage of the supply chain, from the extraction and transport of coal and other ores to the factories, to the hurried transport of finished goods to wholesalers, distributors, and retailers.

The dramatic increase in the flow of commerce was matched by the equally impressive decrease in transaction costs. This was achieved, in large measure, by dint of the new vertical economies of scale. Mass-producing products in giant, centralized factories reduced the cost per unit of production, allowing manufacturers to pass the savings along the entire supply chain to the end user. The mass production of cheap goods encouraged more consumption, which allowed more factories to produce greater volumes of goods at ever cheaper prices.

Vertical economies of scale became the defining feature of the incipient industrial age and gigantic business operations became the norm. New businesses patterned after the railroad and telegraph organizational structures began to proliferate. Mass wholesalers emerged after the Civil War, followed by mass retailers, like Marshall Field's in Chicago, Macy's in New York, and Wanamaker's in Philadelphia. Mail-order houses like Montgomery Ward and Sears, Roebuck and Co. appeared around the same time.

The first national grocery chains—Grand Union, Kroger, Jewel Tea Company, and the Great Western Tea Company—took advantage of the new continental rail links and began consolidating their power over the food chain. By the early 1900s, small farms serving local markets began to give way to the first agribusiness operations, transforming food production into a factory system.

Brand products like Quaker Oats, Campbell soups, Pillsbury flour, Heinz, Carnation, American Tobacco, Singer Sewing Machine, Kodak, Procter and Gamble, and Diamond Match made their debut and quickly became a dominant new force, edging out small, local, cottage-run family businesses. The new brands established predictable pricing of products and standardized product quality, transforming consumption into a rational process that guaranteed uniformity across national markets.

The rationalization of production and distribution of products required a rationalization of the workforce itself. Frederick Taylor became the first management expert. His theory of scientific management was designed to recast the persona of the worker to comport with the operational standards that were used to maintain new, centralized, corporate bureaucracies. Taylor used efficiency principles already developed by engineers and applied them to workers with the expectation of turning them into living machines, whose performance could be optimized, much like the continuous production processes churning out standardized products.

Taylor believed that the best way to optimize worker efficiency was to separate thought from action and place total control over how a task was to be accomplished in the hands of management. "If the workers' exertion is guided by their own conception," according to Taylor, "it is not possible . . . to enforce upon them the methodological efficiency or the working pace desired by capital."[7]

Taylor took the core idea of executing rationalized authority in a centralized, top-down management scheme and imposed it on every worker. He wrote:

> The work of every workman is fully planned out by the management at least one day in advance, and each man receives in most cases complete written instructions, describing in detail the task which he is to accomplish, as well as the means to be used in doing the work. . . . [T]his task specifies not only what is to be done but how it is to be done and the exact time allowed for doing it.[8]

The principles of scientific management quickly crossed over from the factory floor and commercial offices into the home and community, making efficiency the cardinal temporal value of the new industrial age. Henceforth, maximizing output with the minimum input of time, labor, and capital became the *sine qua non* for directing virtually every aspect of life in contemporary society.

Nowhere were the new rationalizing principles of the modern business enterprise more welcomed than in the public school system, first in America and Europe and, later, the rest of the world. Turning out productive workers became the central mission of modern education. Schools took on the dual task of creating a literate workforce and preparing them to serve authoritarian and centralized businesses, where they would take orders from the top and optimize their output at the bottom in the most efficient manner possible, while never questioning the authority under which they labored.

The schools became a microcosm of the factories. One-room schoolhouses gave way to giant, centralized schools that, in appearance, could easily have been mistaken for factories. Students learned never to challenge the teacher's authority. They were given daily work assignments, along with detailed instructions on how to carry them out. Their tests were standardized and their performance was measured by the speed and efficiency of their responses. They were isolated into autonomous units and informed that sharing information with fellow students was cheating and a punishable offense. They were graded on the basis of objective criteria and promoted to the next grade on the basis of merit. This educational model has remained in force to the present day and is only just now coming into question with the emergence of the Third Industrial Revolution, whose distributed and collaborative nature requires a concomitant educational model.

The centralized and rationalized business model established during the First Industrial Revolution carried over to the Second Industrial Revolution. In 1868, John D. Rockefeller founded the Standard Oil Company of Pennsylvania. Eleven years later, he controlled 90 percent of the refining operations in the United States.[9] After the US Supreme Court ordered the breakup of his holding company in 1911, forcing Standard Oil to reorganize into smaller companies in states where they were conducting business, other oil companies jumped into the market. Each of the companies sought to aggregate every aspect of the oil supply chain into a single integrated business, allowing them to control oil fields, pipelines, and refineries, as well as the transport and marketing of the products, all the way to the neighborhood gas station.

By the 1930s, twenty-six oil companies, including Standard Oil of New Jersey, Gulf Oil, Atlantic Refining Company, Phillips 66, Sun, Union 76, Sinclair, and Texaco, owned two-thirds of the capital structure of the industry, 60 percent of the drilling, 90 percent of the pipelines, 70 percent of the refining operations, and 80 percent of the marketing.[10] In 1951, oil overtook coal as the leading energy source in the United States.[11]

Automobile companies followed suit. Dozens of car companies formed in America and Europe in the first two decades of the twentieth century. But by 1929, the field had narrowed to a handful of giants and a few hangers on. In the United States, the big three automakers—GM, Ford, and Chrysler—dominated the industry.

The telephone companies were even fewer in number at the inception. AT&T seized the field of operation, becoming a virtual monopoly, which it remained until the 1980s when it, too, was broken up.[12]

While many economists and virtually every politician of the past century tirelessly extolled the virtues of the small business entrepreneur—painting a Rockwellian picture of thousands of neighborhood enterprises driving the engine of modern capitalism—a far different history has unfolded in the real world of commerce and trade. The oil age from its onset has been characterized by gigantism and centralization. That's because harnessing oil and other elite fossil fuels requires large amounts of capital and favors vertical economies of scale, which necessitates a top-down command and control structure. The oil business is one of the largest industries in the world. It's also the most costly enterprise for collecting, processing, and distributing energy ever conceived by humankind.

Virtually all of the other critical industries that emerged from the oil culture—modern finance, automotive, power and utilities, telecommunications, and commercial construction and that feed off of the fossil fuel spigot—were, in one way or another, similarly predisposed to bigness in order to achieve their own economies of scale. And, like the oil industry, they require huge sums of capital to operate and are organized in a centralized fashion.

Three of the four largest companies in the world today are oil companies—Royal Dutch Shell, Exxon Mobil, and BP. Underneath these giant energy companies are some five hundred global companies representing every sector and industry—with a combined revenue of $22.5 trillion, which is the equivalent of one-third of the world's $62 trillion GDP—that are inseparably connected to and dependent on fossil fuels for their very survival.[13]

In the 1950s, the president of General Motors, Charles Erwin Wilson, is reported to have said something to the effect of "What's good for General Motors is good for the country."[14] True, but we need to appreciate the deeper reality that the internal combustion engine is a machine designed for turning oil into power and mobility. It is fossil fuels and, in the twentieth century, primarily oil, that is the prime mover of the economy. British politician Ernest Bevin once quipped that, "The kingdom of heaven may be run on righteousness, but the kingdom of earth runs on oil."[15]

It goes without saying that the beneficiaries of the oil era, for the most part, have been the men and women in the energy and financial sectors and those strategically positioned across the First and Second Industrial Revolution supply chain. They have reaped extraordinary fortunes.

By the year 2001, the CEOs of the largest American companies earned, on average, 531 times as much as the average worker, up from 1980 when that figure was only forty-two times greater. Even more startling, between 1980 and 2005, over 80 percent of the increase in income in the United States went into the pockets of the wealthiest 1 percent of the population.[16]

By 2007, the wealthiest 1 percent of American earners accounted for 23.5 percent of the nation's pretax income, up from 9 percent in 1976. Meanwhile, during the same period, the median income for non-elderly American households declined and the percentage of people living in poverty rose.[17]

Perhaps the most apt description of the top-down organization of economic life that characterized the First and Second Industrial Revolutions is the often-heard "trickle-down theory"—the idea that when those atop the fossil fuel–based industrial pyramid benefit, enough residual wealth will make its way down to the small businesses and workers at lower levels of the economic ladder to benefit the economy as a whole. While there is no denying that the living standards of millions of people is better at the end of the Second Industrial Revolution than at the beginning of the First Industrial Revolution, it is equally true that those on the top have benefited disproportionately from the Carbon Era, especially in the United States, where few restrictions have been put on the market and little effort made to ensure that the fruits of industrial commerce are broadly shared.

THE COLLABORATIVE ECONOMY

The emerging Third Industrial Revolution, by contrast, is organized around distributed renewable energies that are found everywhere and are, for the most part, free—sun, wind, hydro, geothermal heat, biomass, and ocean waves and tides. These dispersed energies will be collected at millions of local sites and then bundled and shared with others over intelligent power networks to achieve optimum energy levels and maintain a high-performing, sustainable economy. The distributed nature of renewable energies necessitates collaborative rather than hierarchical command and control mechanisms.

This new lateral energy regime establishes the organizational model for the countless economic activities that multiply from it. A more distributed and collaborative industrial revolution, in turn, invariably leads to a more distributed sharing of the wealth generated.

The partial shift from markets to networks brings with it a different business orientation. The adversarial relationship between sellers and buyers is replaced by a collaborative relationship between suppliers and users. Self-interest is subsumed by shared interest. Proprietary information is eclipsed by a new emphasis on openness and collective trust. The new focus on transparency over secrecy is based on the premise that adding value to the network doesn't depreciate one's own stock but, rather, appreciates everyone's holdings as equal nodes in a common endeavor.

In industry after industry, networks are competing with markets, and open-source commons are challenging proprietary business operations. Microsoft, a traditional market-based company with tight proprietary control over its intellectual property, was unprepared for the likes of Linux. The first of many open-source software networks, the Linux community is made up of thousands of software programmers who collaborate together, devoting their time and expertise to correct and enhance software code being used by millions. All of the changes, updates, and improvements made to the code are kept in the public domain, available without charge to everyone in the Linux network. Hundreds of global companies like Google, IBM, the US Postal Service, and Conoco have joined the Linux open-source network and become part of its ever expanding global community of programmers and users.

Similarly, the major encyclopedia companies like Britannica, Columbia, and Encarta, which traditionally paid academics to write scholarly articles for their extensive sets of hardcover books containing the condensed knowledge of the world, were unable, in their wildest imaginations, to anticipate Wikipedia. Twenty years ago, the very idea that hundreds of thousands of professional and amateur scholars from all over the world would collaborate with one another to create academic and popular essays on virtually every conceivable topic, in every discipline, without pay, and make the information available to everyone on the planet, would have been unthinkable. Incredibly, the English version of Wikipedia has more than 3.5 million entries—and is almost thirty times the size of Encyclopedia Britannica.[18] Even more amazing is the fact that tens of thousands of people fact-check and reference the articles, keeping the accuracy of the contributions competitive with conventional encyclopedias. Today, Wikipedia is the eighth most visited site on the Internet, attracting around 13 percent of Internet visitors every day.[19]

Networks exist for sharing music, videos, medical information, travel tips, and thousands of other interests. Lateral search engines like Google and social networking sites like Facebook and Myspace have changed the way we work and play. Tens of thousands of social media networks, with communities reaching into the millions and hundreds of millions of members, have bloomed in less than fifteen years, creating a new distributed and collaborative space for sharing knowledge and spurring creativity and innovation across every field. Many of these open source platforms serve as hothouses for the incubation of new enterprises, some of which remain on the commons in cyberspace, while others migrate to the marketplace or nonprofit sectors.

REINVENTING THE WAY WE DO BUSINESS

Nothing is more suggestive of the industrial way of life than highly capitalized, giant, centralized factories equipped with heavy machines and attended by blue-collar workforces, churning out mass-produced products on assembly lines. But what if millions of people could manufacture batches or even single manufactured items in their own homes or businesses, cheaper, quicker, and with the same quality control as the most advanced state-of-the-art factories on earth?

Just as the TIR economy allows millions of people to produce their own energy, a new digital manufacturing revolution now opens up the possibility of following suit in the production of durable goods. In the new era, everyone can potentially be their own manufacturer as well as their own power company. Welcome to the world of distributed manufacturing.

The process is called 3-D printing; and although it sounds like science fiction, it is already coming online, and promises to change the entire way we think of industrial production. The process is amazing.

Think about pushing the print button on your computer and sending a digital file to an inkjet printer, except, with 3-D printing, the machine runs off a three-dimensional product. Using computer aided design, software directs the 3-D printer to build successive layers of the product using powder, molten plastic, or metals to create the material scaffolding. The 3-D printer can produce multiple copies just like a photocopy machine. All sorts of goods, from jewelry to mobile phones, auto and aircraft parts, medical implants, and batteries, are being "printed out" in what is being termed "additive manufacturing," distinguishing it from the "subtractive manufacturing," which involves cutting down and pairing off materials and then attaching them together.[20] Industry analysts forecast that millions of customers will routinely download digitally manufactured, customized products and "print them out" at their business or residence.

3-D entrepreneurs are particularly bullish about additive manufacturing, because the process requires as little as 10 percent of the raw material expended in traditional manufacturing and uses less energy than conventional factory production, thus greatly reducing the cost. As the new technology becomes more widespread, on site, just in time, 3-D printing of customized manufactured products will increasingly reduce logistics costs, with the possibility of huge energy savings. The energy saved at every step of the digital manufacturing process, from reduction in materials used, to less energy expended in making the product, and the elimination of energy in transporting it, when applied across the global economy, adds up to a qualitative increase in energy efficiency beyond anything imaginable in the First and Second Industrial Revolutions. When the energy used in the process is renewable and also generated on site, the full impact of a lateral Third Industrial Revolution becomes strikingly apparent.

In the same way that the Internet radically reduced entry costs in generating and disseminating information, giving rise to new businesses like Google and Facebook, additive manufacturing has the potential to greatly reduce the cost of producing hard goods, making entry costs sufficiently low to encourage hundreds of thousands of mini manufacturers—Small and Medium Sized Enterprises (SMEs)—to challenge and potentially outcompete the giant manufacturing companies that were at the center of the First and Second Industrial Revolution economies.

Already, a spate of new start-up companies are entering the 3-D printing market with names like Within Technologies, Digital Forming, Shape Ways, Rapid Quality Manufacturing, and Stratasys, and are determined to reinvent the very idea of manufacturing in the Third Industrial era. Manufacturing is going lateral, with immeasureable consequences for society.[21]

The democratization of manufacturing is being accompanied by the tumbling costs of marketing. Because of the centralized nature of the communication technologies of the first and second industrial revolutions—newspapers, magazines, radio, and television—marketing costs were high and favored giant firms who could afford to devote substantial funds to market their products and services. The Internet has transformed marketing from a significant expense to a negligible cost, allowing startups and small- and medium-sized enterprises to market their goods and services on Internet sites that stretch over virtual space, enabling them to compete and even out-compete many of the giant business enterprises of the twenty-first century.

To get a feel for how radically different distributed and collaborative business models are from the conventional centralized business models of the nineteenth and twentieth centuries, consider Etsy, a brash, web start-up company that has taken off in less than four years. Etsy was founded by a young New York University graduate, Rob Kalin, who made furniture in his apartment. Frustrated that he had no way to connect with potential buyers interested in hand-crafted furniture, Kalin teamed up with a few friends and put up a website designed to bring individual craftsmen of all kinds, from around the world, together with prospective buyers. The site has become a global virtual showroom, where millions of buyers and sellers from more than fifty countries are connecting, breathing new life into craft production—an art that had largely disappeared with the advent of modern industrial capitalism.

Textiles and other crafts fell victim to industrial production at the outset of the First Industrial Revolution. Local cottage industries could not compete with centralized factory production and the economies of scale made possible by large investments of financial capital. Factory goods were simply cheaper, which forced craft production to near extinction.

The Internet has changed the nature of the game by flattening the playing field. Connecting millions of sellers and buyers in virtual space is almost free. By replacing all of the middlemen—from wholesalers to retailers—with a distributed network of millions of people and eliminating the transaction costs that are marked up at every stage of the supply chain, Etsy has created a new global craft bazaar that scales laterally rather than hierarchically, and acts collaboratively rather than top-down.

Etsy brings another dimension to the market—the personalization of relationships between seller and buyer. The website hosts chat rooms, coordinates online craft shows, and conducts seminars, allowing sellers and buyers to interact, exchange ideas, and create social bonds that can last a lifetime. Giant, global companies mass-producing standardized products on assembly lines operated by anonymous workforces can't compete with the kind of intimate one-to-one relationship between artisan and patron. Kalin says that "this human-to-human relationship of the person who's making it with the person who's buying it is at the core of what Etsy is."[22]

Lateral peer-to-peer scaling and virtually nonexistent transaction costs—except for shipping—allow craft production to compete in price with mass production. Although still in its infancy, Etsy is a quickly growing enterprise. In the first half of 2009, when durable goods sales were flat around the world in the aftermath of the collapse of the global economy, the Etsy bazaar rung up $70 million in sales and added a million new sellers and buyers to its network. In 2011, sales topped nearly $500 million.

In a recent conversation, Kalin told me that his mission is to help foster "empathic consciousness" in the global economic arena and lay the foundation for a more inclusive society. His vision of creating "millions of local living economies that will create a sense of community in the economy again" is the essence of the Third Industrial Revolution model.[23]

Etsy is only one of hundreds of global Internet companies that are bringing together producers and consumers in virtual marketing spaces and, in the process, democratizing marketing costs across the global economy.

Just as network sites like Etsy give small craft producers access to a global market with nearly zero entrance costs, local generation of green energy will similarly reduce their production costs. As more and more craftsmen and small- and medium-sized businesses convert their small workshops to micro power plants, their production costs will fall precipitously, giving them a greater edge in the new, networked economy.

As the new 3-D technology becomes more widespread, on site, just-in-time customized manufacturing of products will also reduce logistics costs with the possibility of huge energy savings. The cost of transporting products will plummet in the coming decades because an increasing array of goods will be produced locally in thousands of micro-manufacturing plants and transported regionally by trucks powered by green electricity and hydrogen generated on site.

The lateral scaling of the Third Industrial Revolution allows small- and medium-sized enterprises to flourish. Still, global companies will not disappear. Rather, they will increasingly metamorphose from primary producers and distributors to aggregators. In the new economic era, their role will be to coordinate and manage the multiple networks that move commerce and trade across the value chain.

Recall that in the First and Second Industrial Revolutions, the cost of extracting, processing, and distributing fossil fuels was so expensive that only a few big, centralized players could amass the financial capital to manage the energy flow. Big oil required big banks.

Today, microfinance operations like the Grameen Bank, ASA, EKI, and other lenders disburse a total of more than $65 billion in loans to more than 100 million borrowers in the poorest regions of the world.[24] Micro-lending is increasingly being used to finance local green energy generation in places that have never before even had electricity. Grameen Shakti (GS), an offshoot of the Grameen Bank, provides small microloans for the installation of solar home systems and other renewable energy technologies for

thousands of rural villages. By the end of 2010, GS had financed the installation of half a million solar home systems at a rate of around 17,000 installations every thirty days. The company has trained thousands of women
as technicians, providing them with employment and assuring the proper
vocational expertise to maintain the installations.[25]

By distributing microloans to the poorest entrepreneurs on Earth, the
Grameen banking model successfully combines conventional, commercial
banking practices with the unconventional mission of eliminating the cycle
of poverty. Kiva, a nonprofit facilitator of microloans, takes the financing
process a step further by establishing a purely distributed and collaborative
banking model. Founded in 2005, Kiva's philosophical premise couldn't be
more different than the one that drives commercial banking. Its founders
believe that "people are generous by nature, and will help others if given
the opportunity to do so in a transparent, accountable way."[26] To advance
its mission, Kiva "encourages partnership relationships as opposed to bene-
factor relationships."[27] Every prospective entrepreneur has a profile page,
with a personal photo and description of what their loan would be used
for. Lenders choose the loan request that they would like to finance and the
amount—as little as a $25—and then team up with other lenders to fund
the full amount of the loan. All the lenders receive monthly updates on the
loan repayment.

The organizational process by which loans are made is truly distributed
in nature. Over one hundred field partners in various regions of the world
make the loans weeks before the loan requests are posted on Kiva's website.
The field partners then receive the loans from Kiva to replenish the loans
they have just made. The field partners set the interest rates for the loans.
Kiva does not charge any interest to its field partners, nor does it pay interest to its lenders. After the loan is paid back in full, the Kiva lender has a
choice to re-lend the funds to another entrepreneur, donate the funds to
Kiva, or withdraw the funds.

Using this innovative approach to microfinancing, Kiva has matched up
more than half a million lenders in 209 countries with 469,076 small entrepreneurs in fifty-seven countries. It has made loans totaling $178,338,325,
of which 81 percent have gone to women. Kiva's average loan is $380 and
the repayment rate is 98.9 percent.[28] All the loans go to small entrepreneurs
whose businesses tend to have a marginal ecological footprint.

New collaborative business practices are reaching into every aspect of
economic life. Community Supported Agriculture (CSA) is a good example

of the impact that new TIR business models are having on how food is grown and distributed. After a century of petrochemical-based agriculture, which led to the near demise of the family farm and gave birth to giant agrifarm businesses like Cargill and ADM, a new generation of farmers is turning the tables by connecting directly with households to sell their produce. Community supported agriculture began in Europe and Japan in the 1960s and spread to America in the mid-1980s.

Shareholders, usually urban households, pledge a fixed amount of money before the growing season to cover the farmer's yearly expenses. In return, they receive a share of the farmer's crop throughout the growing season. The share usually consists of a box of fruits and vegetables delivered to their door (or to a designated drop-off site) as soon as they ripen, providing a stream of fresh, local produce throughout the growing season.

The farms, for the most part, engage in ecological agriculture practices and utilize natural and organic farming methods. Because community supported agriculture is a joint venture based on shared risks between farmers and consumers, the latter benefit from a robust harvest and suffer the consequences of a bad one. If inclement weather or other misfortunes befall the farmer, the shareholders absorb the loss with diminished weekly deliveries of certain foods. This kind of peer-to-peer sharing of risks and rewards binds all of the shareholders in a common enterprise.

The Internet has been instrumental in connecting farmers and consumers in a distributed and collaborative approach to organizing the food supply chain. In just a few years, community supported agriculture has grown from a handful of pilots to nearly three thousand enterprises serving tens of thousands of families.[29]

The CSA business model particularly appeals to a younger generation that is used to the idea of collaborating on digital social spaces. Its growing popularity is also a reflection of the increasing consumer awareness and concern about the need to reduce their ecological footprint. By eliminating petrochemical fertilizers and pesticides, CO_2 emissions from long-haul food transport across oceans and continents, and the advertising, marketing, and packaging costs associated with conventional Second Industrial Revolution food production and distribution chains, each shareholder comes to live a more sustainable lifestyle.

An increasing number of CSA farmers are beginning to convert their farm properties to micro–power plants, harnessing wind, solar, geothermal, and biomass on site, thereby radically reducing their energy costs. The savings are passed along to their shareholders through cheaper annual membership and subscription rates.

Again, like so many of the other new, collaborative business practices that are taking hold across every commercial sector, the new, lateral scaling can, and often does, trump the traditional, centralized approach of creating gigantic organizations that scale vertically and organize economic activity hierarchically.

Some of the businesses most associated with conventional centralized market capitalism are now being challenged by the introduction of new distributed and collaborative business models. Take, for example, the car, the lynchpin of the Second Industrial Revolution. The shift into a Third Industrial Revolution economy, with its emphasis on increasing energy efficiency and reducing carbon footprint, has given rise to nonprofit car-sharing networks all over the world.

In America, car-sharing operations are sprouting up across the country. City Wheels in Cleveland, HourCar in Minneapolis/St. Paul, Philly Car Share, I-Go in Chicago, and City Car Share in San Francisco are among the new breed of nonprofit networked organizations providing mobility for hundreds of thousands of users. For a nominal membership fee, users join the car-sharing network and receive a smart card that gives them access to parking lots and vehicles. Users pay for the miles driven, but because most of the car-sharing organizations are nonprofit organizations, the cost is less than what is charged by the major car rental companies. Many of these automobile fleets are also made of the most energy-efficient vehicles available on the market.

I-Go in Chicago even provides an innovative Internet service that allows its members to integrate their trips from point A to point B by connecting multiple modes of transport along the route. A user might begin on commercial rail or bus, switch to a bike share, and pick up a car share for the remaining part of his or her journey. The goal is to minimize automobile miles traveled and, by so doing, significantly reduce each user's carbon footprint.

It is estimated that each car sharing vehicle takes up to twenty cars off the road. Car sharers report that they typically reduce the miles they drive by about 44 percent. The reduction in CO_2 emissions can be dramatic. Communauto, the Canadian car sharing service in Quebec, reports a 13,000-ton reduction in CO_2 emissions by its 11,000 members. A study in Europe found that car sharing cut CO_2 emissions by as much as 50 percent.[30]

Zipcar, the world's largest car-sharing business is a for-profit operation founded in 2000. In just ten years, the company has grown to hundreds of thousands of members. There are several thousand Zipcar locations around the world and more than eight thousand vehicles to choose from. The company, whose revenue topped $130 million in 2009, is growing at a phenomenal rate of 30 percent a year. In 2010, Zipcar launched a hybrid electric vehicle pilot project in its San Francisco location. The brand has become popular among the environmentally conscious millennium generation who refer to themselves as "zipsters."[31]

As renewable energy and the TIR infrastructure become more widespread, car-share lots, like Zipcar, will be able to provide green electricity on site to power electric plug-in vehicles. Car-share commons are likely to become a significant alternative to the conventional model of purchasing cars in markets, especially in dense urban areas where the cost of maintaining a car that is used only infrequently makes little practical sense.

I had the occasion to meet Robin Chase, the founder and former CEO of Zipcar, at the 2011 OECD International Transport Forum in Leipzig, Germany. I was there to give an opening address on the need to create an integrated post-carbon transport and logistics network—pillar 5—across each continent between now and 2050 in order to advance the creation of seamless continental markets. Robin participated in the transport panel immediately following my presentation. In her remarks, she emphasized that the new car-sharing business model represented a disruptive revolution in the nature of mobility, transforming the automobile from a private possession to a collective convenience and from an autonomous experience to a collaborative enterprise.

After the session, Robin and I sat down and talked in greater detail about an emerging distributed capitalism that was shaking the foundation of the conventional market economy. Robin is currently developing a new car-share business, Buzzcar, whose aim is to extend the notion of distributed and collaborative mobility to the next level—a fully lateral business model. She noted that millions of automobile owners use their vehicles less than one or two hours a day, and they remain idle the rest of the time. She told me that she hoped to put those millions of cars to use, making them part of a vast fleet of shared vehicles that can be accessed by others, allowing the owners to make income off their cars while giving others easy access to mobility in neighborhoods around the world. The critical missing link is convincing insurance companies to insure individuals rather than automobiles so that both the owner and the user are covered against liability. Robin said that she is in communication with a number of insurance companies and hoped to sign deals in the very near future.

A younger generation is beginning to share more than cars. Couch Surfing is an international nonprofit association that is reinventing the travel and tourism sector and, in the process, reducing the carbon footprint of hundreds of thousands of tourists. The global network is connecting travelers with local hosts who open up their homes and provide free accommodation and hospitality. Already, more than one million couch surfers have visited one another in 69,000 cities around the world.

Members can access information on each other's interests and perspectives, as well as find out how other members evaluated their experiences with local hosts. Participants are encouraged to correspond with one another prior to visits and to stay in touch afterward. This distributed and collaborative social commons is designed to bring people from diverse cultures together to share their lives. The goal is to help "unify people through honest and empathic communication."[32] Couch Surfing's mission is to advance the notion that we are all members of an extended global family.

The network has enjoyed surprising success since its inception in 2003. Members report 4.7 million positive experiences, or 99.7 percent of all couch surfing experiences.[33] Even more impressive, members say that their experiences have resulted in more than 2.9 million friendships, of which 120,000 are described as being close.

Part of the responsibility that goes with global citizenship is stewarding our common biosphere by living more sustainably. By providing free lodging in local homes for more than a million travelers, Couch Surfing helps to significantly reduce the carbon footprint that would occur if travelers stayed in more energy-intensive hotel accommodations.

The emerging TIR economy is spawning collaborative business practices that would have been unheard of just a few years ago, and even the big global companies are getting into the game. Some of the new business models are so wild and unconventional that they require a complete rethinking of the nature of commercial transactions. "Performance contracting" is a good case in point.

A company like Philips Lighting will contract with a city to install a new generation of highly energy-efficient LED lights in all public and outdoor lighting facilities. Philips's bank finances the project and the city, in turn, pays back Philips over a series of years through energy savings. If Philips fails to achieve the energy savings projected, the company takes the loss. This is the kind of collaborative partnership that will increasingly become the norm in a Third Industrial Revolution economy.

"Shared Savings Agreements" is another TIR business model that enjoys some common ground with performance contracting, but is designed to meet different ends. The new business practice is beginning to be used in the residential real estate market in several countries, with some success. While in America nearly 68 percent of families own their own homes, a majority of families rent in many other countries. For example, in Spain and Germany, more than half of the families live in flats.[34] In places where renting exceeds owning, there is little incentive for the real estate owners to retrofit their buildings and convert them to micro–power plants because the utility bills are paid by the renters. In Switzerland, where only 30 percent of households own their own homes and most families rent, some landlords are entering into shared savings agreements with their lessees. Under the terms of the contract, the landlord agrees to convert the building to a green micro–power plant, and the tenants agree to share some of the savings from their electricity bill with the landlord over a period of time sufficient to recoup his investment. The landlord ends up with a building that has appreciated in value because it is now generating its own green electricity. The value added can be used to increase rental rates for new lessees, but at a price that's less than the savings on their future electricity bills, creating a win-win deal for both the landlord and the tenants.

If the global economy is to transition successfully into a Third Industrial Revolution infrastructure, entrepreneurs and managers will need to be educated to take advantage of all the cutting edge business models, including open-source and networked commerce, distributed and collaborative research and development strategies, and sustainable low-carbon logistics and supply chain management.

SOCIAL ENTREPRENEURSHIP

The collaborative nature of the new economy is fundamentally at odds with classical economic theory, which puts great store on the assumption that individual self-interest in the marketplace is the only effective way to drive economic growth. The Third Industrial Revolution model also eschews the kind of centralized command and control associated with traditional

Soviet-style socialist economies. The new model favors lateral ventures, both in social commons and in the market place, on the assumption that mutual interest, pursued jointly, is the best route to sustainable economic development. The new era represents a democratization of entrepreneurship—everyone becomes a producer of their own energy—but also requires a collaborative approach to sharing energy across neighborhoods, regions, and whole continents.

The TIR economy embodies the spirit of the social entrepreneurial movement sweeping the globe. Being both entrepreneurial and cooperative is no longer considered a contradiction but, rather, a prescription for reordering economic, social, and political life in the twenty-first century.

Social entrepreneurs are streaming out of universities all over the world and creating new businesses that bridge the for-profit and not-for-profit sectors—hybrid enterprises that will likely become more commonplace in the years to come.

Have you heard of TOMS? This business, which has both a profit-making and nonprofit component, makes shoes—not any kind of shoes, but shoes made from sustainable, organic, recycled, and even vegan materials. But that is just the beginning of the story of what might be the most unorthodox shoe company in the world. The canvas or cotton fabric shoes are based on a traditional shoe called *alpargata* that has long been worn by farmers in Argentina. The company is the creation of Blake Mycoskie, a young social entrepreneur from Arlington, Texas, who founded the business in 2006. TOMS shoes are sold in more than five hundred stores in the United States and abroad, including Neiman Marcus, Nordstrom, and Whole Foods.

Mycoskie's profit-making operation, which is located in Santa Monica, California, has already sold more than a million pairs of shoes. But here is where it gets interesting. For every pair of shoes sold, his nonprofit subsidiary, Friends of TOMS, distributes a pair of shoes free to a child in need somewhere in the world. Over a million free shoes have been given to kids in the "one-to-one movement" in poor communities in the United States, Haiti, Guatemala, Argentina, Ethiopia, Rwanda, and South Africa.

Why give away a pair of shoes for every pair of shoes sold? Mycoskie points out that without shoes, children are not allowed to attend schools in many of the poorest regions of the world. Walking barefoot exposes youngsters to a debilitating disease called podoconiosis or "mossy foot," a soil-transmitted fungus that gets into the pores on the bottom of feet and destroys the lymphatic system. It is reported that more than one billion people are at risk of contracting soil-transmitted diseases. The simple solution: shoes.

And what happens to all of the millions of shoes when they wear out? TOMS Community Wall website invites its customers to post creative ideas for recycling the shoes into useful second-generation products including bracelets, soccer balls, plant hangers, and coasters. TOMS is illustrative of the new social entrepreneurial business models that are emerging in a Third Industrial Revolution era.

THE SHIFT in the way the world does business has triggered a struggle of epic proportions between the old guard of the Second Industrial Revolution, who are determined to hold on to their shrinking vestiges of power, and the young entrepreneurs of the Third Industrial Revolution, who are equally committed to advancing a lateral, sustainable economic game plan for the world. At stake is the very basic question of who will control power in the global economy of the twenty-first century. Both forces are jockeying for market advantage and lobbying to secure favored status, including government subsidies and tax incentives worth billions of dollars.

The real question to be asked is, "Where does industry and government want to be twenty years from now: locked into the sunset energies, technologies, and infrastructures of a failing Second Industrial Revolution, or moving toward the *sunrise* energies, technologies, and infrastructure of an emerging Third Industrial Revolution?"

The answer is obvious, but ushering in the new era of distributed capitalism is likely, nonetheless, to be a difficult journey. The problem, at this point, is not the lack of a plan to get there—we have it. The Third Industrial Revolution is a common sense approach to transitioning into a post-carbon era. The wildcard is public perception. And here is where we are running up against a wrong-headed idea of how economic revolutions occur that borders on the delusional.

HOW ECONOMIC REVOLUTIONS ARE REALLY MADE

Many Americans have long harbored the notion that the great economic advances are always the result of the government getting out of the way and allowing the invisible hand of capitalism free reign in an unfettered market. Europeans, and other societies around the world, are far less convinced of the virtues of wide-open, libertarian capitalism and have historically shown a preference for proactive government involvement in the economic process in order to maintain a more balanced social market model. Still, even among the more temperate social welfare economies, there is a growing populist sentiment—but still a minority—for pushing back on the government's traditional role in the economy, right at the time when we need more activist government involvement with the private sector to regrow commerce and trade.

Faced with record government deficits and high taxes, millions of disgruntled voters are rightfully concerned about mortgaging their future in a heap of unpayable debt and saddling their children with a bankrupt society. But believing somehow that if the government were to stand down, the entrepreneurial spirit would be unleashed, new economic opportunities would abound, and the general welfare of the human race would be vastly improved does not square with the historical record.

Reality check! While the market has been an unrivaled commercial engine for promoting inventiveness and entrepreneurialism, it has never, on its own, created an economic revolution. Quite simply, this is a myth that continually rears its head in the American psyche, attracting converts among the disaffected. The sham is tolerable in good times. But in this critical moment in human history, when our very survival and the future of our planet are at stake, we can no longer afford to dwell in a mystical land of magical thinking.

Economic revolutions don't just emerge from the ether. The laying down of a new communications and energy infrastructure has always been a joint effort between government and industry. The cherished laissez-faire idea that economic revolutions flow inexorably from the partnering between inventors and entrepreneurs—with the first risking his or her time to come up with a new technology, product, or service and the second willing to invest his or her capital to get the new idea to market—is only part of the story. Both the First and Second Industrial Revolutions required a large-scale government commitment (in terms of public funds) to build the infrastructure. Government also established the codes, regulations, and standards to manage the new flow of economic activity, and it created generous tax incentives and subsidies to assure the growth and stabilization of the new economic order.

As I'm writing this book, a debate is raging between Wall Street and 1600 Pennsylvania Avenue over how much government involvement is desirable in the affairs of the American economy. That debate has now spilled over onto Main Street. A populist backlash against "big government' is gathering steam as taxpayers blame the White House and Congress for the dismal state of the American economy. Millions of Americans have come to question the legitimacy of government tinkering in the commercial life of the country. Thomas J. Donohue, the president of the US Chamber of Commerce, has implied that President Obama's administration is bad for business, which is perhaps the worst epithet that can be hurled against a politician in the USA. This is a strange accusation coming just months after the Obama administration and Congress bailed out Wall Street and averted a free fall into a great depression.

The fact is the Chamber of Commerce's position is disingenuous, while the widespread populist belief—that an unencumbered marketplace, free of the heavy hand of government, has always been the winning formula for commercial success—is just plain misinformed. Government and business have shared the same bed, if not from the very beginning of the country's existence, then at least since the end of the Civil War, when the railroads required massive federal assistance in their efforts to lay down a continental rail infrastructure.

It was at that time that the term *lobbyist* was coined by President Ulysses S. Grant to characterize the pack of bankers and railroad men who would stalk the lobby of the majestic Willard Hotel, across from the White House, hoping to bend the ear of a cabinet member or member of Congress on behalf of sweetheart legislation. It wasn't long before the bankers and railroad men were joined by the oil men. Together, they became an ever-present unelected force in the nation's capital, lobbying for taxpayers' money to grease the wheels of commerce.

Our European friends have always been more up front about the close relationship between government and industry. Central governments financed much of the energy and communications infrastructure in Europe, as well as the public transport for the First and Second Industrial Revolutions. In the United States, the federal and state governments provided less direct aid but extended vast sums of indirect public assistance.

While there is nothing inherently wrong with singing the praises of the marketplace, the outright denial of the continuous interplay of the public and private sectors that, in large part, facilitated and guaranteed the commercial success of every developed nation, can have negative consequences for society. First, it encourages government and business to take their relationship underground and out of sight, where they hide their transactions in a veil of secret deals buried deep inside arcane pieces of legislation. In return, elected officials are smothered with generous campaign contributions that assure their reelections. Second, this lack of transparency allows the business community to continue to proffer the myth that America's success is attributable solely to the virtuous workings of the free market, while simultaneously giving it the upper hand in criticizing prospective legislation that might regulate its abuses or reign in its inordinate power over the affairs of the economy and society.

In times of crisis, like the present moment, when the full creative potential of the country needs to be harnessed to ease the economy off of a dying energy/communications infrastructure and give birth to a new commercial paradigm, only an open, transparent, and comprehensive partnership between business, government and civil society will provide the traction to make the transition possible. That kind of relationship exists in the European Union, where the social/market model is strong enough to win public support for a new public/private partnership. In America, however, when we hear about the need to bring government and industry together to advance a new economic vision and game plan for the country, the reaction of many Americans is to cry "socialism" and decry the loss of American freedom.

The public seems to be of two minds about the relationship between business and government. On the one hand, local constituents rarely complain and generally applaud when their senator or congressperson is able to steer federal government appropriations and projects worth millions of dollars to the state and local congressional district, especially if it's likely to create new employment opportunities. In fact, if their elected representatives were not able to "bring home the bacon," chances are they would not be reelected. On the other hand, politicians in other states and congressional districts are lambasted for earmarking pet projects in pieces of national legislation designed to bring "the pork" to their regions. Apparently, whether people are thrilled or upset depends on whether the pork is going to their district or someone else's.

The problem is that the political system is rigged from the outset to represent large commercial interests, leaving the average voter and taxpayer little choice but to root for their representatives to grab the trimmings for their district before it gets dispersed somewhere else.

What I have described is the real "American exceptionalism." We are virtually alone among the mature democracies in allowing corporate contributions to buy election campaigns. Most European Union member states restrict or forbid such practices and require publicly financed elections. According to the Center for Responsive Politics, the average cost of winning a House race in 2008 was nearly $1.1 million. It cost almost $6.5 million to win a Senate seat. Presidential elections are even more expensive. The Center reported that more than $1.3 billion were spent by the candidates in the 2008 presidential election.

How important are campaign funds to winning elections? According to a post-election analysis of the 2008 elections by the Center for Responsive Politics, in 94 percent of the Senate races and 93 percent of the House of Representatives races that had been decided within twenty-four hours after the polls closed, the highest-spending candidate won.

Ending the practice of private funding in elections and mandating public financing would go a long way to restoring the democratic process in the United States. Yet, the American public has shown little interest in making the case for the public financing of elections. The issue is never among the major concerns of voters when they are polled.

To make matters worse, by a five-to-four majority, the US Supreme Court ruled in 2010 that it is unconstitutional to restrict anyone, even a company, from donating money to an election campaign, as it violates Americans' basic right to express their political choices as they see fit.

What we are left with is a strange paradox. Millions of Americans want government to keep its hands out of the commercial arena, but are unwilling to mobilize sufficient public response to end the practice of private commercial interests buying elections and directing taxpayers' money to their pet commercial projects and industry interests.

So, while many Americans profess to be zealous in their determination to separate the market and the state—even more than their desire to separate church and state—in truth, they would rather get at least some of the commercial spoils of the unholy alliance between corporate America and the federal government than be left out of the feast altogether.

A vast majority of Americans have what might be called a quasi-religious relationship with business. Their Calvinist faith in the marketplace and hatred of big government—to the point of equating it with godless socialism—blinds them to corporate greed, allowing businesses to get away with creating a form of socialism for the select and pauperism for the people. Many Americans mistakenly believe that the American dream flows inexorably from an unhampered free market, and they close their eyes to the long history of corporate-government collusion. As long as Americans continue to believe that markets perform best for society when unencumbered by government, while they wink at a political process in which elected officials allow business trade associations to draft legislation that would benefit them at the expense of the rest of society, we are likely doomed as a nation.

The solution begins with acknowledging that all of the great leaps forward in American economic history have occurred only when government helped finance the critical energy and communications infrastructure and continued to underwrite its performance so that thousands of new businesses could grow and flourish. Indeed, I cannot conceive of any practical way to advance a new economic era for the country, absent a full and robust partnership between government and business at every level—city, county, state, and federal.

Second, we need to learn valuable lessons from the tawdry history of corporate-government relations in the past to ensure that the Third Industrial Revolution is of a different nature—that is, an open and transparent collaboration between government, business, and civil society, which represents the interests of all the American public, not just those of a corporate elite.

Coming to grips with the real history of the relationship between industry and government will not be easy. I recall a television debate I had several years ago with a prominent libertarian from a highly respected Washington think tank. At one point in the discussion he asserted that whenever the government meddled in the marketplace, the economy suffered. He then turned to me and asked, rather pointedly, whether I could think of any "concrete" example of where a federally sponsored effort in the commercial arena had a salutary effect on commerce and trade that could not have been more effectively accomplished by private industry. Taking advantage of the metaphor, I raised the specter of the Interstate Highway Act, the most costly public works project in history, which laid down highways of "concrete" across America and led to an unprecedented boom in economic prosperity that spanned a generation.

The $25 billion plan called for setting aside a whopping 1,600,000 acres of land for the 41,000 mile network of superhighways.[35] More than 42 billion cubic yards of earth were removed in the process of laying down the roadbed.[36] Tens of thousands of miles of drainage pipes were embedded beneath the road. The road itself constituted a thin surface coating atop a concrete base paved over steel reinforcement bars. To ensure that no vehicle would ever have to stop en route, 54,663 bridges and 104 tunnels were built along the interstate.[37]

The building of the interstate highway infrastructure had both an immediate stimulus effect on the industries that participated in its creation, as well as a multiplier effect on the economy as a whole that would finally peak in the late 1980s. Oil companies, general contractors, cement manufacturers, steel companies, heavy equipment companies, lumber companies, paint manufacturers, lighting companies, landscaping companies, and rubber companies were among the dozens of industries involved in the building of the great interstate highway system.

President Eisenhower's dream of "ribbons across the land" employed millions of workers, took forty years to complete, crossed three time zones, and came to be seen as America's greatest economic accomplishment in the post–World War II era.

Nor was the mammoth government project to create an interstate highway infrastructure an anomaly. From the very outset of the Second Industrial Revolution, the critical industries that made up the infrastructure—oil, automotive, telecommunications, electric utilities, construction, real estate, and so on—banded together in a mega lobby to ensure that every level of government would provide the necessary financial underwriting, as well as industry-friendly codes, regulations, and standards to ensure market success. The creation of a fossil fuel energy regime, the installation of an integrated telecommunication grid, the establishment of a national electricity power grid, and the build-out of the nation's suburban housing, all of which rode atop the oil curve for the better part of the twentieth century, were made possible by the generous, but often disguised or hidden, enablement of government.

The fossil fuel industry and nuclear power have been subsidized by American taxpayers for generations. Even long after the energy industries had matured, the federal government was pumping tens of billions of dollars into their R&D efforts. Between 1973 and 2003, the US government paid out $74 billion in energy subsidies to promote R&D in fossil fuels and nuclear power, despite the fact that these industries were flush with income and boasted corporate giants that were among the biggest companies in the world.[38]

It was the federal government that conspired with AT&T at the beginning of the twentieth century, transforming it into a quasi-public telecommunication monopoly, which allowed the company to reap billions of dollars of revenue under the regulatory cover of the government, without having to compete in the open marketplace.

The state governments followed suit with the regulation of power and electric utility companies, making them quasi-public monopolies and guaranteeing them high electricity rates, the right of public domain, and other advantages normally associated with government-run utilities.

While nominally overseen by state governments, in practice, many utilities effectively policed themselves, ensuring handsome revenues at the expense of their customers and taxpayers. They did this by putting in place effective professional lobbies in the state capitals and creating the infamous "revolving door," by which government officials in the oversight agencies would periodically leave their government posts for lucrative jobs as lobbyists in the companies they were previously overseeing, while others from the same companies were quickly appointed by the government to take the very seats that had just been vacated.

The electrification of America made possible the lighting of American cities, the powering of factories, the heating and cooling of buildings, and the use of household electrical appliances. Even more important, electrification brought with it a new communications revolution to manage a more complex Second Industrial Revolution economy.

Nowhere has the federal government's enablement of the commercial market been more pronounced, but less acknowledged, then in the great suburban construction boom of the twentieth century. The Federal Housing Administration (FHA), set up in 1934 by the US government, virtually underwrote the construction industry—America's largest commercial sector— for the remainder of the century. FHA loan guarantees to mortgage lenders, backed up by the US Treasury, coupled with a tax law allowing homeowners to deduct interest rates on their mortgage payments, stimulated the greatest housing construction boom in all of history. By the 1960s, the FHA was underwriting the financing of four and a half million suburban homes a year, nearly one-third of all the houses financed in the country.

Commercial developers were provided with equally generous government subsidies. The US Congress amended the IRS code, allowing developers to write off the cost of a new building in seven years, rather than the standard forty-year depreciation schedule. The subsidy, worth billions of dollars, spurred the building of thousands of shopping malls and strip malls off the new interstate highway exits and alongside suburban housing developments.

The government helped finance virtually every stage of development of the critical infrastructure of the Second Industrial Revolution, as well as subsidize the many commercial opportunities that flowed from it. The expenditure of government funds to activate, deploy and maintain the industrial system amounted to trillions of dollars—the biggest public investment in the marketplace in all of recorded history. The government's involvement in the commercial arena helped make the United States an unrivaled economic superpower.

For those who doubt the critical role that government has played in America's commercial success, I have included a separate essay on our website that chronicles this unacknowledged relationship, with the hope that it will put to rest, once and for all, the libertarian myth about how the United States became the greatest economy on Earth.

SEEING THE BIG PICTURE

The most difficult task in the transformation from the Second to a Third Industrial Revolution is conceptual rather than technical in nature. The movers and shakers of the Second Industrial Revolution quickly came to understand, at least intuitively, that a new communication medium and energy regime created a single indivisible economic paradigm. One could not develop without a relationship with the other. They also realized that the new infrastructure being created by this convergence would fundamentally reconfigure the temporal and spatial orientation of society, requiring new ways to organize and manage commercial activities and living patterns.

It didn't take long for the emerging oil companies, auto companies, telephone companies, power and utility companies, and construction and real estate companies of the Second Industrial Revolution to figure out that each of their pursuits reinforced the commercial opportunities of the others, and that they would never create the economies of speed and scale that would allow them to optimize their full commercial potential by going it alone. Processing oil, manufacturing automobiles, laying down roads, installing telephone lines and electrical utilities, building suburban communities and institutionalizing modern business practices are not separate commercial entities, but components of a single enterprise—a Second Industrial Revolution.

The entrepreneurs understood this from the very beginning and pooled their mutual interests, creating a powerful lobbying force both in the United

States and Europe and, later, in the rest of the world, to advance their common cause. While that lobbying force was often predatory and unsavory, consumed by self-interest and unconcerned with the public welfare, it did perform a public service that too often goes unrecognized. The lobbyists connected the dots. That is, they brought together all of the disparate commercial forces and melded them into a set of relationships that became an embryonic template for a new economic organism.

The lobbyists then cajoled, manipulated, and exploited the full power of the government to help gestate the new economy. To their lasting credit, it is fair to say that the inventors, entrepreneurs, and financiers of the Second Industrial Revolution understood the system they were creating before the intellectual community could describe and categorize it, or government could properly regulate it.

Although we think of entrepreneurship as isolated commercial accomplishments—in the form of new inventions or business ideas—the truly great entrepreneurial contributions are more systemic in nature. They occur when the business community comes to see how their individual commercial pursuits fit into a broader economic vision. When that happens, new economic eras arise. It's only later that those new economic paradigms are given a name and made into a compelling story that captures the public's imagination, providing a frame of reference for the full mobilization of society. (Arnold Toynbee, the acclaimed British historian, first popularized the concept of the "Industrial Revolution" in a series of lectures he delivered in the late 1880s, well after the First Industrial Revolution was underway.[39])

Today, we are witnessing the convergence of a new communications media and energy regime—a Third Industrial Revolution. Businesses across widely divergent fields—clean energies, green construction, telecommunications, micro-generation, distributed grid IT, plug-in electric and fuel cell transport, sustainable chemistry, nanotechnology, zero-carbon logistics and supply-chain management, and so on—are developing an array of new technologies, products, and services.

Until recently, these new commercial opportunities have attracted only modest interest in the investment community and with the public at large. That's because we human beings live by stories, and stories are always about the relationships and interactions between characters. Just as individual words don't tell a tale, individual technologies, product lines, and services don't make a new economic narrative. It's when we discover how they all relate to each other and create a new economic conversation that heads start to turn. That's now beginning to happen as TIR visionaries co-author the opening chapters of a new story for the global economy.

THE EMERGING THIRD INDUSTRIAL REVOLUTION is not only changing the way we do business, but also the way we think about politics. The struggle between the older hierarchical power interests of the Second Industrial Revolution and the nascent lateral power interests of the Third Industrial Revolution is giving rise to a new political dichotomy, reflective of the competing forces vying for dominance in the commercial arena. A new political script is being written, recasting the very way people will view politics as we move deeper into the new era.

CHAPTER FIVE
BEYOND RIGHT AND LEFT

When was the last time you heard anyone under the age of twenty-five rant about his or her ideological beliefs? Something very strange is happening out there. Ideology is disappearing. Young people aren't much interested in debating the fine points of capitalist or socialist ideology or the nuances of geopolitical theory. Their political leanings are configured in an entirely different way.

Our global policy team began picking up on this phenomenon as we became more engaged in the political process in Europe, the United States, and other countries. We have come to discover what we suspect is a new political mindset emerging among a younger generation of political leaders socialized on Internet communications. Their politics are less about right versus left and more about centralized and authoritarian versus distributed and collaborative. This makes sense.

The two generations whose sociability has been formed, in large part, by Internet communications are far more likely to divide the world into people and institutions that use top-down, enclosed, and proprietary thinking, and those that use lateral, transparent, and open thinking. As they come of age, they are affecting a shift in political thinking—one that will fundamentally alter the political process in the twenty-first century.

HOW THE INTERNET SLAYED MACHISMO

The Presidential Palace in Madrid is surrounded by a lush lawn and shaded by trees. Clusters of flowering plants and tropical bushes greet visitors at

every turn. Pathways connect the president's quarters to other annexes housing the presidential entourage. The grounds exude a serene atmosphere.

I was anxious to meet José Luis Rodríguez Zapatero, the young, forty-
eight-year-old career politician who now commanded the most powerful
country in the Spanish-speaking world. When he came out in the anterior
room to greet me, the first thing that caught my attention was his warm
smile and relaxed demeanor. He seemed quite comfortable in his own skin.
We began our conversation—which would last more than two hours and
cover a wide range of subjects from philosophy and cultural anthropology
to the rough-and-tumble realities of a complex global economy—with an
admission on my part. I confided that my wife, Carol, and I had been following his political career with great interest. We were particularly taken
by his surprise announcement upon assuming the presidency that one of his
top priorities would be to end machismo in Spain. I leaned in a bit closer
and asked, rather delicately, "What would dispose you to begin a presidency on such a note—especially in Spain?"

His response was revealing. He reminded me that for centuries in Spain
the Catholic Church and the monarchy kept a tight hold on the affairs of society and that machismo had become the cultural narrative that allowed hierarchical forms of control to descend from the pinnacle of ecclesiastical and
governmental authority all the way down into the domestic relations in every
home. Machismo was the social glue that conditioned successive generations
to accept the unbridled exercise of authority, whether practiced by the church,
the state, or one's employer, without questioning or challenging its legitimacy.

The president then paused for several moments. I sensed that he was
digging deeper to find the words that could express what animates his own
life's mission. He chose them carefully. "Machismo," he told me, "is what
keeps the old order going. It's what poisons the human drive for dignity. It
locks up the human spirit and kills personal freedom. We Spaniards have
experienced firsthand the devastating toll it takes on the human psyche,
generation after generation. We have to make a clean break if we are to
have a meaningful future as a people." Then he added a last thought on
the subject. "For a younger generation growing up on the Internet and
comfortable interacting in social media, the hierarchically organized flow
of authority and power from the top down is old school." Machismo has
run up against Facebook and Twitter.

Zapatero is among the first of a younger generation of political leaders whose sensibilities reflect a deep change in consciousness. The older
hierarchical way of organizing social relations is giving way to networked

ways of thinking, and posing a challenge to the operating assumptions of our most basic institutions, including our family relationships, religious practices, educational system, business models, and forms of governance.

Zapatero and I talked about applying network thinking to the economic arena. We discussed, at length, the need to transition the Spanish economy from a Second to a Third Industrial Revolution model, and how the democratization of energy was the critical pathway that would move society from authoritarian structures to collaborative ones.

As we finished what would be the first of many meetings and discussions in the ensuing years, Prime Minister Zapatero turned to me and said, "You know, Jeremy, Spain completely missed the First Industrial Revolution, and sat out most of the Second Industrial Revolution. I want to give you my personal pledge that we won't let the Third Industrial Revolution pass us by. Our government is determined to lead the way into a sustainable and democratic economic future."

Prime Minister Zapatero made the Third Industrial Revolution economic model the centerpiece of his vision for the country. Under his leadership, Spain shot from the bottom of the pack to become the second-leading producer of renewable energy—behind Germany—in Europe.

Unfortunately, Prime Minister Zapatero's administration lost focus halfway into his last term in office, undermining many of the gains that were pushing Spain to the forefront of the Third Industrial Revolution. Spain got caught up in the debt contagion that had already claimed Greece, Ireland, and Portugal. The collapse of the Spanish housing bubble transformed the country overnight from the poster child of the new commercial Europe—for fifteen years Spain's growth exceeded Germany's—to the bad boy of European market overreach. When I first began advising Prime Minister Zapatero, the Spanish economy was booming, employment was high, social programs were among the most generous in Europe, and the government boasted a healthy surplus. By 2007, the housing market had collapsed, unemployment was running in excess of 20 percent—among the highest in Europe—and the government was awash in debt. Prime Minister Zapatero was being pressured by the financial markets to drastically reign in government spending or face a loss of its credit rating and a potentially humiliating bailout by the European Union.[1]

In Zapatero's defense, he inherited a housing bubble that had been metastasizing for more than a decade before he came into office. He was forced to make draconian cuts in social programs or lose the ability to borrow funds and keep the Spanish economy afloat. The austerity budget, which was passed in December 2010, did not go down well with the Spanish public—especially the youth, whose unemployment rate had billowed up to 45 percent, creating widespread unrest across the country.[2]

I met with Prime Minister Zapatero in New York in October 2009, when he was there to address the UN general assembly. He asked me if I would help his administration draft a comprehensive TIR economic plan to restart the Spanish economy. I agreed and said that we would need to concentrate on reviving the housing market by creating the appropriate government codes, regulations, standards, and incentives to convert the nation's moribund real estate sector into millions of green micro–power plants—pillar 2.

Prime Minister Zapatero liked the plan and asked me to work with Bernardino León Gross, the secretary general of the Prime Minister, to move the initiative along quickly. In the succeeding months, however, the government got bogged down in the day-to-day muck of hammering out an austerity program while the international financial community cast a dark and menacing shadow over its every move—effectively creating a siege mentality. The result is that our plan to resuscitate the economy kept being pushed aside.

I met with Prime Minister Zapatero again in March of 2010. We agreed that an austerity program had to be coupled with an equally ambitious economic plan for the country to give a sense of mission, lest the Spanish public lose all hope for an economic recovery. He asked me to immediately sit down with the minister of industry, trade, and tourism, Miguel Sebastián Gascón, and begin the process of developing a comprehensive TIR plan for the country. My subsequent meeting with Sebastián was disappointing. I left with the impression that he was not interested in working together and was even philosophically lukewarm, if not opposed, to a Third Industrial Revolution rollout. I was quite surprised at the apparent difference in Prime Minister Zapatero's urgent plea to move the new economic plan and the polite resistance of his cabinet minister. Despite furtive efforts by Bernardino León Gross over the next year to get the TIR plan back on track, inertia set in, the government reeled back, and Prime Minister Zapatero's grand dream of leading Europe into a Third Industrial Revolution faded.

Whether Spain can regain the momentum it lost in the aftermath of the 2008 economic downturn and recapture a prominent leadership role in the race to a Third Industrial Revolution is problematic at this point. Time will tell.

ALL NODES CONNECT WITH ROME

Prime Minister Zapatero is a socialist and his administration is one of the leading socialist powers in the world today. But the Third Industrial Revolution vision doesn't belong to any particular political party affiliation. In Rome, Mayor Gianni Alemanno is with the People of Freedom party and part of the center-right Berlusconi coalition government. But his vision of a Third Industrial Revolution for Rome aligns him far more closely with Prime Minister Zapatero's thinking than with that of his own prime minister, Silvio Berlusconi.

The mayor's attention is focused on two goals: breathing fresh life into the Rome economy by becoming a leader among the world's great cities in sustainability, and securing the 2020 Olympics games for the city (Rome has not hosted the Olympic games since 1960).

We spent little time on philosophical questions in our first meeting. Rather, the mayor was intent on giving me a brief history lesson as a way of providing context for our discussions. He reminded me that the building we were in—Rome's city hall—was designed and built by Michelangelo at the height of the Italian Renaissance, and was meant to symbolize the reawakening of the human spirit in the arts, literature, and culture in the Western world. He asked me to accompany him to the window. Outside his office lay the excavated remains of the ancient Roman forum. The mayor pointed to a small stone—Lapis Niger—just below and asked if I knew what it was. I shrugged and he explained that what we were looking at is the final yard of the great Roman road infrastructure that stretched out in every direction across the expanse of the European continent. "You know the old saying, all roads lead to Rome?" Pointing to the black stone he said, "That's ground zero."

We talked about Rome inspiring a new Renaissance by way of an information/energy superhighway that would start at the City Hall gate and spread across Italy and all of Europe, the Middle East, and North Africa, following the lines of the old Roman Empire. The new energy highway, however, would not be constructed to facilitate conquest but, rather, to encourage a new form of collaboration between people and foster biosphere consciousness.

In subsequent discussions with the mayor, the question of who would control the generation and distribution of power in the region came up repeatedly. The point was made that if the Internet had been in the hands of a private carrier in every locale, it would have likely thwarted the free flow of information in cyberspace. Because the city owns its own electric utility, however, the power grid already belongs to the citizenry. For Rome, then, the issue was not access to the transmission lines, but the ability to own and control the generation of renewable energy at its source—in the neighborhoods across the city and region.

I told the mayor that I favored the creation of energy cooperatives in every neighborhood to allow small, micro-producers of energy to aggregate their capital and spread their risks so they can become effective players in the distributed energy market. Recall that the creation of rural electric cooperative associations across the poorer rural regions of the United States in the 1930s, '40s, and '50s, brought electricity to millions of homes and small businesses, and is an example of the power inherent in the cooperative model. Because the Third Industrial Revolution communication/energy system is by nature a distributed and collaborative process, it favors a cooperative business model at the nodal sites.

When I first raised the question of neighborhood energy cooperatives with Mayor Alemanno, I wasn't sure how he would respond, given his political party affiliation. Some on the political right in Italy have traditionally opposed cooperatives, regarding them as socialist instruments that undermine the individual entrepreneurial spirit. In reality, it's a bit more complicated than that. The Italian cooperative movement is a huge commercial force in Italy, as it is in the rest of Europe and much of the world. In Italy, there are three main cooperative movements: Legacoop, coming out of the communist left wing; Confcooperative, affiliated with the Catholic Church; and a third co-op, AGCI, which is associated with the noncommunist left. So, in a sense, cooperatives have historically crossed the conservative-liberal spectrum and enjoyed widespread popular support.

Mayor Alemanno allayed my concerns by informing me that as the former National Agricultural Minister for the Berlusconi government, one of his more important accomplishments was to help establish rural agricultural cooperatives across the country. He said that as far as he was concerned, energy cooperatives in the neighborhoods of Rome were the way to go and that we should bring the well-established cooperative associations into the TIR planning process at the early stages, which we did.

THE GREAT POLITICAL SWITCH

Okay. I grant you that Italian politics is a bit unorthodox. But how do we account for the great political switch of 2010 in the United Kingdom? How could it be that the party of Margaret Thatcher has suddenly gone lateral? The iron lady was the closest thing to a patriarch in heels we are ever likely to see. She was the epitome of the kind of top-down, heavy-handed politician that dominated the twentieth century—the Lyndon Johnsons, Winston Churchills, and Charles de Gaulles of the world (and I say this with affection). Back then, we looked up to our political leaders as father figures who would watch over the motherland while we tended to our work and day-to-day lives.

Now we have David Cameron, who definitely calls himself a conservative, but appears to be using a different playbook that political scientists have yet to dissect and categorize. The 2010 national elections brought this to the fore for me through some rather bizarre encounters. It all started when I met David Miliband in London in March of 2009.

At the time, Miliband was serving as the environmental minister in Tony Blair's Labour Party cabinet. He later went on to become foreign secretary in the Gordon Brown administration. I was in town to deliver the Ralph Miliband lecture at the London School of Economics (LSE). The lecture was named after David's father, a prominent Marxist scholar. (The Miliband family enjoys a long history in the British socialist movement.) David was a whiz kid who, at the tender age of twenty-nine, became the head of policy for Prime Minister Blair. His boyish appearance belied his forty-three years.

David was expected to attend my afternoon lecture and introduce me. I dropped into his office in the morning hours to pay a courtesy call. It was obvious from the time I arrived that the young minister was preoccupied and even a little annoyed at having to set aside a few moments to chat. He told me that he would not have time to attend the afternoon lecture and introduce me, as previously arranged, because of pressing business. When I began discussing the virtues of micro-generation of renewable energy and peer-to-peer sharing of green electricity, it became clear that he was uncomfortable with the vision of a Third Industrial Revolution.

A debate had been raging within the British Labour Party over its long-standing opposition to nuclear power. The nuclear industry had launched a public relations lobbying campaign in Europe and America arguing that nuclear power needed to be resurrected as a primary source of energy generation in the fight against global warming because it did not emit CO_2 and was, therefore, a clean energy technology. Prominent policy makers in the United Kingdom, like Sir David King, the chief science advisor to the government, were championing the return of nuclear power along with Labour Party leaders, most notably Tony Blair and Gordon Brown.

Miliband, as environmental minister, was caught in the crossfire between the pro- and anti-nuclear voices in the party, and had made overtures in recent weeks suggesting that he was open to the idea of enlisting nuclear power in the battle against global warming—thereby setting off a heated protest within party ranks.

I reminded David that there were only 442 nuclear reactors in the world, and they only generate about 6 percent of our total energy. To have even a minimal impact on climate change, according to the scientific community, nuclear power would have to take up 20 percent of the world's energy generation. That would mean replacing every aging nuclear power plant and building an additional one thousand. To accomplish this task would require the construction of three new plants every thirty days for the next forty years—a total of about fifteen hundred nuclear power plants at a cost of $12 trillion.[3] I asked him if, from a policy perspective, he really believed that a commitment on that scale was politically practical and commercially feasible, at which point he became a bit testy, saying he was not all convinced that the new renewable energies alone could get us to a low-carbon economy—even if aggregated and scaled up with grid IT management. He said he now believed that nuclear power would have to play a considerable role in mitigating climate change. He then apologized for not being able to continue with the conversation but needed to get to a meeting. It was, to say the least, an unsettling visit. I had expected someone of his age, with his socialist family roots, to be more enthusiastic about the prospect of democratizing energy.

Later that afternoon, I had just completed my presentation on the Third Industrial Revolution before the LSE faculty and student body, when a woman rushed up to me. She said she was thrilled with the vision of a Third Industrial Revolution but warned that the British government was taking a U-turn back to the old, centralized power sources of the twentieth century, especially with the reintroduction of nuclear power, which she regarded as dangerous to the future welfare of humanity. She pleaded with me to do a documentary opposing nuclear power that would have widespread visibility like Al Gore's film, *An Inconvenient Truth,* did for global warming. She offered her assistance. Seeing that she was visibly shaken and distraught, I asked her name. She said, "Marion Miliband," the wife of the late Ralph Miliband, for whom the lecture I had just given is named. I said, "I was just with your son a few hours ago, and he appears committed to the idea of bringing back nuclear power. Shouldn't you be talking with him?" She said, "He won't listen! It's hopeless." I later read that Mrs. Miliband refused to endorse either David or his younger brother Edward, who were running against each other to assume the mantle of leadership of the British Labour Party in the wake of Gordon Brown's defeat to David Cameron, the Conservative Party leader. Ed Miliband later went on to edge out his brother in a razor-thin election, becoming the new titular head of the party.

The afternoon took an even more unusual turn. As I was leaving the school, a young man came up to me in the street and introduced himself as part of the team that was crafting the energy and climate change policy for the Conservative Party and said that David Cameron was quite taken with the Third Industrial Revolution. He mentioned that a colleague, Zac Goldsmith, was the party's unofficial gadfly on climate change and energy issues. I told the young man that I was an old friend of Zac's father, the late Sir James Goldsmith, and his uncle, Teddy Goldsmith, and asked him to convey my warm regards to Zac. Sir James was the eclectic billionaire and "bad boy" politician whose views were continually shaking up the UK political landscape, and Teddy was the founder and publisher of the *Ecologist,* one of the world's leading environmental journals. He asked if I had an extra copy of my presentation that he could share with the Conservative Party's environmental group, and I obliged. I didn't hear from him again.

A few months later, a UK member of Parliament by the name of Greg Barker contacted me. He said he was the shadow climate change minister for the UK Conservative Party and that the party had just formulated its energy and economic sustainability policy, which closely followed the Third Industrial Revolution vision and game plan. He wondered if it might not be possible to arrange a meeting and joint press conference with myself and Mr. Cameron to announce his party's intention to adopt the Third Industrial Revolution plan, if elected to govern the country. I said I was game if we could work out some of the particulars, including deliverables and scheduling. Over the next several months, Barker and I chatted several times by phone and kept in touch by email. In the end, we weren't able to make the event happen.

Shortly after Cameron became prime minister, I ran into Barker in Lisbon, where I was delivering the opening address at a conference put together by the *International Herald Tribune* on sustainable economic development, which was attended by some of the world's leading players in green finance. Greg had recently been appointed as minister of state of the Department of Energy and Climate Change for the Cameron government. His immediate boss, Chris Huhne, secretary of state for Energy and Climate Change, was openly calling for a transformation into a Third Industrial Revolution economy, as a way to advance economic recovery and spawn millions of new jobs, while simultaneously addressing the issue of climate change and energy security.

While Cameron's party, like Miliband's, had included nuclear power in its future energy mix during the electoral campaign, his partners in the new coalition government, the Liberal Democrats, were vehemently opposed to building new nuclear power plants in the UK. This might have been a stumbling block preventing the two parties from creating a coalition government were it not for a deal they struck agreeing that no public subsidies would be extended to the nuclear industry for putting a new generation of nuclear power plants online—essentially putting an end the prospect of a nuclear renaissance. To ensure the kill-off of nuclear power, the new Cameron government appointed Chris Huhne, a leader of the Liberal Democrats and a staunch opponent of nuclear power, as the Secretary of State for Energy and Climate Change.

Cameron and Huhne are fierce champions of distributed green power, making it the lynchpin of their future economic vision for the country.[4] Their advocacy of a Third Industrial Revolution puts them out in front of David Miliband and some of his colleagues in the Labour Party in advancing a new vision of lateral power for the country.

In all fairness to David Miliband, the Labour Party has likewise supported green energy, feed-in tariffs, "pay as you save" energy efficiency programs, and even smart grids. The difference is that David, and his brother Ed, who served as the last environmental minister in the Gordon Brown administration, have never publicly outlined a vision of a distributed power revolution and have preferred to cast their initiatives as stand-alone projects, much as President Obama has done in the United States. The Cameron government, at least, has taken a more systemic approach, understanding that the five pillars of a Third Industrial Revolution make up a seamless infrastructure for establishing a new economic paradigm.

Barker is the man responsible for coming up with a detailed TIR economic road map. He asked if representatives from our global policy team and Third Industrial Revolution Global CEO Business Roundtable might be willing to assist his ministry, and said that the Cameron government was on a fast track to put together a comprehensive economic plan by the spring of 2011. I agreed and we followed up with a meeting of six of our key policy people and corporate experts, and a like number of the UK government's point people to discuss the various elements that would need to be integrated into a TIR road map for the United Kingdom, including barriers to entry into the market, scale-up, and commercial penetration. The Cameron team was also interested in the kinds of codes, regulations, and standards, as well as incentives and financial leveraging that would be required to effectively usher in a Third Industrial Revolution economic development plan. We later provided a more detailed report covering the particulars for use by the ministry in crafting their final road map report. Barker assured me that the Cameron government is fully aware of the "complexities of integrating and harmonizing the five critical pillars of the Third Industrial Revolution infrastructure," and encouraged a continued dialogue between his government and our global team as they advanced a TIR agenda.[5]

What I found fascinating about the UK experience is that here were two young politicians, Miliband and Cameron, one partially stuck in the old top-down approach to energy and economic development and the other hitching his political fortunes to the distributed-network approach, each defying the conventional party labels. Whether the Cameron government will, in fact, follow through on its assurances rather than slip back into the kind of siloed incremental approach to a green future that is so typical of other governments is still an open question.

The shift in how political leaders and parties identify themselves along the new spectrum will likely be the subject of much debate in the years to come by political scientists, psychologists, and sociologists. Why do George Papandreou, the prime minister of Greece and president of the Socialist International, and Angela Merkel, the most powerful conservative head of state in the world, essentially agree on the basic question of how power should be managed and distributed in the emerging new economic era?

Papandreou invited me to present an address to the plenary session of the Socialist International biannual conference in June 2008. I only later found out that he had taken the unusual step of violating policy at the Socialist International, which forbade anyone but socialist party leaders from addressing their biannual convention. Papandreou is deeply committed to moving the community of nations into a green future, characterized by the democratization of energy.

So, too, is Chancellor Merkel. At the dinner of German business leaders that Chancellor Merkel hosted (referenced in chapter 2), she made clear her government's intention on the future direction of the German economy. Merkel is known for holding her cards close to the chest. She is that rare politician who prefers to work quietly and methodically, outside the limelight, to create a consensus that will allow her to move the government's political agenda forward. That said, I was taken by surprise at the end of the dinner by the chancellor's closing remarks to the assembled business leaders. Merkel said that she was firmly committed to establishing the five pillars of the Third Industrial Revolution infrastructure for Germany and believed that Europe's future and the world's lie with a transition into a sustainable, green era.

The new political orientation is not only making for strange bedfellows among politicians, but is also beginning to bring together economic forces whose interests have not always coincided. We're witnessing the first inkling of a new political movement in Europe. In the late summer of 2010, Angelo Consoli was in touch with Guglielmo Epifani, the powerful Secretary General of CGIL, Italy's largest trade union, with a membership of six million workers representing 60 percent of the entire unionized workforce. Epifani expressed an interest in meeting with me the next time I was in Rome to discuss his union throwing its support behind the Third Industrial Revolution. I was already scheduled to be in Rome a few weeks later on September 27 to deliver a speech before members of the Italian Parliament on the need to lay the groundwork for an empathic civilization and biosphere consciousness. Gianfranco Fini, the moderate center-right speaker of the lower house of the Parliament, had read my book, *The Empathic Civilization,* and was taken by the alternative narrative of the history of human consciousness and anxious to give the book a wider political audience. I decided to combine my visit with a face-to-face meeting with Epifani. So, I spent September 27 with Italy's center-right parliamentary leader and the leader of the Italian trade union movement—whose political affiliations couldn't be more different.

I met with Epifani and Susanna Camusso, the president-elect of the union, in the morning. In attendance were three senior officials of the union. They told me the union was ready to put its full force behind the Third Industrial Revolution game plan for Italy. Moreover, the union was willing to work with regional and local elected officials from across the spectrum—without a political litmus test—as long as they were committed to advancing the five-pillar infrastructure in their regions or locales.

For Epifani, the primary consideration was securing green jobs for millions of Italian workers. Did that mean that CGIL would support the rollout of a Third Industrial Revolution for Rome even though the mayor's political affiliation was right wing? The answer was yes.

I suggested that the trade union movement join forces with the two other powerful economic players in Italy, the small- and medium-sized enterprise associations and the producer and consumer cooperatives, to create a single economic voice representing the businesses, consumers, and workers of Italy. Epifani agreed and within days contacted the other groups, who expressed a keen interest in the new initiative. The advance work for the new political marriage had already been done. I had been meeting with local SME associations all over Italy for a half decade, talking of the vast commercial benefits that a distributed and collaborative green economy would mean for their businesses. The cooperative associations were equally enthusiastic. Just one year earlier Legacoop, Italy's largest cooperative, had been instrumental in bringing the country's other major cooperatives on board in support of the TIR. Together the trade unions, SMEs, and cooperatives would be a powerful force in reshaping politics in Italy—a prospect very much on the minds of my Italian friends.

On January 24, 2011, I joined CGIL in Rome to announce the formal alliance between the labor union, the Italian SME associations, and the Italian cooperative associations to transition Italy into a Third Industrial Revolution economy. The new coalition drew national headlines and created a stir in political circles. Politicians began to reposition their party platforms to accommodate the new reality of a lateral power movement that was beginning to assert itself on the national stage.

The new TIR political force quickly crossed the Italian border and spread throughout Europe. The European Association of Craft, Small, and Medium-sized Enterprises (UEAPME) brought its clout to the new movement. The giant umbrella organization is made up of national SME associations across the EU member states and represents twelve million enterprises and fifty-five million employees. Coops Europe also weighed in. The Europe-wide association is made up of 161 separate national cooperative organizations in thirty-seven countries. All together, these cooperatives represent the interest of 160,000 cooperative enterprises, 5.4 million jobs, and 123 million members.[6] The European Consumers' Organization (BEUC), comprising forty consumer groups from thirty European countries, brought the voice of hundreds of millions of European consumers to the budding TIR alliance.

On February 1, 2011, these three European-wide associations, representing the vast majority of businesses and consumers in Europe, joined forces with all five of the major political party groups of the European Parliament in the signing of a declaration, calling on the European Commission to prepare a comprehensive plan for the implementation of the Third Industrial Revolution five-pillar infrastructure in the twenty-seven EU member states.

A month later, on March 7, Spain's two powerful trade unions joined forces with the nation's SME association, the national association of cooperatives and nonprofit enterprises, and the country's consumer federation, to push for a TIR rollout across the Spanish economy. The coalition is united in the belief that the Third Industrial Revolution offers the only practical long-term economic plan to regrow the Spanish economy, spur new business opportunities, and create new jobs. Similar coalition initiatives are being readied across Europe.

The coming together of this unlikely coalition of businesses, labor organizations, cooperatives, and consumer associations could potentially be a game changer in European politics. The SMEs have traditionally tilted somewhat to the right and the labor unions to the left, with cooperatives and consumer associations split across the spectrum. The Third Industrial Revolution brings these groups together in a new and powerful lateral force. Since the Third Industrial Revolution is distributed and collaborative in nature, it scales best to millions of small micro-entrepreneurs and consumers who pool their collective interests in cooperative enterprises. And because the laying down of a five-pillar Third Industrial Revolution infrastructure over forty years requires millions of local labor-intensive jobs, the new economy becomes the salvation of a unionized workforce that has increasingly been marginalized by globalization.

The timing for such a political realignment is propitious. Many companies have outgrown national markets in the mature economies and have turned to the emerging markets, setting up shops throughout the developing world. What they are leaving behind are millions of underemployed and unemployed workers, and thousands of small businesses whose revenues are shrinking because they are no longer able to depend on the morsels that fell from the table when big corporations were still native.

But make no mistake about the potential economic clout if millions of little players were connected in distributed networks, and collaborated together across sectors and industries. In the European Union, 80 percent of the new employment in recent years has been generated in small- and medium-sized firms of 250 or fewer employees. Similarly, in the United States, 65 percent of the new jobs over the past fifteen years have been generated by small businesses. If these businesses were to connect with one another along the five-pillar infrastructure of the TIR economy and collaborate in embedded commercial networks across continents, the long-term lateral economic multiplier effect could conceivably eclipse the economic gains made by the centralized, hierarchical business organizations that dominated the Second Industrial Revolution—in much the same way that distributed and collaborative social media are trampling the conventional, top-down communications media of the twentieth century.

WHY THE INTERNET PRESIDENT DOESN'T GET IT

I suspect at this juncture my American readers are asking, "What about President Obama?" Obama is the man who most reflects, in the public mind, the generational shift taking place in the world. The young president has confessed that the most difficult thing he had to give up on assuming high office was not his privacy but his precious BlackBerry. He surely would be attracted to the idea of a distributed and collaborative energy revolution patterned after the Internet model—right?

Obama has made green energy a part of his economic recovery plan. But when we look at the fine print, we see that his administration is even more deeply committed to bringing back nuclear power, offshore oil drilling, and experimental technologies to clean up coal emissions, allowing for a vast expansion of coal-fired power plants. And even his green economic recovery program is formulated more along the lines of centralized management and distribution of renewable energies than a distributed model, reflecting the top-down organizational thinking that governed the First and Second Industrial Revolutions. How do we account for his policies?

Let me take you back to 2003 to give you some background on how Washington has come to think about sustainable economic development. Out of the blue, I got a phone call from a senior science fellow in Senator Byron Dorgan's office asking if I would come in to meet with the senator. Word had gotten back to Washington, DC, about the spadework the European Union was doing to establish an infrastructure for green energies and a low-carbon economy. The senator was particularly keen on hearing more about pillar 3, advancing hydrogen storage. The *New York Times* had run an article mentioning President Prodi's hydrogen research initiative, and Dorgan wanted to know more. The senator was the head of the Democratic Policy Committee and responsible for bringing new ideas to the attention of Senate Democrats.

Dorgan, who hails from North Dakota, a conservative coal-producing state, had nonetheless been one of the leading progressive advocates for green energies in the US Senate. He wanted to know what we were doing in Europe and asked my thoughts on what we might possibly do here in the United States. I was candid with him and said that Europe was leaving the United States behind on the way to a green economy, and that catching up might be difficult with a climate change skeptic president in office (President Bush) and the Republican Party controlling both houses of Congress. Nonetheless, he asked me if I would put together a memorandum that he could circulate to his Senate colleagues, similar to the plan I had worked on with President Prodi at the European Commission. I agreed. He then invited me to make a presentation on the Third Industrial Revolution to all of his Senate colleagues at their traditional Thursday lunch session.

The lunch was set for March 20, just hours after the United States began its bombing campaign over Iraq. The senators were clearly preoccupied as they filed into the room and I wondered how I was going to keep their attention long enough to talk about a future hydrogen economy and how it related to the other pillars that make up the infrastructure of a new commercial era.

Here we were in another war in the Middle East with the prospect of mass casualties and years of occupation. The media in other parts of the world, if not America, were already calling it an "oil war." Iraq has the fourth-largest oil reserves in the world, a fact not lost on political pundits who questioned whether we would have invaded the country if it had not been an oil treasure trove.

To my surprise, the discussion was lively. A number of senators seemed genuinely interested in the prospects of a hydrogen economy. I noticed Senator Hillary Clinton in the back of the room listening intently to the conversation and taking down an occasional note. She was the very last to speak, but it was clear from her remarks that she was aware of the deeper, unexamined ramifications of what we were discussing.

Clinton went straight for the hard-nosed practicalities. With the Congress controlled by the Republicans, a president steeped in the oil industry and a country now knee-deep in war in the Middle East, the best prospect for moving a hydrogen R&D agenda—pillar 3—was to lock it into the defense appropriation budget. Senators Clinton and Dorgan subsequently cosponsored legislation.

I didn't see Senator Dorgan again until February of 2009. By that time the European Parliament had formally endorsed the Third Industrial Revolution, and various departments and agencies of the European Commission were readying initiatives. Member states—Germany, Spain, and Denmark, among others—were well on the way to laying out the five-pillar infrastructure of the Third Industrial Revolution, and the term itself had become part of the vernacular among CEOs of European and global companies and small- and medium-sized enterprises.

After seven years, the election of President Obama and the takeover of both houses of Congress by the Democrats provided an opportunity to again test the waters in Washington. I sat down with Senator Dorgan and briefed him on the EU progress in the years since we met. Like Clinton, he understood the disruptive economic implications of moving to a distributed and collaborative energy regime and cautioned me that Congress, the White House, and much of American industry weren't ready—not by a long shot. He offered to arrange a meeting with the new secretary of energy, Steven Chu, and said he would have a conversation at the next opportunity with the president. I thanked him and said that our group, which now numbered more than one hundred global companies and trade associations, was ready to meet with the president, the secretary of energy, and Congress to talk about how the Third Industrial Revolution infrastructure could be the foundation for a long-term economic recovery for the country. I didn't hear from him again while he was in office—although I'm sure he tried his best to make the appropriate connections; they just weren't interested.

I found this out firsthand in 2009 when I did a joint presentation with Henry Kelly, principal deputy assistant secretary for the Department of Energy, at a business seminar hosted by the Wharton Fellows in Washington. After my presentation, Kelly was questioned by a Wharton professor, Jerry Wind, on his thoughts on the likelihood that the United States would embark on a distributed Third Industrial Revolution game plan similar to the one unfolding in Europe. Professor Wind offered up the analogy of a baseball game and asked, "Would our players be on first base, second base, third base, or on the way to home plate?" The secretary responded by saying, "We're just coming up to bat."

What Kelly left unsaid is that the US team is playing a different game altogether—betting on the installation of giant, centralized wind and solar parks in the midwestern and southwestern states. The idea is to pass federal legislation that would mandate the creation of a super high-voltage grid that could send the electricity generated in these more sparsely populated regions back to customers in the more populated eastern regions of the country. The cost for creating the high-voltage grid would be spread among millions of electricity customers.

This centralized approach to harnessing renewable energy and distributing electricity has not gone over well with eastern governors and power companies. In July 2010, eleven New England and mid-Atlantic governors sent a letter to the US Senate's majority leader, Harry Reid, and minority leader, Mitch McConnell, opposing the national electric transmission policy. The governors argue that centralizing wind and solar energy generation in the western region of the country "would harm regional efforts to promote local renewable energy generation . . . and hamper efforts to create clean energy jobs in our states."[7] The governors were particularly alarmed by the $160 billion price tag to create a national transmission corridor from the West to the East.

Fourteen power companies—many of whom operate in the regions that would be deleteriously affected by centralized power generation—joined the mid-Atlantic and Eastern governors, calling on Congress to allow every region of the country to exploit its own renewable energy resources. The power companies argued that "national policy should not be biased toward building remote generation resources connected to population centers with long multi-state transmission lines." The companies, which included Entergy, Northeast Utilities, DTE Energy Company, and Southern Company, said that transmission planning should remain regional.[8]

New York Times reporter Matthew Wald put his finger on what is shaping up to be a pivotal battle around the future of the Third Industrial Revolution, noting that "the basic conflict remains distant energy versus local energy."[9] Yes, but with a caveat. The question is whether renewable energy production will be centralized in one part of the country and then distributed to the rest of the United States or generated locally everywhere and shared across the continent. In other words, does the United States commit itself to a centralized supergrid and a one-way flow of renewable energy to end users, or to a distributed smart grid that allows thousands of local communities to generate their own energy and distribute electricity peer-to-peer in a national power grid.

The challenge that faces our TIR companies at the federal level is two-fold. First, the conventional energy sector, built around fossil fuels and nuclear power, thinks in a centralized manner, and organizes from top to bottom. The Third Industrial Revolution is bucking up against such an ingrained management style, that it is virtually impossible for executive leadership at the corporate suite level to imagine the alternative.

Second, the corporate mindset is mirrored in Congress. The committee chairpersons, senators, representatives, and legislative staff work so closely with the energy industry in drafting legislation that the accustomed thinking in Congress about how one promotes and regulates energy and electricity reflects the thinking in the corporate board room. In this case, the proposed legislation mandating a unidirectional high-voltage grid from west to east, at a cost of $160 billion, subsidized by millions of electricity consumers who will have to pay more for their electricity, locks the country into the same kind of centralized command and control over power that occurred during the First and Second Industrial Revolutions and, in the process, gives one region an advantage over the others.

If, however, the federal government were to install a distributed national power grid that connects the entire continent and allows every local producer to feed electricity unto the network, it would create the kind of lateral scaling that we've seen with distributed Internet businesses. The price of electricity for every business and consumer would continue to drop as it did in the case of sharing information.

President Obama has been out on the political circuit talking up the need to replace a half-century-old servomechanical power grid with a digital, state-of-the-art smart grid and is pushing for thousands of miles of new power lines to meet America's future electricity needs. But why would the president favor this centralized approach to organizing renewable energy resources that are, by their nature, broadly distributed and locally available?

THE OLD ENERGY LOBBY MAKES ITS LAST STAND

Follow the money. The big energy companies can legitimately claim to have the most powerful lobby in Washington—an army of more than six hundred registered lobbyists—a force so influential that, up to now at least, it could dictate the energy "choices" for the country.[10] Who are these lobbyists? According to one study, three out of every four lobbyists who represent oil and gas companies were previously members of Congress who served on the committees that oversee and regulate the industry, or worked for various federal agencies responsible for regulating the energy industry.[11] There is a Chaplinesque quality to the infamous "revolving door," with energy executives and government officials changing hats and desks in a kind of perpetual blur.

Senators and congressmen on key committees are rewarded with campaign contributions for their pro-industry leanings and for writing up the appropriate legislation, and then rewarded again after leaving office with lobbying positions inside the industry.

What does the energy industry get in return for their generosity? Plenty. Their return on investment would be the envy of any banker. From 2002 to 2008, federal energy subsidies to the fossil fuel industry totaled more than $72 billion. Renewable energy subsidies that same period were less than $29 billion.[12]

To ensure that the politicians toe the line, the energy lobby pours billions of dollars into public media campaigns and finances its own educational institutes, providing grants to pro-industry researchers and underwriting grassroots campaigns whose missions are to convince voters that America's best hope lies with supporting big oil. And the fact is, their strategy is fairly successful.

Much of the efforts by big oil in recent years have focused on sowing public doubt and skepticism on climate change. In the short period between 2009 and 2010, the oil, coal, and utility industries spent $500 million to lobby the government against the passage of climate-change legislation.[13]

Groups like Americans for Prosperity and Freedom-Works, financed, in large part, by oil industry interests, have been particularly successful in getting the burgeoning Tea Party movement to embrace their message in election campaigns across the country. A *New York Times*/CBS poll conducted in the fall of 2010, on the eve of the off-year elections, found that a mere 14 percent of Tea Party supporters believe that global warming is an environmental problem, compared to nearly 50 percent of the general public.[14]

The growing public skepticism on climate change has gotten the attention of political candidates, especially in close elections where a few percentage points can spell victory or defeat. The *National Journal* reported that nineteen out of the twenty Republican senatorial candidates in the 2010 elections questioned climate change and opposed legislation to address global warming.[15]

The fossil fuel energy lobby in the United States has fought the introduction of renewable energy into the electricity mix for decades. And in the few instances where big oil companies have entered the renewable energy market, they have followed the traditional route of centralizing production and feeding the electricity into a unidirectional power grid.

There are signs, however, that the Second Industrial Revolution energy lobby is beginning to lose its once iron-clad grip over energy policies in Washington. David Callahan, a senior fellow at Demos, the Washington-based public policy research group, wrote a provocative essay in *The Washington Post* suggesting that the "dirty rich," by which he means the wealthiest Americans who made their fortunes in the polluting, extractive industries of the Second Industrial Revolution, are diminishing, in comparison to the "clean rich," whose fortunes are derived from the new, high-tech information industries of the Third Industrial Revolution. He points out that in 1982, 38 percent of the wealthiest Americans in the Forbes 400 came out of the oil industry and related manufacturing industries, while only 12 percent came out of technology and finance. By 2006, the tables had turned, with 36 percent of the richest Americans coming out of tech and finance, and only 12 percent from oil and related manufacturing.[16]

Many of the high-tech billionaires, like the founders of Google, Larry Page and Sergey Brin, are transforming their facilities into low-carbon emission operations, and investing millions of dollars in the new distributed renewable energy technologies of the Third Industrial Revolution.

While still the most powerful lobbying force in Washington, the old energy lobby—and the Second Industrial Revolution industries surrounding it—may be on its last legs. What hasn't yet happened, however, to any significant degree, is the coming together of a powerful renewable energy lobby with the accompanying industries that make up the five-pillar infrastructure of a Third Industrial Revolution. Part of the reason for this is that many of the key industries that have long been a part of the Second Industrial Revolution juggernaut find themselves caught between two energy regimes and economic eras, and two very different business models. It's not unusual to see the same industry lobbyists from the auto industry, the construction sector, the power and utility industry, and IT and transport sectors lobby for competing Second and Third Industrial Revolution legislative initiatives and regulatory policies at the same time, with confusing and sometimes comical consequences.

A distributed and collaborative TIR network needs to model its lobbying efforts to comport with its mission to create a transparent, democratic, sustainable, and just world. Paying knowledgeable lobbyists to make the case in the state Houses, Congress, and the executive agencies for a Third Industrial Revolution vision and game plan should be encouraged. Financing election campaigns and rewarding government personnel with private sector jobs in return for their support should be strictly prohibited.

The struggle over laying down a centralized supergrid or a distributed smart grid will likely determine the kind of economy and society our children and grandchildren inherit for the rest of the century. At this time, there is nothing to suggest that the Internet president is likely to stray much from the conventional wisdom and the long arm of the fossil fuel industry. However, an emerging Third Industrial Revolution lobby in Washington, the state capitals, and municipalities could launch a powerful counterforce, pushing the country toward a new economic agenda. The question is whether we will seize the moment or lose it.

THE TRANSFORMATION OF THE ECONOMY and the change in political values is forcing a commensurate power shift in governing institutions. While the First and Second Industrial Revolutions were accompanied by national economies, nation-state governance, and a centralized, top-down geopolitical division of the world, the Third Industrial Revolution, because it is distributed and collaborative by nature and scales laterally along contiguous landmasses, favors continental economies and political unions. We are moving from "globalization" to "continentalization."

CHAPTER SIX

FROM GLOBALIZATION TO CONTINENTALIZATION

I first heard the term *continentalization* at a small gathering in a secluded hotel in the countryside outside of Paris. It was in late May 2008. CEOs of the leading postal companies, representing much of the logistics traffic of the global economy, were settled in for a soul-searching talk about the future of the global economy.

A sense of uncertainty hung in the air. The attendees were very worried. In the business community, a rule of thumb is that a drop in shipments is a warning sign of storm clouds on the economic horizon. Global transport was grinding to a halt—something these CEOs had never seen in their lifetime. Purchasing power was plummeting around the world and factory inventories were piling up in the warehouses, yards, and ports. It looked like the entire economic engine of the global economy was shutting down.

I was at the meeting, convened by the International Post Corporation, the umbrella association of the world's postal companies, to give an address on the European Parliament's new long-term economic vision and game plan.

During my presentation, I explained that just as information likes to "run free" on the Internet, distributed renewable energy likes to run uninhibited across national borders. When millions of people generate their own energy on or around their homes, factories, and offices, sharing their energy from neighborhood to neighborhood and region to region, everyone becomes a node in a borderless green electricity network that scales laterally across entire continents. I noted that the First and Second Industrial Revolution energies and communications media gave rise to national markets and nation-state governments. The Third Industrial Revolution energies, communications media, and infrastructure, by contrast, spread out to the edge of contiguous landmasses. In the green-powered Third Industrial Revolution, continents become the new playing field for economic life, and continental political unions, like the European Union, become the new governing model.

Immediately after my talk, Peter Bakker, the CEO of TNT (the former Dutch postal company that was privatized and is among the leading logistics companies in the world), took the floor. To my surprise, he turned to the group and said, "Globalization is dying." In his opinion, the dramatic rise of the price of oil on the world market makes it increasingly problematic to send freight by air across the oceans, and government pressure to tax CO_2 emissions would only add to logistics costs. The economic current, he said, is shifting from globalization to continentalization. He argued that growth in commerce and trade is going to become increasingly drawn to continental markets. The logistics business, he said, is already redirecting much of its focus to a continental world.

If Bakker is right, the partial repositioning of commerce and trade from globalization to continentalization, coupled with the Wi-Fi–like spread of a TIR logistics infrastructure across continental landmasses, will likely speed the formation of continental economies and political unions.

The attendees at the meeting agreed to endorse the European Union's plan to implement a Third Industrial Revolution infrastructure. But as they voted, I couldn't help but notice the silence in the room as we each sank into our own thoughts about what might lie ahead.

RETURN TO PANGAEA

Although I had been talking for some years about how Third Industrial Revolution infrastructure favors continental markets, continental political unions, and transcontinental connectivity, the profound spatial implications didn't really register until just recently. I was on a night flight coming into Dakar in June of 2009. Looking out the window, I could see the twinkling lights coming from the infamous Island of Gorée, one of several collection points in Senegal for the transatlantic African slave trade. Dakar is the furthest western point of continental Africa, and as a result, became an embarkation point for transporting slaves to the Americas.

A few days later I was having lunch on the beach with Moustapha Ndiaye, a personal advisor to President Abdoulaye Wade of Senegal, about the possibility of his country pioneering a Third Industrial Revolution economic development plan that might serve as a model for the rest of West Africa. Every time I looked up from our conversation, I couldn't help but see the Island of Gorée immediately off the beach—a constant reminder of the gruesome toll that slavery and colonialism exacted on the African continent and its people.

At one point the conversation turned to the unique features of the West African coastline and I mentioned, in passing, how interesting it was that the curvature of the African coast fits almost identically with South America's eastern coastline, like two parts of a jigsaw puzzle.

Scientists have long suspected that at one time early on in the Earth's history, the two continents might have been a single landmass, and that a geological process, over time, could have separated them. In the 1960s, geologists were abuzz about new theories of tectonic plate shifts and continental drift. A consensus was emerging among scientists that as late as two hundred million years ago, in the Mesozoic era, the continents were connected in one extended landmass—what geologists called *Pangaea*. Scientists believe that a shift in the Earth's tectonic plates caused Pangaea to break up into the continents that currently exist. Now, for the first time, there is some talk of rejoining the continents again in a single global landmass, marking a return to Pangaea. Let me explain.

TIR infrastructure is just beginning to spread across continents in tandem with the creation of nascent continental markets and continental governing unions. The European Union is the first continental economy and political union to begin transitioning into a Third Industrial Revolution. Continental unions have recently been formed in Asia (the ASEAN Union), Africa (the African Union), and South America (the Union of South American Nations). In North America, the North American Free Trade Agreement (NAFTA) is a precursor to a continental union. While localities, regions, and national governments will not disappear in the coming century—they will actually be strengthened—continental unions provide an overarching political jurisdiction for regulating integrated continental markets. The new continental unions, in turn, are beginning to make plans to physically connect their landmasses, to create a seamless geographic space for conducting global commerce in the twenty-first century. In effect, continentalization is fostering a return to a single global continent—a second Pangaea, this time engineered by human hands.

The European Union has recently entered into a partnership with the African Union to begin laying the infrastructure for a Third Industrial Revolution, which will eventually join the two continents. For example, plans are being developed for a multibillion dollar project, called Desertec, which will bring energy generated from solar and wind technologies from the Sahara desert, via interconnector cables, to Europe—providing more than 15 percent of the European Union's total energy needs by 2050.[1]

At the same time, Spain and Morocco have been in discussions about building a transport tunnel below the Strait of Gibraltar that will link Europe and Africa. Like the Channel Tunnel that connects the United Kingdom to Europe, the new tunnel would carry passengers and freight between Europe and Africa, bringing the two continents together in a single logistics grid.

Discussions are also underway between Russia and the United States to construct a sixty-four-mile tunnel under the Bering Strait, linking Siberia and Alaska, for an estimated cost of between $10 and $12 billion. The tunnel will feature a high-speed rail system to link Eurasia and the Americas for commerce, trade, and tourism, creating a connected, land-based logistics network that stretches three quarters of the way around the world—from London to New York.[2] The tunnel will serve a dual purpose, allowing both continents to share electricity harnessed from the vast amount of renewable energy in Siberia and Alaska.

Laying down underwater high-voltage cables to exchange green electricity between Europe, Africa, Asia, and the Americas is easier, from an engineering standpoint, than constructing deep-ocean tunnels and, for that reason, will likely come to pass in the near future. Tunnel connections will take longer, with policy analysts projecting more than twenty years to complete.

For those who find the possibility of connecting the continents hard to believe, recall the widespread skepticism when the ideas of the Suez and Panama canals were first bandied about. Although the technical and engineering challenges, not to mention the costs involved, cast doubt on their feasibility, the commercial advantages were just too great to ignore. We found ways to build both canals in record time.

The Suez Canal, which cut across Egypt to connect the Mediterranean Sea and Red Sea, opened up an artificial water route between Europe and Asia without having to navigate all the way around the Horn of Africa. The 101-mile canal was begun in 1859 and completed just ten years later. Over 1.5 million people were employed over the course of the project and thousands lost their lives in the undertaking.[3]

The Panama Canal, first begun by the French in the 1880s and abandoned shortly thereafter, was picked up and completed by the United States. The canal cut across Central America, connecting the Atlantic and Pacific Oceans, thereby eliminating the long journey around the Strait of Magellan at the southern tip of South America. The American Panama Canal was begun in 1904 and completed just ten years later, at a cost of 5,609 human lives.[4]

While the engineering challenges involved in connecting the world's great continental landmasses are equally daunting, the commercial opportunities are enormous. Although far from certain, it's quite possible that the continents of the world will reconnect in a Third Industrial Revolution infrastructure well before mid-century, paving the way for a return to Pangaea.

Just as the Internet connected the human race in a single distributed and collaborative virtual space, the Third Industrial Revolution connects the human race in a parallel Pangaean political space. What will this political space look like? Because the TIR infrastructure, which is the centerpiece of continental markets and continental governance, scales laterally and is distributed, collaborative, and networked, continental and global governance is likely to be as well. The idea of a centralized world government might have been a logical fit for the Second Industrial Revolution, whose infrastructure scaled vertically and whose organization was hierarchal and centralized, but it is bizarrely out of place and out of sync in a world where the energy/communication infrastructure is nodal, interdependent, and flat. Networked communication, energy, and commerce spread across the planet invariably gives rise to network governance at both the continental and global levels. The engineering of an interconnected, intercontinental living space creates a new spatial orientation. In an increasingly integrated global society, people begin to see themselves as part of an indivisible planetary organism.

THE WORLD'S FIRST CONTINENTAL UNION

Medieval scholars could not have imagined the concept of a nation—a secular governing authority that ruled by the consent of the citizenry rather than by holy mandate. Today, the European Union notwithstanding, most people in the world would have a difficult time imagining being a citizen of a continental union and feeling like they were part of an extended political family that stretched from ocean edge to ocean edge. The thought of each continent being governed by a political union would seem odd. Yet, barring some unforeseen circumstances, this is likely where society is headed. It is strange to hear policy analysts and journalists speculate about all the various new political power realignments—G20, G8, G2, BRIC—but never mention a more fundamental political realignment beginning to take place all over the world in the form of continental governance.

The Third Industrial Revolution not only brings with it a new generation of political leaders who think in a manner that is distributed and collaborative, but also new governing institutions that are likewise distributed and collaborative. The European Union is the first continental union. It was born in the aftermath of two devastating world wars and was conceived with the idea that traditional geopolitics, in which each sovereign state competed both in the marketplace and on the battleground to achieve its self-interests, needed to give way, at least in part, to a new continental politics in which nations collaborated with each other to advance their collective security and economic interests. While national self-interest didn't disappear with the creation of the European Union, each generation of Europeans has become increasingly comfortable identifying itself, at times, as Europeans.

The European Union initially came together around the sharing of energy. The European Coal and Steel Community Pact (ECSC) in 1951 was the brainchild of Jean Monnet, who is regarded by most Europeans as the father of the European Union. Monnet argued that the long-standing economic rivalry between Germany and France might best be attenuated by merging their coal resources and steel production, especially along the long-disputed industrial corridor that bordered the Ruhr and Saar rivers. The ECSC Treaty of Paris was signed by France, Germany, Italy, Belgium, the Netherlands, and Luxemburg. In 1957, the six member countries signed the Treaty of Rome, expanding the idea of cooperation to include the creation of the European Economic Community. The countries also entered into a separate agreement to create the European Atomic Energy Community (Euratom), a cooperative venture to develop nuclear power across their regions.

Today, the European Union encompasses twenty-seven member states with a total population of five hundred million citizens in an area that extends from the Irish Sea to Russia.

Now, as the EU enters its second half century, energy again has become central to the next stage of continental development. While the European Union is potentially the largest internal commercial market in the world, with its five hundred million consumers, and an additional five hundred million consumers in its associated partnership regions stretching into the Mediterranean and North Africa, it has not yet created an integrated single market.

The Third Industrial Revolution makes possible the establishment of a distributed continental energy and communication infrastructure that will create a seamless economic space, so that the billion plus people in the EU region can engage in commerce and trade with efficiency and ease, and with a low carbon dioxide footprint, allowing Europe to become the largest integrated single market by 2050. This is the critical unfinished business of the European Union.

Asian, African, and South American nations are beginning to follow the European Union's lead by forming their own continental unions with the same goal in mind—creating a single integrated market. And like the European Union, they are bringing distributed Internet communication media together with distributed renewable energy to create an infrastructure for a Third Industrial Revolution economy—one that can host a fully integrated power grid, telecommunications network, and transport system for continent-wide commerce and trade. A distributed and collaborative energy/communication infrastructure that crosses entire continents will spur the maturation of continental forms of governance.

THE ASEAN UNION

The process is already well under way in Asia, where ten Southeast Asian nations—Indonesia, Malaysia, Philippines, Singapore, Thailand, Brunei Darussalam, Myanmar, Vietnam, Laos, and Cambodia—have created the Association of Southeast Asian Nations or ASEAN. Three other countries—China, Japan, and the Republic of Korea—have affiliated with ASEAN to form ASEAN Plus Three, or APT.

ASEAN was established back in 1967 to facilitate "economic growth, social progress and cultural development in the region through joint endeavors."[5] It wasn't until 2003, however, that the member states agreed to create an ASEAN community, patterned along lines similar to the European Union. In 2007, the member states met on Cebu Island in the Philippines and took a giant step forward by signing the Cebu Declaration on the Acceleration of the Establishment of an ASEAN community by 2015. The ASEAN community is made up of three pillars: the ASEAN Political-Security Community, ASEAN Economic Community, and ASEAN Social-Cultural Community.[6]

An ASEAN charter entered into force in 2008, committing the member countries to operate within a common legal framework and create formal organs to facilitate the building of a cohesive continental community.[7]

At the Cebu Philippines East Asian Summit in 2007, the ASEAN member states signed a second accord, a Declaration on East Asian Energy Security, that would serve as a basis for the creation of a continental energy infrastructure and lay the foundation for a TIR economy across the Asian land space. The energy agreement was also signed by ASEAN's regional partners, the People's Republic of China and the Republic of India, both of whom are on the Southeast Asian continent, and the Pacific nations of Japan, the Republic of Korea, Australia, and New Zealand.

The signatories acknowledged "the limited global reserve of fossil energy, the unstable world prices of fuel oil, the worsening problems of the environment and health, and the urgent need to address global warming and climate change."[8] Given these constraints, the question looming for the ASEAN nations is how to continue growing their economies at a brisk speed without compromising the environment or contributing to global warming. To fuel their economic growth, they will need clean energy on a grand scale, which will require a collective commitment to bring renewables online quickly across the continent and the Pacific Rim.

The parties therefore agreed to "reduce dependence on conventional fuels . . . increase the capacity and reduce the costs of renewable and alternative energy sources through innovative financing schemes" and "ensure availability of a stable energy supply through investments in regional energy infrastructure such as the ASEAN power grid."[9]

The last provision of the Cebu Declaration—the creation of the ASEAN power grid—is pivotal to the transition into a Third Industrial Revolution continental economy and the solidification of an ASEAN continental governing space. ASEAN, whose moniker is "ten nations, one community," has laid out a comprehensive long-term energy plan for the continent and launched its initial five-year agenda, which it calls the ASEAN Plan of Action for Energy Cooperation (APAEC) 2010–2015. The centerpiece of the plan is the ASEAN power grid—a "flagship program" that was inaugu-

rated in 2004 by the ASEAN heads of state. The goal is "a totally integrated Southeast Asian power grid."[11]

Establishing a common electricity power grid across the Southeast
Asian continent provides the nervous system for the creation of a single,
integrated market and a continental political union. Currently, there are
four interconnection power grid projects underway and eleven more in the
planning stage, with an estimated cost of $5.9 billion.[12]

ASEAN clearly understands the importance of transitioning to renewable energies, and the critical role that an interconnected continental power
grid will play in creating an ASEAN community. ASEAN states, in unequivocal terms, that it "views the need for ASEAN countries to move beyond
independent energy policies and planning[,] to . . . inter-dependent, inter-
country, and outward looking policies for greater economic integration."[13]
The speed at which ASEAN countries create an integrated, single market
and continental political union will ultimately hinge on how fast they can
build out a green smart grid to connect the region.

Although the ASEAN community is quickly moving from vision to political reality, there are a number of open questions that could undermine
its efforts to create a continental union. The first is the imposing presence
of China. With 1.3 billion people and an economy that has already eclipsed
Japan as the engine of Asia, China is the great unknown in the Asian arena.[14]
Will it remain on the sideline as an associated partner region, especially if
ASEAN becomes a single political community? A political union of 605 million Southeast Asians, while only half the population of China, would still
be a force to reckon with. If Japan, the Republic of Korea, Australia, and
the Philippines were to shift from partner status to formal members of the
ASEAN community, that would bring on board additional economic clout
and almost three hundred million more people to boot, making the union a
strong counterplayer to China in the region.

If India, the world's other fast-growing Asian giant, with nearly 1.2 billion people, were to become a full-fledged member of the ASEAN community, it, too, might overwhelm the rest of the member states and dominate
the political game.

The reason the European Union has been able to succeed in its efforts
to create a single, continental political space is that no single government
can completely dictate the terms of political engagement. While Germany
is the economic engine and the most powerful single player in the union, its
power doesn't overwhelm the rest of the pack.

The EU community stops at the doorstep of Russia. That's not to say that Russia couldn't justifiably claim that it is part of Europe as much as it is part of Asia, and that it ought to be included in the European Union. Up to now, however, it has enjoyed only a special partnership status, and few observers think that's likely to change in the foreseeable future.

I broached the subject of membership in the European Union at dinner once with Mikhail Gorbachev. He said that his country was just too big to fit into the EU room, and that instead Russia would likely enjoy an ever-closer partnership with the union, even to the point of being connected in an integrated continental electricity, communication, and transport grid—in effect, becoming part of a single market but not a single political space.

The same may happen in Asia with respect to China and India. The centralized command and control infrastructure of the Chinese government makes it less likely than India to engage in the kind of distributed and collaborative relationships that are the defining characteristic of continental union politics. India, on the other hand, with its far more decentralized and democratic power structure, might fare better in forging closer partnership ties, and even possible membership, in the ASEAN Union. All of this is purely speculative at this point in time. A younger generation coming of age in China is far more comfortable with a distributed and collaborative approach to economic, political, and social organization, and could quickly change the dynamics of the game, with consequences that are difficult to predict at this early stage of continentalization.

A final point ought to be raised, which is relevant to the creation of continental unions on every continent—that is, the increasing power exercised by localities and regions that are no longer as constrained by national boundaries.

This shift in political power was unanticipated when the European Union was first getting off the ground. The only real debate at the time was whether the European community would be more of a common market or a centralized federal state. The British favored the former, hoping to maintain their national sovereignty while enjoying the commercial advantages of becoming part of a larger integrated market. The French were disposed to a more centralized architecture, which they hoped they could direct or at least influence, without too much loss of national sovereignty. In the end, the European Union developed along altogether different lines, ultimately becoming far more than a common market and far less than a centralized federal state. What the EU experience shows is that when nation-states come together to create a common political community with integrated markets and open borders, commercial and political relations tend to flatten and extend across previous national boundaries, creating a new power configuration that is more nodal and distributed than centralized and top-down. EU governance more resembles a network of nation-states, regions, and municipalities, in which no single force determines the direction of the union, forcing all of the political players to engage in collaborative efforts to reach consensus on common goals.

The creation of a continental market and continental governance with open borders also allows regions to bypass their national governments and create their own commercial relationship with other regions, sometimes contiguous to but just across national boundaries, and other times far removed in geography from their home country. Contiguous cross-border EU regions are increasingly involved in commercial partnerships of all kinds and often enjoy closer commercial ties with each other than each region has with its own national government or more distant countrymen.

The Third Industrial Revolution communication/energy paradigm, because of its lateral orientation, flourishes in borderless open spaces. What this means is that as the ASEAN Union becomes more of a reality, open borders will allow contiguous regions to interconnect and jointly build out the five-pillar infrastructure of the TIR, much like Wi-Fi communications spread from neighborhood to neighborhood and quickly developed into vast, interconnected webs that span contiguous landmasses.

If China and India, both of whom have signed the Cebu Energy Declaration, would open their borders, thereby allowing neighboring regions to connect and build out shared TIR infrastructure, the spreading network could whittle away at the sovereign power each government previously enjoyed over the generation of energy and distribution of electricity within their borders. This would fundamentally alter the political configuration of power, much as it is doing on the European continent.

China and India may find they have no choice but to become part of a continental union if they want to remain relevant in the world economy of the twenty-first century. At present, both countries are moving quickly to develop the various TIR technologies. China, in particular, is within striking distance of taking over the commanding lead that the European Union has long enjoyed in the development and marketing of some of its key technological components. But China has siloed each of the technological pillars as if they were stand-alone items. So while it is fast becoming the leader in renewable energy technology and beginning to construct zero-emission and positive-power buildings, developing hydrogen and other storage technologies, creating smart power grids, and producing electric and fuel cell vehicles, it does not yet fully understand the social impact these advances will have when connected in a single, interactive system. Together, they require a flat, open, and shared continental political space to develop, scale, and fully optimize their economic potential. Ironically, China may end up developing the very software and hardware components that take down its present form of top-down governance. And that is what truly qualifies as "a contradiction," to use a favorite Marxist phrase.

THE AFRICAN UNION

In 2002, the heads of state of the fifty-four nations on the African continent, with a combined population of more than 1 billion people, launched the African Union (AU) with the goal of accelerating "the political and socio-economic integration of the continent."[15] The mechanics of getting the AU off the ground were bogged down in bureaucratic delays until 2008, when the African Union and the European Union entered into the Africa-Europe Energy Partnership (AEEP). The aim of the partnership is to promote the development of renewable energy and create an electricity master plan for Africa, connecting its one billion people in an integrated grid that will crisscross the continent.

Africa has the least developed electricity infrastructure of any continent in the world. Seven out of every ten people in Sub-Saharan Africa have no access to electricity, while many others have only spotty and irregular access.[16] The fact that much of Africa is without even a Second Industrial Revolution infrastructure may turn out to be an asset. Some policy analysts argue that Africa could "leapfrog" into a Third Industrial Revolution without having to address the thorny issue of how to manage the expense and ease the pain of transitioning out of a dying Second Industrial Revolution infrastructure. With this in mind, the European Union earmarked €376 million to seventy-seven projects, mostly to promote renewable energy sources and grid extension, with an additional €588 million pledged to future projects not yet on the drawing board.

The EU/AU energy partnership set two specific short-term targets: first, to bring modern and sustainable energy services to at least an additional hundred million Africans; second, to greatly increase the use of renewable energy on the African continent by building 10,000 megawatts of new hydropower facilities, 5,000 megawatts of wind power, and expanding other renewable energy by 500 megawatts.[17] Like ASEAN, there is a growing realization that a distributed and collaborative renewable energy regime will invariably be accompanied by the formation of a networked, continental governing space.

Still, Africa faces a significant obstacle. Because the Second Industrial Revolution did not take hold across much of Sub-Saharan Africa, there is a lack of professional and technical expertise and vocational skills to support the industries that would need to be developed to get the job done. That's why the EU/AU partnership is as much about sharing knowledge and technical expertise as it is about capital expenditure and technology transfer. The idea is to create a close, collaborative partnership between the two continental unions that will allow Africa to grow their businesses and train a skilled work force that can build and manage a TIR infrastructure. The hope is that the joint energy initiatives to create a green electricity grid across the African continent will open up "significant new areas for industrial trade and business cooperation between Africa and Europe" and help establish a powerful intercontinental market.[18]

The EU/AU partnership has won praise from around the world. TIR advocates point out that unlike the First and Second Industrial Revolutions, which relied on elite fossil fuel energies found only in select places and required large military investments and geopolitical manipulation to secure, all of which favored the interests of the more powerful northern nations, renewable energies are found everywhere. They are particularly abundant, however, in the developing countries below the equator. Because renewable energy is widely distributed, a Third Industrial Revolution is just as likely to take off in the developing world as the developed world. Africa, in particular, has barely begun to exploit its renewable energy potential. Energy analysts say that solar, wind, hydro, geothermal, and biomass sources could more than supply the energy needs of every continent. The key is providing a favorable playing field, and that means financial aid, technology transfer, and training programs to assist developing nations, like the ones being advanced by the EU/AU partnership.

Already however, such efforts are raising eyebrows. Skeptics question whether these programs might constitute a new kind of "eco-colonialism." They point to the controversial Desertec Industrial Initiative in the Sahara as a possible harbinger of this.[19] A fierce debate is unfolding between those who advocate centralizing energy production for export versus those who champion generating electricity from locally available renewable energy and sharing it regionally across distributed smart grids. The debate is similar to the one in the United States over centralizing wind and solar production in the West and exporting electricity via super high-voltage power lines to the eastern states, versus those in other parts of the country who prefer to produce electricity locally from renewable energy sources and share it across a distributed, national smart grid.

Backers of the Desertec Industrial Initiative argue that "if you enable large-scale investments into power generation and power transmission in North Africa, then this will automatically lead to local industry, transfer of technology, and the transfer of knowledge." Some African officials agree. Aboubakari Baba Moussa, director of infrastructure and energy of the African Union Commission, says the Desertec project is a win-win for both the European Union and for Africa. "In Africa, we don't have a shortage of solar radiation, we don't have a shortage of land. The Europeans don't have the same resources." Baba Moussa hopes that similar projects can be marshaled for the Kalahari Desert in South Africa and the Ogaden desert in East Africa. He asks critics to "imagine how many hundreds of thousands of jobs could be created and how much energy could be produced."[21]

Others are far more guarded. They wonder whether the potential jobs will merely be for temporary, unskilled labor, with most of the skilled workforce brought in from Europe to build and maintain the facilities. The late Hermann Scheer, the chairman of the World Council for Renewable Energy and a member of the German Parliament, argued that transporting solar energy over vast distances is inefficient and a waste of money, and that Africa should be focusing its efforts on local generation of renewable energies instead. Greenpeace comes down in the middle on the debate. Sven Teske, Greenpeace's international renewable energy director, supports Desertec, but with the qualification that it should be developed alongside local renewable energy generation initiatives across the continent.[22]

The struggle over centralized versus distributed generation of renewable energy is intensifying around the world. For my part, while I don't oppose some centralized applications of solar, wind, hydro, geothermal, and biomass power, they are likely to make up a small portion of the renewable energy generated to power a Third Industrial Revolution economy. The reality is that renewable energies are, by nature, universally distributed, and the new, distributed communication technologies make it possible to harness and store these energies locally and distribute them across intelligent utility networks that span entire continents. The potential to produce more distributed power more efficiently and more cheaply far exceeds the conventional centralized approach to harnessing these energy sources.

Lateral power is already beginning to transform the developing world. Electricity is now coming to remote areas in Africa, which never before had access to a centralized power grid. Not surprisingly, the introduction of cell phones has helped precipitate the development of a nascent TIR infrastructure.

Virtually overnight, millions of Africa's rural households have scraped together enough money—from selling an animal or surplus crops—to purchase a cell phone. The phones are used as much for carrying on commercial activity as for personal communications. In rural areas, far removed from urban banking facilities, people are increasingly relying on cell phones to facilitate small money transfers. The problem is that without access to electricity, cell phone users often have to travel on foot to get to a town with electricity in order to recharge their phones.

Elisabeth Rosenthal, writing in the *New York Times,* recounts the story of a rural woman living in Kenya who had to walk two miles once a week to get a motorcycle taxi and drive for three more hours to a town to recharge her cell phone battery for a 30 cent fee. Recently, her family sold some farm animals to buy an $80 solar power system. A single solar panel now affixed on the tin roof of her hut provides enough electricity to not only charge the cell phone but also power four overhead electric lights.[23] Although the statistics are still spotty, it appears that families across Africa are installing solar panels and analysts predict a quick scale-up as millions of others follow suit into the Third Industrial Revolution. What's going on in Africa heralds a historic transformation as households leapfrog from the pre-electricity era directly into the TIR age.

Besides solar, other green micro-generation energy technologies are quickly coming online, including small biogas chambers that make electricity and fuel from cow manure, tiny power plants that make electricity from rice husks and small hydroelectric dams that generate power from local streams. Still missing is a smart, distributed power grid that will allow stand-alone micro-generators to share electricity with others across entire regions. That is likely to come as millions of families begin generating their own electricity from on-site renewable energies. This process represents the democratization of energy in the world's poorest communities.

THE SOUTH AMERICAN UNION

The South American union is a latecomer to continentalization. Two earlier regional associations—the Andean Community of Nations, formed in 1969, made up of Bolivia, Chile, Columbia, Ecuador, and Peru; and Mercosur, founded in 1991 and comprising Brazil, Paraguay, Uruguay, and Argentina—were both designed to create a common free-trade area.

In May 2008, heads of state representing twelve South American nations agreed to join together and establish the Union of South American Nations (UNASUR). The union, which absorbs the two existing customs unions, Mercosur and the Andean Community, and includes Guyana, Suriname, and Venezuela, covers a region of 6,845,000 square miles, with a combined population of 388 million people and a gross domestic product of $4 trillion. The fledgling South American union will have a common defense. Its first secretary general, the former Argentine president, Néstor Kirchner, was appointed in 2010, but died shortly thereafter. The current secretary general is Maria Emma Mejia Vélez, the former Columbian foreign minister. The member nations have also agreed to establish a South American Parliament, issue a single passport, create a common currency, and move toward an integrated, single market by 2014.

The treaty creating the union puts energy at the top of the agenda, committing the member nations to a build-out of a continental infrastructure for sharing energy and electricity. The Energy Council of South America, established in April 2007 by the twelve heads of state, was made a formal part of UNASUR and given the responsibility for developing a South American Energy Strategy. The council has put a priority on developing the continent's abundant renewable energy because "it plays an important role in the diversification of the primary energy matrix, energy security, the promotion of universal access to energy, and environmental preservation."[24]

In practice, many South American countries have been slow to wean themselves off fossil fuels. Brazil, the continent's economic powerhouse, is an exception. It generates 84 percent of its electricity from renewable hydroelectric power, and domestic ethanol makes up between 20 and 25 percent of every liter of petrol used in transport.[25] The strong reliance on hydroelectric power and plant-based ethanol makes Brazil one of the most advanced renewable energy economies in the world.

Still, Brazil's love affair with renewable energy could change. The discovery of vast oil reserves in deep waters off the coast in recent years has catapulted Brazil to the front lines of the world's major oil producers—

it now ranks number twelve—raising the question of whether its energy policies, both domestically and internationally, will continue to move in the direction of a Third Industrial Revolution, or backtrack into the older oil culture.[26]

An unknown in Brazil is the country's future hydroelectric capacity. While water is a renewable resource, global warming is forcing a dramatic change in the planet's hydrological cycle, triggering more violent floods and longer periods of drought. The Amazon, which is the principle source of hydroelectric power, is among the regions of the world already affected by climate change–induced drought. In 2001, the country experienced a record drought, significantly reducing its hydroelectric capacity. The result was that the country's transmission grid experienced brownouts and blackouts throughout the year.

More serious droughts in the future could also diminish sugar cane yields and drive the price of ethanol higher. Brazil has an abundance of solar energy, however, which has yet to be harnessed and could pick up the slack.

Venezuela is another interesting anomaly. The country is awash in heavy oil, making it the ninth largest oil-exporting country. Hugo Chavez has used oil revenues strategically in the geopolitical arena to promote his ideological agenda, and on the domestic front to advance his unique brand of populist-socialism. With oil revenue accounting for about 30 percent of the country's total GDP, one would think that Chavez would be the last to champion a shift to renewable energy and a Third Industrial Revolution.[27] Yet, in a world where uncertainty has become the norm, political behavior and policy choices are often just as unpredictable.

It was September 17, 2006. My wife and I had just sat down for our ritual Sunday breakfast, with the *New York Times* spread out on the table. I flipped to the "Ideas and Trends" section, where an entire page was dedicated to Hugo Chavez's favorite books. The spin on the article was to try and dig into the mercurial leader's inner psyche and get a fix on the way he thinks. I scanned down the list of his all-time top reads: Victor Hugo's *Les Misérables,* Miguel de Cervantes's *Don Quixote,* Michael Moore's *Dude, Where's My Country?,* Fritjof Capra's *The Turning Point,* John Kenneth Galbraith's *The Economics of Innocent Fraud,* and Jeremy Rifkin's *The Hydrogen Economy.* I did a double take. I'd never met Mr. Chavez nor even corresponded with him. I glanced over to the article itself to see if I could glean any information on why Chavez was so taken by my book—after all, it was all about the sunset of the oil era, the lifeblood of his Venezuelan economy. Chavez remarked in the article that Fidel Castro, the president of Cuba, had been pushing him to read the book, and he did. (I had never met Fidel Castro either.)

The press reported that in July of 2006, on a state visit to Iran, Chavez had made a speech warning his Iranian audience to prepare themselves for a very different energy future after oil. Chavez referenced *The Hydrogen Economy* and informed his audience that "the book is based on something which is no longer a hypothesis—it is a thesis . . . oil will run out one day."[28] Most old hands in the Middle East didn't need an American citing global peak oil studies to tell them something they already knew in their very marrow. There is a saying in the Middle East that goes something like this: "My grandfather rode a camel, my father drove a car, I travel on a jet, and my grandchild will ride a camel."

Not necessarily. The deserts of the Middle East and North Africa have more solar potential per square inch than any other region in the world—more energy potential, in fact, than all of the oil ever extracted from deep beneath its sand dunes. The United Arab Emirates, the fifth-largest oil producing power, is already preparing for a post-oil era. Abu Dhabi is investing billions of dollars in the construction of a new city rising from the desert. It's called Masdar, a post-carbon city that will be run exclusively by the sun, wind, and other forms of renewable energy. It's a Third Industrial Revolution urban space, the first of thousands of such cities that will be nodes in the distributed networks that will crisscross every continent. I visited Masdar in 2009 and watched as engineers and construction crews were putting up the first building. The structure was like nothing I'd ever seen before. The design, building material, and facade all looked like something out of a futuristic movie. It took my breath away.

So, what's the takeaway from Chavez's speech? Begin transitioning now into a Third Industrial Revolution economy—don't delay until the oil spigot runs dry because then it will be too late.

I heard that very same message for the first time in the summer of 2002 from still another unexpected person—one of the world's leading oil company CEOs. My wife and I were in Los Cabos, in Baja Mexico, for the Asia-Pacific Economic Cooperation (APEC) CEO Summit, the annual meeting of the heads of state of the Pacific region. I was sharing a plenary session panel with Raúl Muñoz Leos, the director general of Pemex, Mexico's state-owned oil company. At the time, Mexico was the fifth largest oil-producing country in the world. I had just delivered my remarks on the coming of peak oil, urging government leaders to begin preparing for a transition into a post-carbon economy. I expected Mr. Muñoz Leos to politely disagree with me and give a more optimistic forecast. Instead, he told the assemblage that Pemex's own internal studies showed that Mexico's oil production would likely peak around 2010. The audience was stunned. One could hear a pin drop in the hall. A Mexican business leader rose from the floor and asked Muñoz Leos what this would mean for Mexico, given that Pemex's oil revenue accounted for a significant portion of the country's GDP and government revenue.

Muñoz Leos's response was circumspect. He said that he agreed with me that Mexico and the world needed to begin immediately planning for a new, renewable energy era. Mexico's best course of action, he said, was to use a sizable portion of its existing oil revenue to lay down an infrastructure for a renewable energy economy. He reminded the group that Mexico enjoyed extensive renewable energy resources with year-round solar irradiation and wind across the entire coastline.

The next year, I was invited down to Mexico by the federal government's Energy Ministry to discuss the prospect of Pemex transitioning into renewable energies and investing in the pillars that make up a TIR economy. To my knowledge, little came of the meeting. Muñoz Leos subsequently left Pemex. Still, every country, whether it is an importer or exporter of oil, would do well to heed his prescient remarks. Time is running out for the Second Industrial Revolution, as well as for laying down a Third Industrial Revolution infrastructure.

I'm reminded that America, once the leading oil power in the world, peaked in oil production in the early 1970s and, since that time, has increasingly had to rely on ever more expensive oil imports to maintain its own economy. Like Muñoz Leos at Pemex and President Chavez in Venezuela, US president Jimmy Carter tried to warn the American people that we needed to find alternatives to oil more than thirty years ago.

In 1979, during the dark days of the second oil crisis, when Iranian oil fields were all but shut down because of the disruption caused by the Iranian revolution, oil shortages resulted in long lines of cars queuing up for blocks at local filling stations in the United States like what happened in 1973 during the first oil crisis. Americans were angry and looking for a solution to a problem that seemed beyond their control. Sensing the mood of the country, President Carter delivered the most important speech of his presidency, although at the time it was not well-received and continues to be a source of derision among political pundits to this day.

The White House called the speech "The Crisis of Confidence," while the popular press dubbed it the "Malaise Speech." Reading it now, more than thirty years later, I am taken by how prophetic his address was. Carter realized that we were becoming more dependent on foreign oil and that the price of energy was likely only to increase in the decades ahead. He said that the oil crisis represented the culmination of a series of events that over twenty-five years had begun to erode the faith of the American people in a better tomorrow—the hallmark of the American dream. The assassination of President Kennedy, his brother, Robert Kennedy, and Martin Luther King Jr.; the long, torturous Vietnam War that had divided America; the growing inflation and unemployment; and the decline in wages were chipping away at the American psyche, creating a "crisis of confidence." The long lines at the fuel pumps and the increasing cost of gasoline and other oil-derived goods and services were exacerbating the crisis of confidence and turning America from a nation of hope into one of despair.

The president called on his fellow Americans to join him in a great crusade to claim our energy independence, put America back on track and restore our faith in the future: "Energy will be the immediate test of our ability to unite as a nation, and it can also be the standard around which we rally. On the battlefield of energy we can win for our nation a new confidence, and we can seize control again of our common destiny."[29]

The president led by example, installing the first solar panels on the White House roof and a wood-burning stove in his living quarters. He set forth bold new initiatives to cut dependence on foreign oil in half by the end of the following decade, establish energy conservation, and develop alternative sources of fuel. He proposed legislation for a solar bank to help the United States "achieve the crucial goal of 20 percent of our energy coming from solar power by the year 2000." He asked Americans to turn down their thermostats and use carpools and public transport. He called for an energy board similar to the War Production Board of World War II to oversee a complete mobilization of the country, with the goal of winning the war of energy independence.[30]

When the price of oil on the world market began to fall, the American business community and the public lost interest in the great energy crusade. Carter's successor, Ronald Reagan, removed the solar panels from the White House roof and scrapped the wood-burning stove in the living quarters. America went back to business as usual, buying even larger gas-guzzling vehicles, and using ever greater volumes of energy to support a wasteful, consumer-driven lifestyle.

Although Carter's warnings faded from the public mind in the ensuing decade, vast changes in the global economy were laying the groundwork for the first tentative forays into North American continentalization and, once again, energy would come to play a critical role.

A BACKDOOR NORTH AMERICAN UNION

The recession of 1990–1991 turned the nation's attention to restoring economic growth. In Washington, both Republicans and Democrats were championing globalization, the elimination of trade barriers, and deregulation of the market as the best route to grow the domestic economy and put Americans back to work. Eager to lead by example, George H. W. Bush successfully negotiated the North American Free Trade Agreement (NAFTA) with Canada and Mexico. Although some political observers wondered whether this was meant to be a precursor to the foundation of a North American political union, President Bush made it crystal clear that it was not the intention of any of the three countries to form a political union like the European Union. Rather, their sights were strictly fixed on the creation of a commercial zone to advance the mutual economic interests of the respective countries.

Energy policy was a key consideration from the beginning of NAFTA, but the focus was on the conventional energies—coal, oil, natural gas, and uranium—and, for good reason, at least as far as the United States was concerned. Canada to the north is the sixth largest oil producer in the world, and Mexico to the south is now the seventh. Sandwiched between two of the world's leading oil producers, the United States was understandably anxious to use NAFTA as an instrument to advance its energy security.

Few US citizens are even aware that Canada is the largest supplier of US oil and refined oil products, representing 21 percent of all US oil imports.[31] Canada also has the second largest oil reserves after Saudi Arabia. In addition, Canada provides 90 percent of all US natural gas imports and represents 15 percent of US consumption. It also has the world's largest high-grade uranium deposits and was the leading producer of uranium in 2008, with 20 percent of total global production. One-third of the uranium used in US nuclear plants is mined in Canada.[32] Canada and the United States also share an integrated electricity grid, all of which makes our Northern neighbor indispensable to the economic well-being of the United States, and our most important trading partner.

A growing number of Canadians, however, question whether NAFTA makes their country a valued partner or a useful appendage to the United States. Many Canadians deeply oppose strengthening NAFTA, arguing that Canada is already being absorbed into the larger US economy and is losing its political sovereignty in the process. Canadians also worry that NAFTA will mean having to go along with the dominant American ideology, which is often at odds with Canada's deeply held cultural and social values. They fear that the new "continentalism" is merely coded language for erasing the border along the forty-ninth parallel. In short, they suspect that NAFTA is a front for a twenty-first century, high-tech American colonialism designed to grab hold of Canada's rich resources and remake its citizenry in the United States' image.

Opponents of the "one container fits all" approach to continentalism also worry that Canada is becoming so dependent on exports to the United States (currently 73 percent of Canadian exports flow south) that the country may eventually be forced to accept whatever commercial and political terms the United States chooses to impose.[33] This is why Canada's NAFTA critics insist on trade, investment, and fiscal policies that encourage the growth of a more robust internal market and overseas trade, reforms to safeguard Canadian industries from US protectionism, and measures to redress the current trade imbalance between Canada and the United States.

While public attention has focused on the benefits and drawbacks of NAFTA, another type of continental political realignment has been quietly gaining momentum over the past twenty years and has the potential to redraw the North American political map. Former Canadian minister of external affairs, Lloyd Axworthy, notes that the 1990s saw the emergence of a spider's web of regional, cross-border, intracontinental networks. In the United States, owing to its tradition of states' rights, the states are mostly free to determine their own economic agreements. During the 1990s, the border states and Canadian provinces took significant steps to increase ties. In 1999, then–Ontario premier, Mike Harris, in a speech to American governors in neighboring states that border Canada, said "We really see you as very strong allies, more so than many parts of Canada, something far more significant than perhaps my national government understands." Cross-border commercial relation-ships have been developing for decades.

The closer commercial ties, in turn, have been accompanied by ever-closer political ties. Regional associations of US governors and Cana-dian provincial premiers now exist from coast to coast to promote and integrate mutual commercial and environmental agendas. In fact, the political integration of Northeastern, upper-Midwest, and Pacific-coast states with Canadian provinces has, in many ways, begun to eclipse the traditional political links each has with political jurisdictions within their own countries.

The Conference of New England Governors and Eastern Canadian Premiers (NEG/ECP), founded in 1973 has been steadily moving toward a regional, transnational approach. The NEG/ECP is made up of six states and five Canadian provinces: Connecticut, Maine, Massachusetts, New Hampshire, Vermont, Rhode Island, Quebec, Newfoundland and Labra-dor, Nova Scotia, New Brunswick, and Prince Edward Island. The gover-nors and premiers meet annually to discuss matters of common interest. Between these summits, the NEG/ECP convenes meetings of state and pro-vincial officials to implement policies, organize workshops, and to prepare studies and reports on issues of regional impact. The conference's many accomplishments include "the expansion of economic ties among the states and provinces; the fostering of energy exchanges; the forceful advocacy of environmental issues and sustainable development; and the coordination of numerous policies and programs in such areas as transportation, forest management, tourism, small-scale agriculture, and fisheries."[34]

Another transnational political region, similar in scope to the NEG/ECP, exists in the Pacific Northwest and is made up of British Columbia, Alberta, the Yukon Territory, Washington, Oregon, Idaho, Montana, and Alaska. Established in 1991, the mission of the Pacific Northwest Eco-nomic Region (PNWER) is "to increase the economic well-being and qual-ity of life for all citizens of the region."[35]

At least as active as its eastern counterpart, the PNWER group is at-tempting to harmonize approaches in the fields of agriculture, environ-mental technology, forest production, government procurement, recycling, telecommunications, tourism, trade and finance, and transportation. PNWER subcommittees are looking to a regional energy strategy, focusing on best practices for sustainable development, as well as exploring meth-ods for states and provinces to reduce soaring health-care costs, tighten border-security issues, expand foreign investment, and share information to upgrade workforce skills.

These transnational political groupings represent a new chapter in North American governance, with both Canadian provinces and US states bringing powerful assets to the partnership. Canada's vast renewable energy reserves provide the kind of energy security that is essential to make transnational political regions semi-autonomous. Canada also sports a highly educated workforce and relatively low production costs. For example, American employers save on health-care costs by locating production facilities in Canada or by outsourcing to Canadian firms because workers in Canada are covered by national health-care insurance.

The border states, in turn, have some of the best universities and research facilities on the planet, giving the budding intracontinental partnership a leg up on other regions of the world in cutting-edge commercial development.

The creation of cross-border regional partnerships in North America are similar to those being formed between regions inside the European Union, and ones that are likely to form on every continent when nation-states begin to ease border restrictions on commerce and trade and form larger commercial trade zones, or even full-fledged continental political unions.

As mentioned earlier in this chapter, continentalization flattens national sovereignty and allows regions to hook up across national borders in wholly new ways that not only create new economic opportunity, but even breed new cultural and political identities. Here is a case in point. Perhaps no contest is more highly charged in terms of national loyalties than bids for the Olympic Games. When Vancouver made its bid for the 2010 Olympic Games, it was supported by every one of the states in the Pacific Northwest Economic Region, creating blowback in other parts of the United States.

It is not surprising that everywhere continentalization is evolving, regions are connecting with one another to create Third Industrial Revolution green infrastructure. Just as elite fossil fuel energies are always harnessed centrally and distributed from the top down, renewable energies are, for the most part, best harnessed locally and shared laterally across contiguous regions.

In the Pacific Northwest Economic Region, Pacific Gas and Electric Company (PG&E) of California, the British Columbia Transmission Corporation (BCTC), and Avista Utility are jointly exploring the erection of a power line that will stretch one thousand miles from southeast British Columbia to Northern California, with the capacity to transport 3,000 megawatts of power from renewable energy harnessed locally and uploaded to the grid along the entire length of the transmission line. Much of the electricity will come from the abundance of wind, biomass, small hydro, and geothermal energy in British Columbia.

Thinking of the Pacific Northwest as a political space is not all that far-fetched. The fact is, the region shares a common history that predates national boundaries but remains alive in the minds of the people who live there. It is not unusual for people living in the Northwest part of North America to think of themselves as being part of Cascadia, a semi-fictional region that includes Alaska, the Yukon, British Columbia, Alberta, Washington, Oregon, Montana, and Idaho. The region is bounded by topography and shares a common past that includes shared ecosystems, the migration patterns of indigenous populations, and European settlement. Thomas Jefferson regarded the region west of the Louisiana Purchase as a potential separate country.

The idea of Cascadia has stuck in the minds of utopian visionaries and has been part of popular lore for as long as anyone cares to remember. If California were to be included—and many inhabitants of Northern California would no doubt consider themselves to be part of Cascadia—the region's sixty million inhabitants would claim a GDP of $2 trillion and rival the size of the Chinese economy.

The Pacific Northwest Economic Region already encompasses much of the region of Cascadia, a fact not lost on regional party leaders. In 2007, the premier of British Columbia, Gordon Campbell, in discussing the enormous economic and social potential of the region, went as far as to say, "I think there is a very strong, natural pull of the region called Cascadia."[36] Because the region's population is among the most environmentally sensitive in North America, Campbell argued that the cross-border political jurisdictions should join together to create a common carbon trading market to address climate change. That year, British Columbia and Manitoba joined with Governor Schwarzenegger of California and other states in signing the Western Climate Initiative to begin working together to implement a regional cap and trade program.

The Conference of New England Governors and Eastern Canadian Premiers are working just as closely to unite their jurisdictions around a common plan to share regionally generated renewable energy in a distributed smart grid network. The governing bodies are quickly putting in place the various pillars of a regional TIR infrastructure and, when that's completed, the region's inhabitants will share far more than energy—they will be part of a regional biosphere connected by post-carbon businesses and workforces. Equally important, they will share a common quality of life in an extended community that bypasses national boundaries, creating their own de facto intracontinental union.

Governor John Baldacci of Maine captured the historic nature of the mission the jurisdictions have set out for themselves in a 2008 meeting of the governors and premiers. On the table was a proposal to construct a 345,000-volt transmission line from central to northern Maine that could connect with a transmission line that had recently been built from Point Lepreau in New Brunswick to the Maine border. The new high-voltage line would be able to accept the flow of electricity generated from locally harnessed renewable energy in Canada and send it across the New England power grid.[37] Speaking in favor of the project, the governor told his Canadian and American peers that:

> New England and Eastern Canada are uniquely positioned to take advantage of tremendous wind, hydro, biofuels, and tidal power to meet our electricity needs. But acting alone, none of us can truly reach our potential. . . . We must develop new transmission capacity that serves both generation projects in New England and improves the capacity to move renewable, green power from Canada into the United States.[38]

There is no doubt that a new intracontinental political realignment is going on, as regions begin to transition their economies into a Third Industrial Revolution, even if it's not overtly acknowledged. Listen to what Massachusetts Governor Deval Patrick had to say at the 2010 Conference of the New England Governors and Eastern Canadian Premiers. He reminded the governors and premiers that "as the region that started the industrial revolution [on North America], the Northeast can also be the region that leads the world in a clean energy revolution." The governor said that he was convinced that "by coming together to announce aggressive regional energy efficiency goals and ramping up renewable energy, we will grow clean energy jobs, enhance our energy security, and improve the air we breathe."[39]

The "we" he referred to is a regional, transnational, and intracontinental political realignment. Washington was absent in his inspirational address, but not far from his mind. That was the very same day Governor Patrick and a group of eleven Mid-Atlantic New England governors sent the letter to Senate Majority Leader Harry Reid and Congress, opposing the plan to create centralized wind and solar power parks in the West and send electricity via high-voltage lines to the East, saying it would "undermine" the potential to harness locally generated renewable energy on the East Coast and "stifle" the economic prospects of the region.

What these transnational regional alliances suggest is that if a continental union does come to North America, it's not likely to be imposed by Washington; rather, it will grow out of the regional political realignment that accompanies a cross-border TIR infrastructure.

FROM GEOPOLITICS TO BIOSPHERE POLITICS

The intercontinental era will slowly transform international relations from geopolitics to biosphere politics. As previously mentioned, the biosphere envelope is the space that stretches from the ocean floor to outer space, within which living creatures and the Earth's geochemical processes interact to sustain life on the planet.

The scientific community's recent insights into the workings of the Earth's biosphere amount to nothing less than a rediscovery of the planet we inhabit. From diverse fields—physics, chemistry, biology, ecology, geology, and meteorology—researchers are beginning to think of the biosphere as operating like a living organism whose various chemical flows and biological systems are continuously interacting with one another in a myriad of subtle feedback loops that allow life to flourish on this tiny oasis in the universe.

This change in how scientists view the Earth is as profound in its implications as the change in thinking in the modern era, when scientists upended the Abrahamic description of the Earth as a creation of God and replaced it with the notion that it was a remnant of the sun, thrown off into space, where it cooled over eons of time and became an inert reservoir of resources for the evolution of life. As life evolved—at least according to the popular misreading of Darwinian theory—a fierce competition for the Earth's resources ensued, locking every species into a relentless battle to prevail and reproduce itself.

The Social Darwinist's view of nature as a battleground, where every creature is fighting with each other to grab as much of the Earth's resources as possible for itself and its progeny, has been taken up by nations and acted out on the grand stage of history in the form of geopolitics. Wars have been waged and political boundaries continually redrawn to secure access to elite fossil fuels—and other valuable resources—the energy lifeline of the First and Second Industrial Revolutions.

The new view unfolding in science, by contrast, sees the evolution of life and the evolution of the planet's geochemistry as a co-creative process in which each adapts to the other, assuring the continuation of life within the Earth's biosphere envelope. Ecologists argue that it is the synergistic and symbiotic relationships within and between species, as much as the competitive and aggressive drives, that help secure each organism's survival.

The shift in energy regimes from elite fossil fuels to distributed renewable energies will redefine the very notion of international relations more along the lines of ecological thinking. Because the renewable energies of the Third Industrial Revolution are ample, found everywhere, and easily shared, but require collective stewardship of the Earth's ecosystems, there is less likelihood of hostility and war over access, and greater likelihood of global cooperation. In the new era, survival is less about competition than cooperation, and less about the search for autonomy than the quest for embeddedness. If the Earth functions more like a living organism made up of layer upon layer of interdependent ecological relationships, then our very survival depends on mutually safeguarding the well-being of the global ecosystems of which we are all a part. This is the deep meaning of sustainable development, and the very essence of biosphere politics.

Biosphere politics facilitate a tectonic shift in the political landscape; we begin to enlarge our vision and think as global citizens in a shared biosphere. Global human rights networks, global health networks, global disaster relief networks, global germ plasm storage, global food banks, global information networks, global environmental networks, and global species protection networks, are a powerful sign of the historic shift from conventional geopolitics to fledgling biosphere politics.

As human populations begin to share green energies across continental ecosystems, engage in commerce and trade in integrated continental economies, and come to see themselves as citizens of continental political unions, the sense of being part of an extended human family is likely to foster a gradual shift in spatial orientation away from geopolitics and toward more inclusive biosphere politics. Learning to share a common biosphere is tautological with biosphere consciousness.

If it is difficult to imagine a change of this kind, think of how preposterous it must have been to a feudal lord, his knights in arms, and his indentured serfs to conjure the possibility of free wage earners selling their labor power in national markets, each a sovereign in his own right in the political sphere, all bound together by a set of agreed-upon rights and freedoms and a sense of national loyalty.

LIKE EVERY OTHER ECONOMIC REVOLUTION that preceded it, the Third Industrial Revolution is going to recast many of our most basic assumptions about the way the world works. While our governing institutions are morphing into new forms, so too are our academic disciplines.

It's been nearly fifty years since I took my introductory class in classical economic theory at the Wharton School at the University of Pennsylvania. I have watched a transformation take place in the workings of the economy over the ensuing half century—most of which has never been integrated into the standard economics textbooks. The once-unquestioned value of unlimited economic growth has given way to the idea of sustainable economic development. The conventional, top-down, centralized approach to organizing economic activity that characterized the fossil fuel–based First and Second Industrial Revolutions, is being challenged by the new distributed and collaborative organizing models that go with a Third Industrial Revolution. The hallowed nature of property exchange in markets has been partially upended by shared access to commercial services in open-source networks. National markets and nation-state governance, once the spatial milieu for all economic activity, are giving way to continental markets and continental governments. The result is that much of economics, as it is taught today, is increasingly irrelevant in explaining the past, understanding the present, and forecasting the future.

Although the term *paradigm shift* has been grossly overused in recent years, I think it's safe to say that when it comes to economic theory, the term is apt. Our children's understanding of economic theory and the governing assumptions of economic practice will be as radically different from ours as the market theorists' ideas are from the "just price" philosophy that governed late medieval commerce and trade.

The biochemist Joseph Henderson once remarked, "Science owes more to the steam engine than the steam engine owes to science." In other words, our intellectual abstractions are often little more than explanations of what we already experience in our technological applications. We might look back fifty years from now and say the same thing about the Third Industrial Revolution technologies and the new economic theory that is likely to accompany them.

PART III
THE COLLABORATIVE AGE

CHAPTER SEVEN
RETIRING ADAM SMITH

The dawn of the market era and the onset of the First Industrial Revolution in the late eighteenth century brought with it a new academic field called economics. In their attempts to understand the new forces let loose by coal-powered steam technology and factory production, the founding fathers of the new discipline—Adam Smith, Jean-Baptiste Say, and the like—looked to the new field of physics for a set of guiding principles and metaphors to fashion their own theories of the workings of the marketplace.

NEWTON'S LAWS AND SELF-REGULATING MARKETS

Sir Isaac Newton's mathematical method for discussing mechanical motion was all the rage at the time. It was being purloined by virtually every serious thinker to explain away the meaning of existence and the ways of the world.

Newton declared that "all the phenomena of nature may depend upon certain forces by which the particles of bodies, by causes hitherto unknown, are either mutually impelled toward each other, and cohere in regular figures, or are repelled and recede from each other." Early on, every schoolchild is introduced to Newton's three laws, which state that

A body at rest remains at rest and a body in motion remains in uniform motion in a straight line unless acted upon by an external force; the acceleration of a body is directly proportional to the applied force and in the direction of the straight line in which the force acts; [and] for every force, there is an equal and opposite force in reaction.[1]

Anxious to ground their musings in the mathematical certainties of physics, Adam Smith and his contemporaries argued that just as the universe, once set in motion, acts automatically like a well-balanced mechanical clock, so too does the marketplace. While God is the prime mover of the universe, man's innate competitive self-interest is the prime mover of the marketplace. Just as the laws of gravity govern the universe, an invisible hand rules over the affairs of the marketplace. Picking up on Newton's observation that "for every action there is an equal and opposite reaction," Smith and others argued that the self-regulating market operated in the same fashion, with supply and demand continually reacting and readjusting to one another. If consumers' demand for goods and services goes up, sellers will raise their prices accordingly. If the sellers' price becomes too high, demand will slacken, forcing the sellers to lower the price to spur demand.

Adam Smith exalted Newton's systematizing of the physics of the universe as "the greatest discovery that ever was made by man," and enthusiastically borrowed metaphors from *Principia* and Newton's other works to fashion classical economic theory.[2]

The problem with using Newton's mechanics to try to understand the workings of the market is that his physics tells us only about speed and location. The great twentieth century scientist and philosopher Alfred North Whitehead once quipped that when it comes to the question of matter in motion, "as soon as you have settled . . . what you mean by a definite place in space-time, you can adequately state the relation of a particular material body to space-time by saying that it is just there, in that place; and, so far as simple location is concerned, there is nothing more to be said on the subject."[3]

Newton's laws of matter in motion don't really help us understand much about how economic activity operates, and are a thin reed by which to anchor the entire discipline. In fact, they actually give us a false sense of how economic activity unfolds because they don't take into consideration the passage of time and the irreversibility of events. In Newton's cosmology, all mechanical processes are, in theory, reversible. For every +T there must be a −T in Newtonian mathematics. Take for example the classical example of billiard balls bumping up against each other on the table. In Newtonian physics, any action on the table is theoretically reversible because the laws of matter in motion make no allowance for the passage of time. But real economic activity is all about the irreversibility of events—how energy and material resources are harnessed, transformed, utilized, used up, and discarded.

WHY THE ENERGY LAWS GOVERN ALL ECONOMIC ACTIVITY

It wasn't until the second half of the nineteenth century, when physicists articulated the first and second laws of thermodynamics—the energy laws—that economists had a scientific basis to accurately describe economic activity. But by that time, economic philosophy was so mired in Newtonian mechanical metaphors that its practitioners were unable to part with these theories, even though they were based on scientific assumptions that were largely inapplicable to economic practice.

The first and second laws of thermodynamics state that "the total energy content of the universe is constant, and the total entropy is continually increasing." The first law, the "conservation law," posits that energy can neither be created nor destroyed—that the amount of energy in the universe has remained the same since the beginning of time and will be until the end of time. While the energy remains fixed, it is continually changing form, but only in one direction, from available to unavailable. This is where the second law of thermodynamics comes into play. According to the second law, energy always flows from hot to cold, concentrated to dispersed, ordered to disordered.

To get a fix on how the first and second laws work in the real world, think about burning a chunk of coal. None of the energy that was contained in the coal is ever lost. Rather, it is transformed into carbon dioxide, sulfur dioxide, and other gases that are dispersed into the atmosphere. Although the energy remains, we can never reconstitute the dispersed energies back into the original piece of coal and use it again. Rudolph Clausius, a German scientist, coined the term *entropy* in 1868 to refer to energy that is no longer usable.

Clausius realized that work occurs when energy goes from a higher concentrated state to a dispersed state—in other words, from a higher temperature to a lower temperature. For example, a steam engine does work because one part of the machine is very hot and the other very cold. Whenever energy goes from a higher to a lower temperature, less energy is available to perform work in the future. If a red-hot poker is removed from a furnace, it immediately begins to cool because heat flows from the hotter surface to the colder surroundings. After a while, the poker is the same temperature as the air around it. Physicists refer to this as the equilibrium state—where there is no longer a difference in the energy levels and no more work can be done.

The question that comes immediately to mind is "Why can't all of the dispersed energy be recycled?" Some of it can, but it would require using additional energy in the recycling process. That energy, when harnessed, increases the overall entropy.

Often, when I do a lecture on thermodynamics, the question arises as to whether I'm not being a bit overly pessimistic, given that the sun, our energy source, is going to burn for billions of more years and provide enough energy for all of our species' needs on Earth for as long as we care to ponder. True enough. But there is another source of energy on Earth that is far more limited—the energy embedded in material form in fossil fuels and metallic ores. These energies are fixed and finite, at least in the vast geological time frame that is important to our survival as a species.

Physicists explain that, from a thermodynamic perspective, the Earth functions as a virtually closed system relative to the sun and the universe. Thermodynamic systems can be divided into three types: open systems that exchange both energy and matter; closed systems that exchange energy but not matter; and isolated systems that exchange neither matter nor energy. The Earth, in relation to the solar system, is a relatively closed system. That is, it takes in energy from the sun, but except for an occasional meteorite and cosmic dust, it receives very little matter from the surrounding universe.

Fossil fuel is a prime example of a materially embedded form of energy, which for all intents and purposes, is a finite resource that is quickly depleting and will likely never reappear on Earth, at least in any time frame of interest to our species. Fossil fuels were formed over millions of years from the anaerobic decomposition of dead organisms. When these fuels are burned, the spent energy, in the form of gases, is no longer able to perform work. While it is theoretically possible that sometime in the distant future—millions of years from now—a similar process might yield a comparable reserve of fossil fuels, the likelihood of that happening is so remote and the time scale involved so distant, that it is all but a moot point.

Rare earths are another example of the inherent thermodynamic limits that we face on Earth. There are seventeen rare earth metals—scandium, yttrium, lanthanum, cerium, praseodymium, neodymium, promethium, samarium, europium, gadolinium, terbium, dysprosium, holmium, erbium, thulium, ytterbium, and lutetium—that are used in a wide range of industrial and technical processes and embedded in technologies and products that are critical to the survival and well-being of society. They are called "rare" because they are limited in availability and many are quickly being depleted to meet the needs of a growing population and globalizing economy.

Albert Einstein once pondered the question of which laws of science were the least likely to be overthrown or seriously modified by future generations of scientists. He concluded that the first and second laws of thermodynamics were most likely to withstand the test of time. He wrote:

> A theory is more impressive the greater is the simplicity of its premises,
> the more different are the kinds of things it relates and the more extended
> its range of applicability. Therefore, the deep impression which classical
> thermodynamics made on me. It is the only physical theory of universal
> content which I am convinced, that within the framework of applicability
> of its basic concepts, will never be overthrown.[4]

Even though the transformation of energy, in all of its various forms, is the very basis of all economic activity, only a tiny fraction of economists have even studied thermodynamics. And only a handful of individuals inside the profession have attempted to redefine economic theory and practice based on the energy laws.

The first effort to introduce the laws of thermodynamics into economic theory was made by the Nobel laureate chemist Fredrick Soddy in his 1911 book *Matter and Energy.* Soddy reminded his economist friends that the laws of thermodynamics "control, in the last resort, the rise or fall of political systems, the freedom or bondage of nations, the movements of commerce and industry, the origin of wealth and poverty, and the general physical welfare of the race."[5]

The first economist to take on his profession directly was Nicholas Georgescu-Roegen, the Vanderbilt University professor whose 1971 landmark book, *The Entropy Law and the Economic Process,* caused a minor ripple at the time, but was quickly dismissed by most of his colleagues. Herman Daly, a student of Georgescu-Roegen and later an economist at the World Bank, and currently a professor at the University of Maryland, built off Georgescu-Roegen's magisterial work, with the publication of his 1973 book, *Toward a Steady State Economy.* The book forced open a discussion at the margins of the economic profession by introducing the ecological sciences into economic thinking and, equally important, laid the foundation for later discussions around applying the operating assumptions of sustainability into the economic field.

In 1980, I published *Entropy*, with an afterward by Georgescu-Roegen, hoping to widen the conversation beyond economics to encompass the totality of the human experience. The book recasts history from a thermodynamic perspective, with particular attention to the entropic consequences brought on by the advances of human civilization. *Entropy* was one of the first books to examine, in depth, the entropic impacts of the industrial revolution on climate change.

Looking back at the past century of efforts to recast economic theory in thermodynamic terms, what stands out is how utterly impenetrable the field has been to rethinking the scientific basis of its own guiding assumptions. Even in the last several years, as more and more business schools around the world have rushed to introduce ecological considerations and sustainability issues into the curriculum, and have started to pay greater attention to the centrality of energy-related concerns and climate change, they have attempted to do so under the auspices of classical and neoclassical economic theory, whose operating assumptions are at odds with the laws of thermodynamics.

As long as Newton's long shadow casts itself over economic theory, it is unlikely that economics, as a discipline, will be able to accommodate the growing schisms that threaten all of its most basic assumptions. Economic historian E. Ray Canterbery notes that taking on the likes of Adam Smith becomes increasingly daunting because he rides on the coattails of the great Sir Isaac Newton. He writes, "From time to time, a cluster of economists consider conventional economics ripe for revolution, but any economic revolutionaries will have to go to the barricades against the genius of Isaac Newton as well as against Adam Smith and his long line of followers."[6] Now however, for the first time, the many cracks in the theoretical foundations of the discipline are threatening to tumble the edifice of classical economic theory.

THE WEALTH OF NATIONS

The fault line that runs through all of classical economic theory is the fundamental misunderstanding of the nature of wealth. John Locke, the English Enlightenment philosopher, argued that "land that is left wholly to nature . . . is called, as indeed it is, waste." Locke turned the second law of thermodynamics on its head by proclaiming that nature itself is useless and only becomes of value when human beings apply their labor to it, transforming it into productive assets. Locke wrote:

> He who appropriates land to himself by his labour, does not lessen but increase the common stock of mankind. For the provisions serving to the support of human life, produced by one acre of inclosed and cultivated land, are . . . ten times more, than those, which are yielded by an acre of Land, of an equal richnesse, lyeing wast in common. And therefore he, that incloses Land and has a greater plenty of the conveniencys of life from ten acres, than he could have from an hundred left to Nature, may truly be said, to give ninety acres to Mankind.[7]

The laws of thermodynamics tell us something quite different. Economic activity is merely borrowing low-entropy energy inputs from the environment and transforming them into temporary products and services of value. In the transformation process, often more energy is expended and lost to the environment than is embedded in the particular good or service being produced.

In this regard, the economic process mirrors the biological processes in nature. When the laws of thermodynamics were first articulated, biologists were at a loss as to how energy continually moves from an ordered to a disordered state while living systems appear to operate in the exact opposite direction, continually remaining ordered.

Harold Blum, the renowned twentieth-century biologist, explained that living organisms don't violate the second law but are merely a different manifestation of its workings. Living creatures, observed Blum, are nonequilibrium thermodynamic systems. That is, every living thing exists far away from equilibrium by continuously feeding off available energy from the environment, but always at the expense of increasing the overall entropy in the environment. Plants for example, take in energy from the sun in the process of photosynthesis, and that concentrated energy is either consumed directly by other animals or indirectly when animals eat other animals. By and large, the more evolved the species, the more energy it consumes to maintain itself in a nonequilibrium state and the more spent energy it spews back into the environment in the process of staying alive.

Erwin Schrödinger, a Nobel laureate physicist, captures the essence of the thermodynamic process by observing that "what an organism feeds upon is negative entropy; it continues to suck orderliness from its environment."[8]

What the biologists are saying conforms with the way we understand the workings of life. We are continuously taking energy into our bodies every time we eat and, in the process of staying alive, are continually depleting energy and contributing to entropic waste. If the energy intake were to stop or if our bodies were no longer able to properly process it because of disease, we would die. At death, our bodies quickly decompose back into the environment. Our life and death are all part of the entropic flow.

Chemist G. Tyler Miller uses an abbreviated food chain to explain how available energy is processed and entropy is created at every stage of expropriation in ecosystems. He begins by pointing out that in devouring prey, "about 80 percent to 90 percent of the energy is simply wasted and lost as heat to the environment."[9] Only 10 to 20 percent of the energy of the prey is absorbed by the predator. That's because transforming energy from one creature to another requires an expenditure of energy and results in the loss of energy.

Miller describes the incredible amount of energy used and entropy created in a simple food chain comprising grass, grasshoppers, frogs, trout, and humans. Miller calculates that "three hundred trout are required to support one man for a year. The trout, in turn, must consume 90,000 frogs, which must consume 27 million grasshoppers, which live off of 1,000 tons of grass."[10]

Now, let's look at the thermodynamic consequences of converting nature's resources into food for human consumption in a complex, industrial civilization and what it portends for how we perceive the wealth of nations. Consider the energy that goes into a beefsteak:

1. It takes nine pounds of feed grain to make one pound of steak.[11] This means that only 11 percent of the feed goes to produce the beef itself, with the rest either burned off as energy in the conversion process, used to maintain normal body functions, or extracted or absorbed into parts of the body that are not eaten—like hair or bones. While we bemoan the energy inefficiency and waste of driving gas-guzzling cars, the energy inefficiency and waste of supporting a grain-oriented meat diet is much worse. Frances Moore Lappé, in her book *Diet for a Small Planet,* points out that an acre of cereal produces five times

the protein of an acre used for meat production.[12] Legumes produce ten times more protein and leafy vegetables produce fifteen times more protein per acre than beef production. Nearly one third of the grain grown in the world today is feed grain for animals rather than food grain for direct human consumption; so while a small portion of the wealthiest consumers luxuriate high up on the food chain, hundreds of millions of other human beings face malnutrition, starvation, and death.[13]

2. Farmers have to use large quantities of fossil fuel–based petrochemical fertilizers, pesticides, and herbicides to grow the feed grain. Additional fossil fuel is expended to operate farm equipment. Trucks, trains, and ships, using even more fossil fuels, must be deployed to transport the grain to giant, mechanized feedlots where it is consumed by the cattle.

3. On the feedlot, the animals are administered a host of pharmaceutical products, including growth-stimulating hormones, feed additives, and occasional antibiotics, again using more energy. The cattle are crammed together in close quarters—feedlots sometimes contain as many as 50,000 or more head of cattle—where they are subject to an infestation of flies that spread diseases like pink eye and infectious bovine rhinotracheitis.[14] To prevent these diseases, highly toxic insecticides derived from fossil fuel, are sprayed from high-pressure hoses, fogging the pens with a cloud of poison.

4. Once fattened, the cattle are transported for hours, and even days, in vans along interstates, on the way to the slaughterhouse—again, expending additional fossil fuel energy.

5. At the slaughterhouse, the animals enter the killing floor, single file, where they are stunned by a pneumatic gun and fall to the ground. A worker hooks a chain onto a rear hoof and hoists the animal upside down over the slaughterhouse floor and then slits its throat, letting the blood drain out.

6. The dead animal moves along an electricity-powered disassembly line, where a machine strips the animal of its hide and organs are removed.

7. Electric power saws are then used to cut the carcass into recognizable cuts, including chuck, ribs, brisket, and steak.

8. The cuts are tossed onto electric-powered conveyer belts, where several dozen boners and trimmers cut off and box the final product.

9. The vacuum-packed cuts of beef are then shipped to supermarkets across the country in air-conditioned trucks.
10. Upon arrival at the supermarket, the cuts are repackaged in plastic made out of fossil fuels, and displayed in air-cooled, brightly lit shelves at the meat counter.
11. Customers drive their cars to the stores to purchase the steak and store it in their freezer or refrigerator, before cooking it on their gas or electric stoves and consuming it.

The energy that goes into the beef at every step of the conversion process is tiny compared to the expenditure of energy used to grow the feed, fatten the animal, transport the steer to market, slaughter the animal, package the cuts, and send them to their final destination on the family table.

That's only part of the energy story. The other part is the entropy bill. Cattle and other livestock are the second leading contributor to climate change after buildings, generating 18 percent of greenhouse gas emissions. This is more than what is produced by worldwide transport. While livestock—again mostly cattle—produce 9 percent of the carbon dioxide derived from human-related economic activity, they produce a much larger share of more harmful greenhouse gases. Livestock account for 65 percent of human-related nitrous oxide emissions—nitrous oxide has nearly 300 times the global warming effect of carbon dioxide. Most of the nitrous oxide emissions come from manure. Livestock also emit 37 percent of all human-induced methane—a gas that has 23 percent more impact than carbon dioxide in warming the planet.[15]

Finally, that one pound beefsteak is only temporary and, upon consumption, is digested by the body and eventually ends up back in the environment in the form of used-up energy or waste.

What, then, are we to conclude about the nature of gross domestic product (GDP)? We think of GDP as a measure of the wealth that a country generates each year. But from a thermodynamic point of view, it is more a measure of the temporary energy value embedded in the goods or services produced at the expense of the diminution of the available energy reserves and an accumulation of entropic waste. Since even the goods and services we produce eventually become part of the entropy stream, for all of our notions of economic progress, the economic ledger will always end up in the red. That is, when all is said and done, every civilization inevitably ends up sucking more order out of the surrounding environment than it ever creates and leaves the Earth more impoverished. Seen in this way, the gross domestic product is more accurately the gross domestic cost, since every time resources are consumed, a portion becomes unavailable for future use.

Despite the incontrovertible fact that all economic activity creates only temporary value, at the expense of the degradation of the resource base on which it depends, most economists don't look at the economic process from a thermodynamic perspective. Enlightenment philosophers, by and large, came to believe that the pursuit of economic activity is a linear process that invariably leads to unlimited material progress on Earth, if only the market mechanism is left uninhibited so that the "invisible hand" can regulate supply and demand. French Enlightenment philosopher and revolutionary Marquis de Condorcet captured the euphoria of the new age of progress when he proclaimed,

> No bounds have been fixed to the improvement of the human faculties . . . the perfectibility of man is absolutely indefinite; . . . the progress of this perfectibility, henceforth above the control of every power that would impede it, has no other limit than the duration of the globe upon which Nature has placed us.[16]

Giddy over the prospect of creating a material cornucopia on Earth, the classical economists, with the exception of Thomas Malthus, were united in their belief that human industriousness could create a utopian paradise. The very idea that an acceleration of economic activity might result in a degraded environment and a dark future for unborn generations would have been unfathomable.

HOW ECONOMIC THEORY BECAME IRRELEVANT

This ideological blind spot shows up in nearly every one of the underlying assumptions of classical and neoclassical economic theory. Perhaps no concept is more highly prized among economists than the notion of productivity. Economists define productivity in terms of output per unit of input. A premium is placed on performing a given task as fast as possible. A more appropriate thermodynamic measure of productivity, however, would emphasize the entropy produced per unit of output.

I recall a study done more than thirty years ago on how much energy is needed to manufacture an automobile. It turns out that much more energy is used than is actually necessary. The extra energy is expended to speed up the process and get the car off the assembly line quicker. This is true across the supply chain. Our obsession with speed of conversion and product delivery comes at a cost—the expenditure of additional energy. And greater use of energy means more energy wasted and a buildup of entropy in the environment.

We have come to believe that by increasing the speed of activity, we somehow save energy, when in thermodynamic terms, the opposite is the case. Not convinced? Have you ever found yourself driving on a back road in the middle of the night only to realize that you are nearly out of gasoline, with no idea how far the next gas station might be? The first inclination of many drivers is to hit the gas pedal and speed up in hopes of finding a gas pump. We rationalize that by going faster we will improve our chances of reaching the gas station before we run out of fuel, which is at odds with the laws of thermodynamics. By driving slower, we increase the distance we can travel and improve our prospects for reaching the gas station.

When neoclassical economists talk about productivity and economic growth as a measure of output per unit of input, the inputs they have in mind are capital and labor. Yet, when economists analyze the actual economic growth in the United States and other industrial countries, the amount of capital invested per worker accounts for only about 14 percent of the increase, leaving 86 percent of the growth unaccounted for. Robert Solow, whose theory of economic growth landed him a Nobel prize, says quite candidly that the missing 86 percent is "a measure of our ignorance."[17]

It took a physicist to explain the apparent enigma. Reiner Kümmel, of the University of Wuerzburg in Germany, constructed a growth model that included energy, along with capital and labor inputs, and tested it against growth data over a period between 1945 and 2000 in the United States, the United Kingdom, and Germany, and found that energy was the "missing factor," accounting for the rest of the productivity and economic growth.[18]

Robert Ayres, a professor of environment and management at the INSEAD business school in Fountainebleau, France, who was trained in physics and devoted much of his professional career to studying energy flows and technological change, and Benjamin Warr, a research assistant, constructed their own three-factor input model and tested it against the economic growth curve during the entire twentieth century in the United States, and then carried out subsequent studies of the United Kingdom, Japan, and Australia. Ayers and Warr found that adding energy to the input model explained "nearly 100% of the Twentieth Century economic growth for each of the four countries." What the Ayres and Warr growth model clearly shows is that "the increasing thermodynamic efficiency, with which energy and raw materials are converted into useful work," accounts for most of the increased productivity gains and growth in industrial societies.[19]

The critical role that energy plays in productivity and profit margins becomes crystal clear when we descend down to the micro level of individual firms. I recently dined with Gabriele Burgio, the visionary CEO of NH Hotels, in one of his hotels in Madrid. NH is the market leader in both Spain and Italy and is Europe's fifth-largest hotel chain, with over 400 properties.

Burgio is on the executive committee of the Third Industrial Revolution Global CEO Business Roundtable. A kind and soft spoken gentleman, whose personal life reflects his passionate commitment to a green future and sustainable economic development, Gabriele is obsessive about energy efficiency. Why? He explained to me over a vegetarian meal that 30 percent of his hotel overhead and operating costs is energy-related, constituting the second biggest cost after human labor. For Gabriele, paying attention to thermodynamic efficiencies and new ways to advance productivity is not an arcane economic concept but, rather, a practical business tool. His success in making the NH Hotel brand a market leader in Europe is in no small part attributable to the tremendous cost savings that he has achieved in reducing energy use and creating more energy-efficient operations—cost reductions that he passes on to his hotel guests in terms of cheaper prices for high-end accommodations.

NH Hotels has introduced an online control system called Datamart, which continuously monitors energy use throughout the hotel, using information to minimize waste while optimizing the comfort of guests. Between 2007 and 2010, NH achieved a dramatic 15.83 percent reduction in energy consumption, a 31.03 percent reduction in CO_2 emission, a 26.83 percent reduction in waste generation, and a 28.2 percent reduction in water consumption.[20]

NH is currently pioneering the concept of "Intelligent Rooms," a real-time monitoring system that can keep up-to-the-moment information on water use, lighting, air conditioning, and heating consumption, and adjust to the changing needs of guests over a twenty-four-hour period. Guests who use less energy than the norm are rewarded for their eco-conscious behavior at check-out time, with credits on their World NH Loyalty cards, which are redeemable for reduced rates during their next stay at an NH Hotel.

NH is also in the early stages of converting its hotels into micro–power plants. In Italy, the company has already installed thermal solar energy in 15 percent of its hotels. Its Vittorio Veneto hotel in Rome is equipped with photovoltaic solar energy, which provides 10 percent of its total energy needs. NH is currently in the planning stages of building the first zero-emissions hotel property in the world. In anticipation of the market introduction of electric plug-in vehicles in 2011, NH has also become the first hotel to include free recharging points at some of its properties.

Wood and paper products used in NH hotels come only from sustainable forests, and all guestroom amenities and accessories are made of "bio" materials with low environmental impact. All waste produced in NH hotels is recycled, and the toilets, showers, and taps use state-of-the-art technology to minimize water use.

The hotel chain has even set up a supplier club—made up of forty or so companies—whose product lines and supply chains are constantly being monitored, evaluated, and upgraded to conform to the energy requirements and ecological prerequisites established by NH Hotels.

By saving energy and creating eco-friendly hotels, NH is profiting and, at the same time, helping to establish a sustainable business operation that provides reasonable room rates for its guests. The guests, in turn, can enjoy their travel accommodations knowing that they are reducing their carbon footprint and doing their part to steward the biosphere. All of NH Hotels' energy-saving technologies and business practices have dramatically increased the company's productivity, allowing it to optimize services with greatly reduced input costs.

Since virtually every economic activity of modern industrial life is made with and run by fossil fuels—petrochemical fertilizers and pesticides for agriculture, construction materials, machinery, pharmaceutical products, fiber, power, transport, heat, light, and so on—it stands to reason that thermodynamic efficiency is central to the story of productivity and economic growth.

But, so, too, is the entropic loss. We need to be continually reminded that whenever we increase the use of energy to accelerate the economic process, the productivity gains must be weighed against the increased entropy that flows into the environment. In the fossil fuel–based industrial age, the burning of coal, oil, and natural gas greatly accelerated economic growth and led to a dangerous buildup of CO_2 (spent energy) in the atmosphere, resulting in a fundamental shift in the climate on Earth. "Haste makes waste" is an age-old adage that reflects an intuitive understanding of the entropy law at work. In terms of thermodynamic efficiency, then, productivity is as much a measure of entropy produced per unit of output as speed per unit of output.

For most of the twentieth century, the price of oil was so low that little attention was given to thermodynamic efficiency in the production and distribution of goods and services. And before scientists understood the relationship between burning carbon fuels and global warming, there was little concern about entropic flow. This has now changed. Peak oil per capita and global peak oil production have been reached, forcing a dramatic rise in the price of energy. At the same time, the accumulated entropic emission of industrial-based CO_2 into the atmosphere has altered the temperature of the planet and put the world into real-time climate change, with dramatic effects on agriculture and infrastructure.

The simple but profoundly disturbing reality is that fossil fuels and rare earths are fast depleting and the entropic debt from past economic activity is mounting at a rate that far exceeds the biosphere's ability to absorb it. This sobering situation calls for a fundamental reassessment of the assumptions that have guided our notions about productivity in the past. From here on, productivity is going to have to be measured in a way that takes into account both thermodynamic efficiencies as well as entropic consequences.

Economists often retort that they do take the entropy bill into consideration by factoring in what they call "negative externalities," or deleterious effects that market activity has on third parties not directly involved in the exchange process. The problem is that the full cost over time to third parties, society as a whole, the environment, and future generations is never taken into account. If it were, the commercial players would, more often than not, have to pay out compensation far in excess of their profits and market capitalism wouldn't survive. Being forced to pay an occasional government fine, tax, or damages resulting from civil suits for the negative effects that commercial activity generates doesn't begin to address the true nature of the entropy bill.

The reason most economists just don't get it is that they fail to understand that all economic activity is borrowing against nature's energy and material reserves. If that borrowing draws down nature's bounty faster than the biosphere can recycle the waste and replenish the stock, the accumulation of entropic debt will eventually collapse whatever economic regime is harnessing the resources.

Every great economic era is marked by the introduction of a new energy regime. In the beginning, the extraction, processing, and distribution of the new energy are expensive. Technological advances and economies of scale reduce the costs and increase the energy flow until the once-abundant energy becomes increasingly scarce and the entropy bill from past energy conversion begins to accumulate. The oil era followed this curve over the course of the twentieth century, peaking in 2006.

But will the TIR energy curve follow a similar trajectory? It depends. While sun, the wind, and other renewable energies are sufficient to provide the energy needs of our species and fellow creatures for as long as our solar system exists, they come with their own entropic constraints. To begin with, renewable energies require material scaffolding. Photovoltaic cells, electric batteries, wind turbines, compact florescent bulbs, and many of the new communications technologies of the Third Industrial Revolution rely, in part, on rare earth materials. A report issued in February 2011 by the American Physical Society and the Materials Research Society, warned that a shortage of some of these rare earth materials could, in the long run, undermine large-scale efforts to deploy the new clean energies.[21] Since many of these rare earth materials are by-products of mining more abundant minerals like copper, there is no immediate concern about shortages. Already, however, there is a heady discussion about finding alternative metals, or even biologically derived substitutes, should we face a shortage sometime in the distant future. Researchers in the burgeoning fields of biotechnology, sustainable chemistry, and nanotechnology are confident that they will be able to find cheaper and more efficient alternatives to these rare earths in the coming decades to service an emergent TIR infrastructure.

A far greater concern in the long run is the potential entropic impact of having available a virtually unlimited supply of clean renewable energy at prices so cheap as to be nearly free, just as in the case with the fall in the cost of information collection and dissemination that occurred as a result of the IT and Internet revolutions in the past two decades. One's first reaction is likely to be, "Great! Unlimited, nearly free renewable energy.

Why worry?" Again, recall that the Earth is a partially closed system that exchanges energy with the solar system but little appreciable matter. If we had a virtually unlimited supply of cheap, green energy, we might be more inclined to convert the Earth's limited low-entropy matter into goods at an ever-accelerating rate, increasing the entropic flow and accumulating more matter chaos—dispersed matter no longer available to do useful work.

Consider, for example, the mining of aluminum. We could extract and manufacture aluminum for commercial purposes using green energy to drive the process. Over a period of time, however, the aluminum rusts and the loose molecules are randomly dispersed back into the environment and become part of the entropic flow. They will never be regathered and reconstituted back to the original aluminum ore from which they came.

This suggests that while we will need to transition into the new, distributed green energies, it will also be necessary to use these energies more parsimoniously to make sure that we do not strip our planet of the low-entropy matter that is equally critical to support life on Earth. From a thermodynamic perspective, the most important lesson we can learn is how to budget our consumption patterns to conform with nature's recycling schedules, so that we can live more sustainably on Earth.

Although there is a worldwide discussion on balancing budgets, when politicians, business leaders, and most of the public consider budget restraints, they give little consideration to the ultimate budget constraint that is dictated by borrowing nature's wealth. Lest we doubt the disconnect, whenever there is the slightest suggestion of taxing gasoline or carbon emissions to encourage energy savings and efficiencies to reduce global warming emissions, much of the public is quick to protest. Yet, the faster we expropriate nature's wealth and the more quickly we consume it, the more scarce resources become and the more pollution we create, making everything more costly across the supply chain. When prices of everything we use and consume go up, the increased costs show up everywhere, including what government needs to spend on public goods and services to maintain our way of life.

Mature ecosystems in nature act quite differently than what we are accustomed to in society. In a climax ecosystem like the one we see in the Amazon for example, the thermodynamic efficiency is as close to a steady state as possible (a perfect steady state is impossible because all biological activity results in some entropic loss). Yet in these climax ecosystems that have developed over millions of years, the consumption of energy and matter does not significantly exceed the ecosystems' ability to absorb and recycle the waste and replenish the stock. The synergies, symbiotic relationships, and feedback loops are finely calibrated to ensure the system's ability to maintain a continuous balance of supply and demand.

I note that biomimicry—the idea of studying how nature operates and borrowing best practices—is becoming an increasingly fashionable pursuit in product research and development, economic modeling, and urban planning. We'd be well-served by studying how climax ecosystems balance their budgets, and applying the lessons to balancing our own budgets within society and between society and nature.

All of this is painfully obvious, which makes one wonder whether economists might be better served by being trained in thermodynamics before they take up their discipline. Frederick Soddy, Nicholas Georgescu-Roegen, Herman Daly, and I previously emphasized the role that thermodynamic efficiencies play in determining productivity and managing sustainability in our own books on the subject, backing it up with anecdotal evidence from across the supply chain throughout history. But what makes the Ayers/Warr analysis particularly pertinent is that it provides evidence over an extended period of time to support the supposition—the kind of hard data that economists could seize, if they chose, to rethink economic theory. For the most part, they choose to ignore the obvious.

Given the central role that thermodynamic efficiency plays in productivity and economic growth, I asked John A. "Skip" Laitner, one of our global team's valued economic analysts from the American Council For an Energy-Efficient Economy (ACEEE), to create a working model that tracked changes in energy efficiency in the twentieth century to see what insights we might glean in preparing the way for a transition to a TIR paradigm. Laitner's study reveals that, while the level of energy efficiency in the United States steadily increased between 1900 and 1980, from 2.5 percent to 12.3 percent, from that time on it has hovered around 14 percent, reflecting the maturation of the Second Industrial Revolution energies and infrastructure. This means that for the past thirty years, we have been wasting 86 percent of the energy we use in the production of goods and services.

While the thermodynamic efficiency has flattened, the entropy bill from past economic activity has climbed dramatically. The estimated cost of air and water pollution and the depletion of nonrenewable resources was $4.5 trillion in 2010, or 34 percent of the nation's GDP—double the percentage

in 1950. These figures don't even take into consideration the escalating entropic bill from global warming gas emissions, which, if measured over the
full duration of their future impact, would dwarf the US and world GDP by
a magnitude too incalculable to measure.

It's a given that 100 percent thermodynamic efficiency is an impossibil-
ity. Laitner's model as well as those of others, however, suggest it's possible
to triple the current level of efficiency to nearly 40 percent over the next
four decades. The US government's National Renewable Energy Laboratory calculates that if all commercial buildings were retrofitted and rebuilt
using state-of-the-art, energy-efficient technologies and practices, it would
reduce energy use by 60 percent. If the installation of rooftop photovoltaic
power systems were added to the mix, it would be possible to achieve an 88
percent reduction in the use of conventional energy. If all new commercial
buildings were green-positive power plants, the increase in energy efficiency
would be even more striking. A comparable push could reduce the conventional energy used in the nation's housing stock by 60 percent.

How much would all of this cost? Implementing the infrastructure improvements in the nation's commercial and residential buildings would cost
approximately $4 trillion over a forty-year period, or about $100 billion a
year, but would generate a cumulative energy bill savings of $6.5 trillion,
or approximately $163 billion per year. Assuming that the infrastructure
improvements are financed and paid for out of the energy savings at around
a 7 percent discount rate, the benefit cost ratio is a robust 1.80. In other
words, for every dollar invested in energy efficiency and/or renewable energy systems, the return on investment would be $1.80.

The reconfiguration of the nation's power grid, from servo-mechanical
to digital and from centralized to distributed, would also significantly increase thermodynamic efficiencies across the economy. The current electricity generation and transmission system only operates at an efficiency
of 32 percent. This level of efficiency has remained unchanged since 1960,
when the current Second Industrial Revolution infrastructure matured.
Amazingly, what the United States wastes in energy in the production of
electricity, is more than Japan uses to power its entire economy. A smart,
distributed power grid that can more efficiently aggregate and route electricity—especially green electricity—would result in significant increases
in energy efficiency. Moreover, a study done by the US government's Lawrence Berkeley National Laboratory reports that current off-the-shelf

waste-to-energy and other recycled energy systems could harness sufficient waste heat from just our industrial plants to produce 20 percent of
our current electricity consumption.

What if we were to factor in the energy efficiency gains in using hydrogen and other storage mediums for renewable energies and the gains in
transitioning the transport fleet from the very inefficient, oil-powered internal combustion engine to super-efficient, electric plug-in and hydrogen-
powered vehicles? The potential uptake in thermodynamic efficiency across
the supply chain and in every sector of society in the emerging Third Industrial Revolution should result in productivity gains far in excess of what we
were able to achieve over the course of the Second Industrial Revolution in
the twentieth century.

RETHINKING PROPERTY IN THE TIR ERA

Nothing is more sacrosanct to an economist than property relations. Classical economic theory is wedded to property exchange in markets as the most
efficient means of generating economic activity and producing prosperity.
This core feature of capitalism brings with it several operating assumptions
that are often regarded as inherent in human nature, but upon reflection,
they are merely social constructs that reinforce a particular way of organizing economic activity that is characteristic of the modern era.

Recall John Locke's belief that private property is a natural right.
Locke wrote,

> whatsoever, then, [man] removes out of the state that nature hath pro-
> vided and left it in, he hath mixed his labor with it, and joined to it some-
> thing that is his own, and thereby makes it his property. It being by him
> removed from the common state nature placed it in, it hath by this labor
> something annexed to it that excludes the common right of other men. For
> this "labor" being the unquestionable property of the laborer, no man but
> he can have a right to what that is once joined to, at least where there is
> enough, and as good left in common for others.[22]

Never mind that for most of human history, our species lived commu-
nally as foragers and hunters and consumed nature's bounty as quickly as
we appropriated it. The idea of property, in the form of stored surplus grain

and domesticated animals, had to await the agricultural era, which didn't commence until 10,000 BC. Paleolithic life was nomadic and followed the changing seasons. The only possessions were the limited attire, ornaments, hand tools, and weapons that could be carried on one's back, and they were regarded as belonging to the community as a whole.

Even with the advent of agriculture, the idea of property was more of a communal concept than an individual possession. Although private property existed, especially with the emergence of the great hydraulic civilizations, its role was limited in scope to the fortunes of kings and traders. As late as the fourteenth century in Europe, lords and serfs belonged to the land, rather than the land belonging to the people. In the Christian schemata, God ruled over the whole of his creation and merely entrusted it to his emissaries on Earth, the Church, who oversaw its stewardship in a descending ladder of trusteeship that reached down from the lords of the feudal estates to the knights, vassals, and serfs in what theologians described as "The Great Chain of Being." The concept of selling and buying land—real estate—didn't take hold until the passage of the great Enclosure Acts in Tudor and Elizabethan England, marking the very end of the feudal economy and the dawn of the market era.

The merchant guilds in the free cities of late medieval Europe also had a limited idea about acquisition of property. They fixed the price and quantity of their production to merely reproduce their way of life, without the intention of acquiring property in excess of what they needed to preserve a steady state of existence.

The First Industrial Revolution quickened the production of goods beyond that of any previous period of history, allowing artisans and laborers to live better than the royalty of just a few centuries earlier. Caught up in the elation, Enlightenment economists began to extol the innate virtues of private property relations in the marketplace, and came to see the acquisition of property as an inherent biological drive, rather than a social proclivity conditioned by a specific communication/energy paradigm.

The market mechanism became the "invisible hand" to regulate the supply and demand of private property and to assure that its distribution was as impartial as the laws of Newtonian physics that governed the universe. The pursuit of self-interest—also regarded as an innate quality of human nature—would guarantee a steady advance of the general welfare and move humankind along the road to unlimited progress. Concepts like "caveat emptor"—let the buyer beware—and "buy cheap and sell dear" created the context for a new, binary social reality, separating the world into "mine" versus "thine."

The emergent Third Industrial Revolution, however, brings with it a very different conception of human drives, and the assumptions that govern human economic activity. The distributed and collaborative nature of the new economic paradigm is forcing a fundamental rethinking of the high regard previously bestowed on private property relations in markets.

The quickening connection of the nervous system of every human being to every other human being on Earth, via the Internet and other new communications technologies, is propelling us into a global social space and a new simultaneous field of time. The result is that access to vast global networks is becoming as important a value as private property rights were in the nineteenth and twentieth centuries.

A generation growing up on the Internet is apparently unmindful of the classical economic theorists' aversion to sharing creativity, knowledge and expertise, and even goods and services in open commons to advance the common good. The classical economists would regard such economic arrangements as inimical to human nature and doomed to fail for the simple reason that human beings are primarily selfish, competitive, and predatory, and would either take advantage of the goodwill and naïveté of their peers, and freeload on the contribution of others, or would go it alone with a far better payoff.

These misgivings seem to have had little impact. Today, hundreds of millions of young people are actively engaged in distributed and collaborative social networks on the Internet, willingly giving their own time and expertise, mostly for free, to advance the good of others. Why do they do it? For the sheer joy of sharing their lives with others in the belief that contributing to the well-being of the whole does not in any way diminish what's theirs but, rather, increases their well-being manyfold.

Social spaces like Wikipedia and Facebook challenge the very basis of classic economic theory, that human beings are selfish creatures, continuously in pursuit of an autonomous existence. Third Industrial Revolution communications and energies bring out a far different set of biological drives—the need for sociability and the quest for community.

Nowhere is this shift in thinking better reflected than in our changing attitudes about property. In the new era, the notion of property, which placed a premium on acquisition of material things in markets and the right to exclude others from their enjoyment, is giving way to a new concept of property as the right to enjoy access in social networks and share common experiences with others. Our ideas about property are so wedded to the traditional notion of ownership and exclusion that it's hard to imagine that there is an older property right individuals enjoyed over the centuries—the right of access to property held in common. For example, the right to navigate rivers, forage in local forests, walk on country lanes, fish in nearby streams, and congregate on the public square. This older idea of property as the right of access and inclusion was increasingly shunted aside in the modern era as market relations came to dominate life and private property came to define the "measure of a man."

In a distributed and collaborative economy, however, the right of access to global social networks becomes as important as the right to hold on to private property in national markets. That's because quality-of-life values become more important, especially the pursuit of social inclusion with millions of others in global communities in virtual space. Thus, the right to Internet access becomes a powerful new property value in an interconnected world.

Google's decision in 2010 to refuse to let the Chinese government censor information on its search engine is part of a dramatic confrontation unfolding in international relations. The showdown began with Secretary of State Hillary Clinton's speech attacking China and other nations for blocking access to parts of Google and other Internet search engines and websites. Clinton warned that "a new information curtain is descending across much of the world" and made it clear that "the U.S. stand[s] for a single Internet where all of humanity has equal access to knowledge and ideas."[23] The Google standoff with China marks a seismic shift from conventional geopolitics, which has governed the affairs of nations from the very beginning of the market economy, to emergent biosphere politics that will increasingly determine the fate of civilization in the global networked economy.

The new conflicts in the biosphere era will increasingly center around access rights. The change reflects the diminishing importance of ownership relative to access in a globally connected and interdependent world.

Young people living in China and other restrictive, authoritarian regimes are struggling to secure the right to access social spaces on global networks with the same fervor that brought young people to the barricades in the eighteenth and nineteenth centuries in the pursuit of property rights.

The Global Internet Freedom Consortium is made up of firewall-busting firms that have created software that breaks through the elaborate systems set up by nations like Egypt, Iran, Libya, Vietnam, Saudi Arabia, and Syria to prevent their populations from getting access to global information networks.[24] Millions of captive people have been able to connect to the global Internet community, for brief moments of time, giving them hope that someday they might enjoy the same right to universal access that so many young people in the developed democracies take for granted.

The power of social media to break down authoritarian rule came into stark relief in Egypt in January and February 2011, when hundreds of thousands of young people defied Hosni Mubarak's brutal control over the country by taking to the streets for eighteen days and bringing the country to a standstill. The youth-led rebellion, symbolized by young Google executive Wael Ghonim, who became their "leaderless" spokesperson, used social media—Facebook, YouTube, and Twitter—to outflank and outmaneuver the state police and military, and eventually bring down one of the most dictatorial governments in the world.

Youth-led street demonstrations using social media also broke out in Tunisia, Libya, Yemen, Jordan, Bahrain, and across the Arab region. The Internet generation is demanding an end to autocratic, centralized governance so they can live in an open, transparent, borderless world that reflects the operating norms and practices of the new social media that has come to define the aspirations of youth everywhere.

The uproar among youth living in authoritarian countries will only grow more intense in the years ahead, as they demand their right to be part of a global family that is beginning to share knowledge, commerce, and social life across national boundaries. The Internet has made the biosphere the new political boundary and, in the process, has made traditional geopolitics appear more like an anachronism.

In a lateral world, even intellectual property, a stalwart feature of capitalism, is unraveling and becoming increasingly marginalized in the commercial arena. Because "information likes to run free" in an Internet world, copyrights and patents are increasingly being ignored or bypassed. When more of the commercial and social life of society is conducted in opensource commons, intellectual property becomes, for all intents and purposes, an outmoded and useless convention. The music companies were the first to feel the full brunt of open-source copyrighted material. When millions of young people began to freely share music with one another online, the companies attempted to protect copyrights by bringing lawsuits against offending music pirates and creating firewalls with new encryption technology—all to little avail.

Book publishers and authors are increasingly making entire chapters of new, copyrighted books available for free on the Internet, hoping readers will be sufficiently interested to purchase the books. The odds are not good. Since there is such voluminous information circulating free on the Internet on every conceivable subject, with new information streaming in with every passing moment, any effort to impose copyright and exact a fee for securing material is likely to be difficult, if not futile. The same goes for newspapers. The younger generation no longer buys daily newspapers and weekly magazines, preferring to log on and access free blog sites like the *Huffington Post* to stay informed. Many of the leading newspapers and magazines have attempted to slow the stampede to free information by making their own content available online, for free, hoping that advertisers will pay for ads on their websites.

For twenty-five years life science companies have been rushing to patent human, animal, and plant genes in an effort to monopolize the genetic blueprints of life on Earth and reap vast commercial gains in fields including agriculture, energy, and medicine. In recent years, however, in the hopes of establishing a more transparent and collaborative approach to scientific research, a younger generation of scientists have countered by making new genetic discoveries freely available on open-source genetic commons on the Internet to encourage the sharing of biological knowledge. It's unlikely that copyrights and patents will survive in their present form in a collaborative, open-source world where the right to universal access trumps the right to exclusive ownership.

Similarly, the right of free and open access to the renewable energies that bathe the Earth—the sun, wind, geothermal heat, ocean waves and tides, and so on—is increasingly becoming a rallying cry of a younger generation committed to sustainable lifestyles and stewardship of the biosphere. The conventional ownership and control of fossil fuel energy in the hands of a few giant corporations and governments, which characterized the First and Second Industrial Revolutions, will appear odd to young people in 2050, who grew up in the TIR economy and assumed that the Earth's energy is a public good—like the air we breathe—to be shared by all of humanity.

Ensuring universal access and guaranteeing every human being on Earth the right to be included in the life of the global commons opens the door to a vast potential extension of human sociability. The individual and collective struggle to secure access rights in the future will likely be as significant as was the struggle to secure property rights in the past.

FINANCIAL CAPITAL VERSUS SOCIAL CAPITAL

Wealth, productivity, balanced budgets, and property rights are not the only features of classical economic theory being rethought. Even the central tenet of capitalism itself is beginning to wobble as a result of the lateral economic opportunities made possible by TIR technologies.

Capitalism was founded on the idea that the accumulation of individual wealth could be harnessed in the form of financial capital to expropriate even more wealth by controlling the technical means by which that wealth is generated and the logistical means by which it is distributed.

The fossil fuel–based industrial revolution required huge up-front costs. Coal-fired steam technology was far more expensive than wood fuel or water and windmill technology. The high costs of the new energies and technologies and the specialization of tasks and skills that went with them favored centralized management and production under a single roof in what would later be called a factory system.

The textile industry in England was the first to be transformed into the new model. Other cottage industries soon followed. A new class of wealthy merchants garnered sufficient financial capital to own the tools of production, which were previously owned by the craftsmen themselves. They were called capitalists. Unable to compete with the economies of scale and speed of the new factory enterprises, craftsmen lost their independence and became hired hands in the factories, and the workforce of the industrial revolution. Historian Maurice Dobb sums up the significance in the shift from craft to industrial production and from cottage industries to capitalist enterprises: "The subordination of production to capital, and the appearance of the class relationship between capitalist and the producers is, therefore, to be regarded as the critical watershed between the old mode of production and the new."[25]

In the new, distributed, and collaborative communication and energy spaces of the Third Industrial Revolution, however, the accumulation of social capital becomes as important and valuable as the accumulation of financial capital. That's because the cost of entering into networks is plummeting as communication technologies become cheaper. Today, nearly two billion people armed with a cheap desktop computer or an Internet-accessible cell phone enjoy access to one another at the speed of light, with more distributed power at their disposal than the global TV networks.[26] Soon, the plunging cost of renewable energy technology will provide every human being with comparable access to energy across distributed energy networks.

The extraordinary capital costs of owning giant centralized telephone, radio, and television communications technology and fossil fuel and nuclear power plants in markets is giving way to the new, distributed capitalism, in which the low entry costs in lateral networks make it possible for virtually everyone to become a potential entrepreneur and collaborator in open Internet and intergrid commons. The upshot is that financial capital is often not as important as social capital, at least at the start-up stage, in the creation of new mega enterprises. Witness twentysomething young men creating Google, Facebook, and other global networks, literally in their college dorm rooms.

It is not that financial capital is no longer relevant. It is. But the way it is used has been fundamentally altered. As the economy flattens and becomes more distributed, favoring peer-to-peer relationships rather than autonomous exchanges, the very nature of how companies derive revenue changes. The production of property for exchange, the very cornerstone of capitalism, becomes increasingly unprofitable in an intelligent economy where exchange costs become cheaper and cheaper, and eventually, virtually free. That process is well under way and will only accelerate in coming decades as the TIR infrastructure matures. As this happens, property exchange in markets will give way to access relationships in collaborative networks, and production for sale will be subsumed by production for just-in-time use. *New York Times* reporter Mark Levine described the new mindset with the astute observation that "sharing is to ownership what the iPod is to the eight track, what the solar panel is to the coal mine. Sharing is clean, crisp, urbane, postmodern: owning is dull, selfish, timid, backward."[27] What I am describing is a fundamental change in the way capitalism functions that is now unfolding across the traditional manufacturing and retail sectors and reshaping how companies conduct business.

In conventional, capitalist markets, profit is made at the margins of transaction costs. That is, at every step of the conversion process along the value chain the seller is marking up the cost to the buyer to realize a profit. The final price of the good or service to the end user reflects the markups.

But TIR information and communication technologies dramatically shrink transaction costs across the supply chain in every industry and sector, and distributed renewable energies will soon do so as well. The new, green energy industries are improving performance and reducing costs at an ever-accelerating rate. And just as the generation and distribution of information is becoming nearly free, renewable energies will also. The sun and wind are available to everyone and are never used up.

When the transaction costs for engaging in the new Third Industrial Revolution communications/energy system approach zero, it is no longer possible to maintain a margin, and the very notion of profit has to be rethought. That's already happening with the communications component of the Third Industrial Revolution. The shrinking of transaction costs in the music business and publishing field with the emergence of music downloads, ebooks, and news blogs is wreaking havoc on these traditional industries. We can expect similar disruptive impacts with green energy, 3D manufacturing and other sectors. So how do businesses make profit when transaction costs shrink and margins disappear?

In a near transaction-free economy, property still exists, but remains in the hands of the producer and is accessed by the consumer over a period of time. Why would anyone want to own anything in a world of continuous upgrades, where new product lines sweep in and out of the market in an instant? In a Third Industrial Revolution economy, time becomes the scarce commodity and the key unit of exchange, and access to services supersedes ownership as the primary commercial drive.

Purchasing CDs has quickly given way to subscriptions in the past decade. Companies like Rhapsody and Napster allow subscribers to access their music library and download their favorite recordings over a month or year.

Ownership of cars, once considered a rite of passage into the adult world of property relationships, has increasingly lost ground to leasing arrangements. Automobile companies like GM, Daimler, and Toyota would rather keep the vehicles and enter into a long-term service relationship with their customers. This way, the user is paying for the driving experience twenty-four hours a day over the period covered by the lease. The auto company gains a captive client and the user enjoys the convenience of mobility and the easy changeover to a new vehicle every two to three years, while leaving the burden of service and repair to the dealer.

Vacation time-shares have also become a hot business model. Rather than buying a second home, millions of vacationers now buy time-shares in vacation property, giving them the right of access to the accommodations for a specific duration of time. They can also use time-share points to access accommodations in thousands of vacation homes around the world.

Still more interesting, in a world where access begins to eclipse ownership and property remains in the hand of the supplier, to be lent out in time segments to users in the form of leases, rentals, time-shares, retainers and other temporal arrangements, the notion of sustainability becomes intimately attached to the bottom line, rather than simply being a socially responsible act of conscience on behalf of enlightened management.

When an automobile remains the property of the automaker from cradle to grave, the company has a vested interest in making a vehicle that is durable, with low maintenance costs, and that is made of material that is easily recyclable, with a low-carbon footprint. When hotels like Starwood build and own time-share properties, they have an interest in using the least amount of energy and the most sustainable resources to provide a quality experience for their time-share users.

The shift from sellers and buyers to suppliers and users, and from exchange of ownership in markets to access to services in time segments in networks is changing the way we think about economic theory and practice. At an even deeper level, however, the emerging TIR energy-communication infrastructure is changing the very way we measure economic success.

THE DREAM OF QUALITY OF LIFE

The Third Industrial Revolution changes our sense of relationship to and responsibility for our fellow human beings. We come to see our common lot. Sharing the renewable energies of the Earth in collaborative commons that span entire continents can't help but create a new sense of species identity. This dawning awareness of interconnectivity and biosphere embeddedness is already giving birth to a new dream of quality of life, especially among the youth of the world.

The American dream, long held as the gold standard for aspiring people everywhere, is squarely ensconced in the Enlightenment tradition, with its emphasis on the pursuit of material self-interest, autonomy, and independence. Quality of life, however, speaks to a new vision of the future—one based on collaborative interest, connectivity, and interdependence. We come to realize that true freedom is not found in being unbeholden to others and an island to oneself but, rather, in deep participation with others. If freedom is the optimization of one's life, it is measured in the richness and diversity of one's experiences and the strength of one's social bonds. A more solitary existence is a life less lived.

The dream of quality of life can only be collectively experienced. It is impossible to enjoy a quality of life in isolation and by excluding others. Achieving a quality of life requires active participation by everyone in the life of the community and a deep sense of responsibility by every member to ensure that no one is left behind.

Enlightenment economists were convinced that happiness and "the good life" were synonymous with the accumulation of personal wealth. A younger generation, at the cusp of the Third Industrial Revolution, however, is just as likely to believe that, while economic comfort is essential, one's happiness is also proportional to the accumulation of social capital.

The change in thinking about the meaning of happiness is beginning to affect one of the key indices for measuring economic prosperity. The gross domestic product (GDP) was created in the 1930s to measure the value of the sum total of economic goods and services generated over a single year. The problem with the index is that it counts negative as well as positive economic activity. If a country invests large sums of money in armaments, builds prisons, expands police security, and has to clean up polluted environments and the like, it's included in the GDP.

Simon Kuznets, an American who invented the GDP measurement tool, pointed out early on that "[t]he welfare of a nation can . . . scarcely be inferred from a measurement of national income."[28] Later in life, Kuznets became even more emphatic about the drawbacks of relying on the GDP as a gauge of economic prosperity. He warned that "[d]istinctions must be kept in mind between quantity and quality of growth . . . . Goals for 'more' growth should specify more growth of what and for what."[29]

In recent years, economists have begun to create alternative indices for measuring economic prosperity based on quality-of-life indicators rather than mere gross economic output. The Index of Sustainable Economic Welfare (ISEW), the Fordham Index of Social Health (FISH), the Genuine Progress Indicator (GPI), The Index of Economic Well-Being (IEWB), and the UN's Human Development Index (HDI) are among the many new quality-of-life economic index models. These new indices measure the general improvement in the well-being of society and include things such as infant mortality, longevity of life, the availability of health coverage, the level of educational attainment, average weekly earnings, the eradication of poverty, income inequality, affordability of housing, the cleanliness of the environment, biodiversity, the decrease in crime, the amount of leisure time, and so on. The governments of France, the United Kingdom, as well as the European Union and the OECD have created formal quality-of-life indexes with the expectation of increasingly relying on these new measurements to judge the overall performance of the economy.

If quality of life requires a shared notion of our collective responsibility for the larger community in which we dwell, the question becomes, where does that community end? In the new era, our spatial and temporal orientation moves beyond arbitrary political boundaries to encompass the biosphere itself.

REDISCOVERING SPACE AND TIME

Enlightenment economists' determination to ground their new theories in the verities of Newtonian mechanics led them to conceive of space and time in a very mechanical and utilitarian fashion. Space was viewed as a container—a storehouse—full of useful resources ready to be appropriated for economic ends. Time, in turn, was a malleable instrument that could be manipulated to speed the expropriation process and create unlimited economic wealth. Human agency was regarded as an external force that acted on the resources scattered across space, transforming them as efficiently as possible, with labor-saving technologies, into productive utilities. The utilitarian approach to space and the efficient use of time became the critical spatial and temporal coordinates of classical economic theory.

The Enlightenment and post-Enlightenment assumptions about space, time, and human agency reflected the thinking of the day. Geologists and chemists believed that the inanimate material of the Earth existed as a kind of timeless, passive reservoir of untapped stock that awaited human activation to set it in motion and transfer it into productive wealth. Now, new scientific discoveries about the workings of the Earth, especially the interaction between geochemical processes and living systems, cast doubt on this last remaining vestige of classical economic thinking.

We touched on the working of the biosphere in earlier chapters. In the 1970s, British scientist James Lovelock and American biologist Lynn Margulis elaborated on the way geochemical processes interact with biological processes on Earth to maintain the ideal conditions for sustaining life on the planet. Their provocative Gaia hypothesis has gained increasing support over the ensuing decades as researchers from a wide range of scientific fields have weighed in, adding additional evidence to bolster Lovelock and Margulis' theory.

Lovelock and Margulis observe that the Earth is a self-regulating system that acts much like a living system. They cite the example of oxygen and methane regulation to make their case. Oxygen levels on the planet have to remain within a very tight range for life to survive. If oxygen levels increase beyond that range, the Earth would erupt in a fireball and terrestrial life would be extinguished. So how does oxygen get regulated?

The two scientists believe that when oxygen in the atmosphere reaches above acceptable levels, it triggers an increase in the production and release of methane from microscopic bacteria. The methane migrates into the atmosphere, where it dampens the oxygen content until it falls back within its proper range. This is but one of countless feedback loops that keep the biosphere a hospitable place for the flourishing of life on Earth.

The new understanding of the workings of feedback loops in ecological networks is paralleled in the modeling of info-energy feedback networks in an emerging Third Industrial Revolution economy. If technology, like art, imitates life, the new networked infrastructure of the TIR economy comes more and more to imitate the workings of the natural ecosystems of the planet. Creating economic, social, and political relationships that mimic the biological relationships of the ecosystems of the Earth is a critical first step in re-embedding our species into the fabric of the larger communities of life in which we dwell.

A new scientific worldview is emerging whose premises and assumptions are more compatible with the network ways of thinking that underlie a Third Industrial Revolution economic model. The old science views nature as objects; the new science views nature as relationships. The old science is characterized by detachment, expropriation, dissection, and reduction; the new science is characterized by engagement, replenishment, integration, and holism. The old science is committed to making nature productive; the new science to making nature sustainable. The old science seeks power over nature; the new science seeks partnership with nature. The old science puts a premium on autonomy from nature; the new science, on participation with nature.

The new science takes us from a colonial vision of nature as an enemy to pillage and enslave, to a new vision of nature as a community to nurture. The right to exploit, harness, and own nature in the form of property is tempered by the obligation to steward nature and treat it with dignity and respect. The utility value of nature is slowly giving way to the intrinsic value of nature.

If all biological organisms are continuously interacting with geochemical processes to maintain a homeostatic condition favorable to the perpetuation of the biosphere and preservation of life on Earth, then securing the long-term well-being of the human species depends on our ability to live in the spatial and temporal restraints under which the Earth functions. Classical and neoclassical economic theory and practice, with their mania for expropriation and consumption, have undermined the feedback mechanisms between the Earth's geochemical and biological processes, impoverished the planet's ecosystems, and led to a dramatic shift in the temperature and climate on Earth.

If we are to survive and prosper as a species, we will need to rethink our concepts of space and time. The classical economic definition of space as a container or storehouse of passive resources will need to give way to the idea of space as a community of active relationships. In the new schema, the geochemical makeup of the Earth is not viewed as a resource or property but, rather, an intricate part of the interactive relationships that sustain life on the planet. That being the case, our economic priorities need to shift from productivity to generativity, and from a purely utilitarian pursuit of nature, to stewarding the relationships that maintain the biosphere.

Similarly, efficiency needs to make room for sustainability in the organization of time. Our very approach to engineering has to be recalibrated to synchronize with the regenerative periodicities of nature rather than simply the productive rhythms of market efficiency.

The shift from productivity to generativity and from efficiency to sustainability places our species back in step with the ebbs and flows, rhythms, and periodicities, of the larger biosphere community of which we are an intricate and indivisible part. This is what the Third Industrial Revolution is really all about and why existing economic theory, as taught in the business schools of the world, is inadequate as a frame of reference for navigating the new economic era and creating biosphere consciousness.

For the skeptics who argue that any attempt to embed human economic activity in the rhythms and periodicities of the biosphere is futile because it conflicts with our biological predisposition to secure autonomy and exercise power over nature from a distance, a quick remedial introduction to chronobiology ought to put any such reservations to rest.

All life forms, from microbes to human beings, are made up of myriad biological clocks that entrain their physiological processes to the larger rhythms of the biosphere and the planet. Living creatures, including human beings, time their internal and external functions with the solar day (circadian rhythms), the lunar month (lunar rhythms), the changing seasons and the annual rotation of the Earth around the sun (circannual rhythms). Psychologist John E. Orme notes that "the physical universe is basically rhythmic in nature. The moon revolves around the earth, the earth around the sun, and the solar system itself changes spatial position in time. All these phenomena result in regular rhythmic changes and the survival of biological species depends on the capacity to follow these rhythms."[30]

Anyone who has ever experienced jet lag from quickly crossing time zones in an airplane understands that the human body is delicately calibrated and choreographed to the rhythms of the planet, and that any disruption throws the body's internal processes into desynchronization. Our body temperature rises and falls in a predictable pattern every twenty-four hours. So, too, does our skin temperature. Women's menstruation cycles tend to follow a lunar cycle. Seasonal Affective Disorder (SAD) generally occurs in the winter months, when sunlight is shortest in duration, and the feeling of lethargy and depression mimics the hibernation process that slows physiological activity among many mammalian species.[31]

Researchers in the field of chronopharmacology are beginning to realize that the time of day a particular medication is given or surgery is performed can influence its effectiveness and are beginning to synchronize treatment to an individual's internal biological clocks.

The fact that human beings, like every other species, are biologically entrained to the periodicities of the Earth changes the way we think about space and time. Our very being is woven into the spatial and temporal coordinates of the Earth. Cells in our physical body are continuously being replaced with each passing moment. Our existence is a pattern of activity, with low-entropy calories of energy flowing into our body from nature, replenishing cells as quickly as they are discarded back to the environment for recycling. We are each an embodiment of the energy currents and the geochemical and biological processes that flow through the biosphere. In the planetary system, life, geochemical processes, and the Earth's periodicities interact in a tightly choreographed set of relationships that assures the functioning of each creature and the biosphere as a whole.

For most of history, our species lived in sync with the rhythms of the planet. The stored fossil fuel energies of the First and Second Industrial Revolutions removed the human race from the periodicities of the Earth for the first time. Today, 24/7 electricity illumination, round-the-clock Internet communication, jet travel, shift work, and a myriad of other activities have dislodged us from our primordial biological clocks. The sun and the changing seasons have become far less relevant to our survival—or at least we thought that was the case. Our increasing reliance on a rich deposit of inert stored sun, in the form of carbon-based fuels, created the illusion that our success on Earth was more dependent on human ingenuity and technological prowess than on nature's recurring cycles. We now know that's not so. The imposition of artificial production rhythms—especially the institutionalization of machine efficiency—has brought great material wealth to a significant portion of the human race, but at the expense of compromising the Earth's ecosystems, with dreadful consequences for the stability of the Earth's biosphere.

The Third Industrial Revolution brings us back into the sunlight. By relying on the energy flows that cross the Earth's biosphere—the sun, wind, the hydrological cycle, biomass, geothermal heat, and the ocean waves and tides—we reconnect to the rhythms and periodicities of the planet. We become re-embedded in the ecosystems of the biosphere and come to understand that our individual ecological footprint effects the well-being of every other human being and every other creature on Earth.

WHETHER IT'S RETHINKING GDP and how to measure the economic well-being of society, revising our ideas about productivity, understanding the notion of debt and how best to balance our production and consumption budgets with nature's own, reexamining our notions about property relations, reevaluating the importance of finance capital versus social capital, reassessing the economic value of markets versus networks, changing our conception of space and time, or reconsidering how the Earth's biosphere functions, standard economic theory comes up woefully short.

On these and other accounts, the changes taking place in the way we understand human nature and the meaning of the human journey are so profoundly disruptive to the way we have thought over the past two hundred years that spawned the first two industrial revolutions, that it is likely that much of classical and neoclassical economic theory that accompanied and legitimized these two earlier industrial eras will not survive the newly emerging economic paradigm.

What is likely to happen is that the still-valuable insights and content of standard economic theory will be rethought and reworked within the purview of a thermodynamic lens. Using the laws of energy as a common language will allow economists to enter into a deep conversation with engineers, chemists, ecologists, biologists, architects, and urban planners, among others, whose disciplines are grounded in the laws of energy. Since these other fields are the ones that actually produce economic activity, a serious interdisciplinary discussion over time could potentially lead to a new synthesis between economic theory and commercial practice and the emergence of a new, explanatory economic model to accompany the Third Industrial Revolution paradigm.

Economics is not the only academic discipline that will need to be transformed. Our public educational system, like our economic theory, has not changed much since its inception at the beginning of the modern market era. Like classical and neoclassical economic theory, it, too, has been a handmaiden for the First and Second Industrial Revolutions, mirroring the operating assumptions, policies, and practices of the commercial order it served.

Now, the shift from a centralized Second Industrial Revolution to a lateral Third Industrial Revolution is forcing a makeover of the educational system. Rethinking the framing concepts that govern education and the pedagogy that accompanies them will not be easy. Teachers around the world are only just now beginning to restructure the educational experience to make it relevant to young people who will need to learn how to live in a distributed and collaborative economy tucked inside a biosphere world.

CHAPTER EIGHT
A CLASSROOM MAKEOVER

I was backstage, fidgeting with my five small note cards, thinking over the key points I wanted to emphasize in my talk. I peeked through the curtain and saw 1,600 high school teachers and state and federal education officials sitting in the audience—and not just any teachers, Advanced Placement teachers, the best high school teachers in America and the ones responsible for preparing the brightest students for college.

It was the annual conference of the College Board, the organization that oversees SAT testing—the standardized test that millions of American high school students must take if their plans include higher education.

Gaston Caperton, the former governor of West Virginia and current president of the College Board, had asked me to deliver the keynote address to the gathering. His only instruction: "Shake them up! Take them into the future. Challenge them to rethink the mission of American education in a globalizing world."

Easily said. But I wasn't sure how the teachers would react if I told them what I really thought needed to be done. To tell the truth, the educational system in America and around the world is a relic of a bygone era. The curriculum is out of date and out of touch with the realities of the current economic and environmental crises. The very methodological and pedagogical assumptions that have guided education for the better part of 150 years—since the beginning of compulsory public education—are a big part of the reason the human race is heading to the edge of the abyss.

Would the teachers waiting patiently in their seats, no doubt expecting an uplifting speech on the value of a sound education, be prepared to hear that much of what we teach and how we teach is dysfunctional and toxic to the future development of the human race?

I walked out onto the floor, took a deep breath, and began with a lament on the state of the world—a sentiment which I hoped would be a liberating reflection by the end of the talk. I scanned the audience, paying close attention to facial expressions and body language as I laid out the breadth of the crisis facing us. I could feel a quietness in the auditorium and I wasn't sure what to make of it. As I began to deconstruct the traditional education system, I detected a slight murmur throughout the room. But it was when I turned to the new, distributed and collaborative teaching methods and learning models that there was a decisive shift in the mood of the audience. Hundreds of teachers became animated and began to nod their approval. As I wrapped up, I realized that a great many of the teachers were well ahead of me, already asking the tough questions in their own classrooms about the future of education and experimenting with new teaching methods and pedagogy to prepare the next generation for living in a distributed and collaborative society.

They stood up and clapped at the end, but as they did, I noticed many were turning to each other and applauding. For many of them, it was a moment of self-affirmation—a feeling that they were on the right track and that their own efforts to rethink American education were well-founded.

We're beginning to hear a new conversation in the educational community. As the Third Industrial Revolution vision takes root in the public imagination and the first tentative steps toward a five-pillar infrastructure materialize, educators, as well as employers and politicians, are starting to ask what changes we'll need to make to prepare future generations for a new economic and political era. Understandably, the first concern is the instrumental realm. There is already significant discussion around the new professional and technical skills that students will have to learn to become productive workers in the Third Industrial Revolution economy.

EDUCATING THE TWENTY-FIRST CENTURY TIR WORKFORCE

Universities and high schools will need to begin training the workforce of the Third Industrial Revolution. Curriculum will need to focus increasingly on advanced information, nano- and biotechnologies, Earth sciences, ecology, and systems theory as well vocational skills, including manufacturing and marketing renewable energy technologies, transforming buildings into mini power plants, installing hydrogen and other storage technologies, laying out intelligent utility networks, manufacturing plug-in and hydrogen fuel cell transport, setting up green logistics networks, and the like.

Aware of the need to prepare students with the professional, technical, and vocational skills they will need to live and work in a sustainable Third Industrial Revolution economy, our global team is working with universities and school systems to transform them into TIR learning environments. In the Rome master plan, for example, we are partnering with Livio de Santoli, the dean of the School of Architecture at La Sapienza University, and his team to reconfigure its campus buildings into a Third Industrial Revolution infrastructure by introducing renewable energies, hydrogen storage technologies, and smart utility networks. The goal is to connect La Sapienza University with other universities, high schools, and primary schools in a TIR grid that will spread out across Rome. This pioneer web can be linked with commercial and residential energy cooperatives in the years ahead, metamorphosing into a fully operable infrastructure.

An equally ambitious effort is underway in school districts across California. High schools and elementary schools are forming partnerships with banks and other commercial enterprises to install solar carports in their campus parking lots. Under the agreements, commercial partners finance the installations and sell the electricity back to the school for a twenty-year period at an agreed-upon price below the cost of securing conventional electricity from the central power grid. The commercial partners, in turn, take advantage of federal and state tax incentives to make a profit on the transaction.

Seventy-five high schools and elementary schools are already generating green energy and administrators predict that the solar carport idea will catch on across the country in the next few years. The administration gives two reasons for the popularity of solar campuses.

First, in a tight economy with diminished school budgets, green electricity provides a significant energy savings. In the Milpitas Unified School District near San Jose, solar panels generate 75 percent of the school district's electricity needs during the regular school year and 100 percent of its electricity needs during the summer school session. The savings on electricity bills can range from $12 million to $40 million over the life span of the solar panels. School-based photovoltaic systems in the San Francisco Bay Area increased by fivefold between 2008 and 2009 and, by 2010, were providing enough power to meet the electricity needs of 3,500 homes.[1]

Second, installing solar infrastructures on campuses allow students to become familiar with the new TIR technology, creating a hands-on learning environment for acquiring the skills they will need in the emerging green economy. "School children are growing up with [green electricity] so that it becomes ingrained in their perception of how a society functions," observes Brad Parker, a solar carport consultant to the San Luis Coastal Unified School District in central California.[2]

Just as schools in the past decade were equipped with personal computers and Internet connections so that students could create their own information and share it with others in virtual space, the current generation of students will need to be equipped with TIR technologies so they can harvest their own renewable energy and share it in open-source energy spaces.

TIR technologies will need to be accompanied by a TIR curriculum. Educators are beginning to introduce smart grid curriculum into elementary and high school classrooms and vocational schools and colleges. With half of America's utility workers slated for retirement in the next five to ten years, the US federal government has allocated $100 million in stimulus funds to promote smart grid curricula in high schools and colleges. In announcing the grants, secretary of energy Steven Chu noted that "building and operating smart grid infrastructure will put tens of thousands of Americans to work."[3] The Department of Energy estimates that the federal grants will train more than thirty thousand workers for the new jobs awaiting them in the TIR era.

Exciting students about electricity and the power grid is priority number one. Lisa Magnuson, the director of marketing for Silver Spring Networks, a company that makes hardware and software to smarten up the nation's power grid, says that America needs to draw on the creativity of a younger generation that has grown up on the Internet. In pilot curricula being tested in school systems in Ohio and California, students are being asked to write essays on topics like, "How will the smart grid change your life or your future career?" Getting the kids to think about producing energy and sharing clean electricity on an Intergrid, the way they now create and share information on the Internet, will open the floodgates to new TIR "killer apps" as they come of age. "We want to make utilities cool again," says Magnuson.

At the university level, state-of-the-art research laboratories are just now being built to provide the next generation of inventors, entrepreneurs, and technicians with the tools they need to create the breakthrough technologies of the TIR era. Ohio State University is now equipped with one of only a handful of high-voltage laboratories in the United States. Researchers and students are using the facility to create virtual platforms that simulate features and functions of the smart grid.

In our San Antonio master plan, we proposed the establishment of a TIR science and technology park adjoining the new Texas A&M University campus to allow for a cross-fertilization of research talent between the various university departments and the companies engaged in TIR technologies and applications. Similar university/private sector partnerships have long existed for Second Industrial Revolution technologies and businesses.

ALTHOUGH PROFESSIONAL AND TECHNICAL SKILLS are critical to transitioning into a Third Industrial Revolution, educators shouldn't put the cart before the horse by emphasizing them at the expense of the deeper changes that must take place. If we change only the skill sets of students but not their consciousness, we will have done little to alter the notion that being productive is the overriding mission of education. What we will end up with is a workforce whose approach to economic activity is still mired in the utilitarian ethos of the earlier two Industrial Revolutions. Students steeped in biosphere consciousness, however, will regard TIR professional skills not merely as vocational tools to become more productive workers but, rather, as ecological aids in stewarding our common biosphere.

THE MOST OUTDATED INSTITUTION IN THE WORLD

The notion that the primary mission of education is to turn out productive workers is grounded on a particular notion of human nature that was spawned in the Enlightenment at the very beginning of the industrial era. The very word *industrial* comes from *industrious,* and refers to a state of mind that accompanied the modern market economy and became essential to its successful deployment. In the late medieval era, economic activity was organized around the idea of maintaining a relatively constant way of life. Young men went through rigorous apprenticeships in their respective crafts before being formally recognized as masters of their trade. While vocational expertise was highly regarded and closely guarded, as mentioned in the previous chapter, economic activity was limited to reproducing a given way of life. To ensure this, prices were fixed and output was limited. The idea of progress did not yet exist in the public consciousness.

The term *industrious* traces its roots back to the cleric John Calvin and the early Protestant reformers who argued that each individual continually strives to improve his or her lot as a sign of personal election and salvation in the next world with Christ. In the early market era, the idea of improving one's lot metamorphosed from a theological prescription to an economic expectation, and a man of "good character" came to be known, judged, and respected for his industriousness. Enlightenment philosophers like John Locke and Adam Smith came to see human nature as acquisitive, utilitarian, and self-interested, and viewed being industrious as an innate capacity that fostered material progress. By the time the First Industrial Revolution was gearing up in the late nineteenth century, employers began to measure a man's industriousness in terms of his productivity, and being productive became the defining characteristic of human behavior itself.

The public school movement in Europe and America was largely designed to foster the productive potential inherent in each human being and create a productive work force to advance the Industrial Revolution. Hundreds of millions of youngsters, stretching over eight generations of history, have been schooled on the Enlightenment assumptions about humanity's core nature.

Our ideas about education invariably flow from our perception of reality and our conception of nature—especially our assumptions about human nature and the meaning of the human journey. Those assumptions become institutionalized in our education process. What we really teach, at any given time, is the consciousness of an era.

Human consciousness, however, changes over history. The way an urban professional thinks today is very different than the way a medieval rural serf thought in the fifteenth century or a forager-hunter twenty thousand years ago. Great changes in human consciousness occur when new, more complex energy regimes arise, making possible more interdependent and complex social arrangements. As mentioned in chapter 2, coordinating those civilizations requires new, more sophisticated communications systems. When energy regimes converge with communications revolutions, human consciousness is altered.

All forager-hunter societies were oral cultures, steeped in a *mythological consciousness*. The hydraulic agricultural civilizations were organized around writing and gave rise to the world's great religions and *theological consciousness*. Print technology became the communication medium to organize the myriad activities of the coal- and steam-powered First Industrial Revolution two hundred years ago, and led to a transformation from theological to *ideological consciousness* during the Enlightenment. In the twentieth century, electronic communication became the command-and-control mechanism to manage a Second Industrial Revolution based on the oil economy and the automobile. Electronic communication spawned a new *psychological consciousness*.

Today, distributed information and communication technologies are converging with distributed renewable energies, creating the infrastructure for a Third Industrial Revolution and paving the way for *biosphere consciousness*. We come to see our species, in all of its diversity, as a single family, and all the other species of life on Earth as our extended evolutionary family, living interdependently in a common biosphere.

BIOSPHERE CONSCIOUSNESS

In the new globally connected Third Industrial Revolution era, the primary mission of education is to prepare students to think and act as part of a shared biosphere.

Our emerging sense of biosphere consciousness coincides with discoveries in evolutionary biology, neurocognitive science, and child development that reveal that people are biologically predisposed to be empathic—that our core nature is not rational, detached, acquisitive, aggressive, and narcissistic, as many Enlightenment philosophers suggested, but rather, affectionate, highly social, cooperative, and interdependent. *Homo sapiens* is giving way to *Homo empathicus*. Social historians tell us that empathy is the social glue that allows increasingly individualized and diverse populations to forge bonds of familiarity across broader domains so that society can cohere as a whole. To empathize is to civilize.

Empathy has evolved over history. In forager-hunter societies, empathy rarely went beyond tribal blood ties. In the hydraulic agricultural age, empathy extended past blood ties to associational ties based on religious identification. Jews began to empathize with fellow Jews as if in an extended family, Christians began empathizing with fellow Christians, Muslims with Muslims, and so on. In the industrial age, with the emergence of the modern nation-state, empathy extended once again, this time to people of like-minded national identities. Americans began to empathize with Americans, Germans with Germans, Japanese with Japanese. Today, at the outset of the Third Industrial Revolution, empathy is beginning to stretch beyond national boundaries to biosphere boundaries. We are coming to see the biosphere as our indivisible community, and empathizing with our fellow human beings and other creatures as our extended evolutionary family.

The realization that we are an empathic species, that empathy has evolved over history, and that we are as interconnected in the biosphere as we are in the blogosphere, has great significance for rethinking the mission of education. New teaching models designed to transform education from a competitive contest to a collaborative and empathic learning experience are emerging as schools and colleges try to reach a generation that has grown up on the Internet and is used to interacting in open social networks where information is shared rather than hoarded. The traditional assumption that "knowledge is power" to be used for personal gain is being subsumed by the notion that knowledge is an expression of the shared responsibilities for the collective well-being of humanity and the planet as a whole.

In schools all over the world, teachers are instructing students, from the earliest ages, that they are an intimate part of the workings of the biosphere and that every activity they engage in—the food they eat, the clothes they wear, the car their family drives, the electricity they use—leaves an ecological footprint that affects the well-being of other human beings and other creatures on Earth. For example, if they eat a hamburger from a fast-food restaurant, it might have come from a steer that grazed on pastureland cut out from a Central American rainforest. The felled trees mean less forest cover and a loss of species that live in the forest canopy. Fewer trees also means less forests available to serve as sinks to absorb industrial CO_2 released into the atmosphere from the burning of coal in centralized power plants. The resulting rise in the Earth's temperature from too much CO_2 in the atmosphere affects the hydrological cycle, leading to more floods and droughts around the world, a diminution in crop yields and a drop in income for poor farmers and their families. A loss in income means greater hunger and malnutrition for at-risk populations—all of which is traceable back to the burger in the bun.

An older generation of skeptics might find the idea of biosphere consciousness a bit over the top, even as their children and grandchildren seem to be quite comfortable identifying with the biosphere as their larger community.

E. O. Wilson, the famed Harvard biologist, says that an intimate relationship with the biosphere is not a utopian fantasy but, rather, an ancient sensibility that is built into our biology but has sadly been lost over eons of human history. Wilson believes that human beings have an innate drive to affiliate with nature—what he calls "biophilia."[4] For example, he cites studies across many diverse cultures that reveal a human propensity for open vistas, lush grasslands, and rolling fields punctuated by small clusters of trees and ponds. Wilson believes that this primal identification with our earliest phase as a species continues to exist deep inside our biological being as a kind of genetic recollection of our biophilic connection. In recent studies of hospital patients, researchers found that when provided a window view of trees, open green landscapes, and ponds, patients more quickly regained their health than those without such exposure, suggesting the restorative value of nature.[5]

Biophilia extends beyond landscapes to our affiliation with our evolutionary relatives. When we observe and interact with other animals, we are continually aware of our similarities. Like ourselves, our fellow creatures have a drive to exist. Each is a unique being. Every creature has its own unrepeatable life journey, each day of which is full of opportunities and risks. We all share vulnerabilities—being alive, whether as a fox navigating the forest or as a human being navigating an urban environment, is fraught with peril. We particularly affiliate with our fellow mammals, who *look* so much like us and *are* so much like us. They are sentient creatures who nurture their young, exhibit emotions, learn from one another, and create rudimentary cultures that are passed on between generations. They create social bonds via play and grooming, and communicate their individual feelings to one another in elaborate social rituals just like us.

Wilson suggests that we emotionally identify with our fellow creatures to the point of experiencing their being as if it were our own. In short, we empathize. Who hasn't had an empathic experience at some point in their life with a fellow creature—whether a companion animal or a chance exposure to a wild creature? When we come across young horses playing and frolicking in open pastures, full of the joy of being alive, or an injured squirrel, writhing in pain and terrified, we feel a deep outpouring of empathy—it is our way of acknowledging the mystery of life that binds us together in fellowship on this Earth. To empathize is to affirm another's struggle to be and flourish. We recognize the intrinsic value of their life as if it were our own. By empathizing we express our kinship with our fellow creatures.

While all of us at one time or another have experienced a biophilia connection, in our urbanized, high-tech society, our exposure to nature and our fellow creatures has steadily diminished. For the first time in history, a majority of human beings lives in artificial environments, virtually cut off from the rest of nature. Wilson and an increasing number of biologists and ecologists worry that the loss of the biophilia connection poses a very real threat to our physical, emotional, and mental well-being, and ultimately stymies our cognitive development as a species.

One thing is for sure, though—if we are not able to recapture our innate biophilia, we will never reach biosphere consciousness. The five pillars of the Third Industrial Revolution are really only tools that can enable us to reintegrate into the natural world. They allow us to reorganize our lives in a way that once again acknowledges the interdependencies of the common biosphere we share with our fellow creatures. But unless the Third Industrial Revolution is accompanied by a change in the way we view and experience the world—biosphere consciousness—it will die prematurely.

RECAPTURING THE BIOPHILIA CONNECTION

How then do we breathe biosphere consciousness into our lives so that we can reestablish our relationship with nature, restore the Earth, and save our species?

Owen Barfield, the late British philosopher, speaks to the present moment facing our species. He observes that humanity has lived through two great periods in its relationship with nature.

For more than 90 percent of our existence on Earth we lived as foragers and hunters. Our ancient ancestors experienced nature directly and intimately. There were few boundaries between the self and the other. Life was lived in a dreamlike state in which living beings and other phenomena interacted, recombined, and exchanged places in bewildering mayhem— what anthropologists call an undifferentiated fog.

Day-to-day life was finely tuned to the periodicities of nature and the changing seasons, as is still the case for every other creature on Earth. "Mother Earth" was less a metaphor than a real primordial being to whom forager-hunters were deeply beholden for their survival. Thus, she was treated with a sense of awe and both loved and feared by humans, befitting their utter dependence on her goodwill.

The great transformation from foraging and hunting to agriculture radically changed human beings' relationship to nature—from one of complete reliance on its goodwill and bounty to increasing control and management of it as a resource. With the domestication of plants and animals, human beings began to detach themselves from the natural world, creating a fictional barrier between human and animal behavior. By the late medieval era, to be civilized was to have rid oneself of a "brutish" animal nature. Successive generations became increasingly self-aware and independent, but at the expense of losing the earlier, intimate participation they enjoyed with nature.

Barfield wrote that the human race is on the cusp of a third period in its relationship to nature—one in which human beings reengage with the natural world, not out of a sense of dependency and fear, as was the case with our species' earliest relationship, but by a deliberate choice to become an intimate part of a broader universal community of life.[6] This is biosphere consciousness. What Barfield leaves unexplored, however, is the underlying historical process by which an increasingly self-aware and individualized species is able to turn the corner and rediscover its interdependent relationship to nature in a volitional way. That understanding is key to rethinking the way we educate present and future generations to foster biosphere consciousness.

Each more complex energy/communications revolution gives rise to a more elaborate differentiation of tasks, which in turn spurs individuation and greater self-awareness. The undifferentiated "we" that characterizes a simple forager-hunter existence, gives way to butchers, bakers, and candlestick makers, each with an awakening sense of his or her own individuality, made possible by the unique task he or she performs in society. Even today, family names harken back to craft skills passed down over the generations: Smith, Tanner, Weaver, Cook, Trainer, and so on.

The growing self-awareness of the human race is the psychological mechanism that allows empathy to grow and flourish. As we become increasingly aware of our own individuality, we come to realize that our life is unique, unrepeatable and fragile. It is that existential sense of our *one and only life* that allows us to empathize with others' unique journeys and to express our solidarity. We do this by engaging in acts of compassion whose purpose is to aid another in the struggle to optimize his or her life. To empathize is to celebrate another's existence.

If our core nature is empathic and we have an innate drive to affiliate with nature, how do we awaken and mature the biophilia connection? Wilson says that "the psychologists have got to be brought in on the act."[7] They need to help us resuscitate the primal biophilia drive that has for so long been buried in our collective subconsciousness. Others agree.

Theodore Roszak, who coined the term *ecopsychology,* was rather disparaging of the psychiatric profession in his 1992 book, *The Voice of the Earth.* Roszak noted that the American Psychiatric Association lists more than 300 mental diseases in the Diagnostics and Statistical Manual, without so much of a mention of the possibility that human beings might suffer mentally from a loss of attachment to nature. He writes, "Psycho-therapists have exhaustively analyzed every form of dysfunctional family and social relations, but dysfunctional environmental relations does not exist even as a concept."[8] Roszak makes the very telling point that the Diagnostics and Statistical Manual "defines separation anxiety disorder as excessive anxiety concerning separation from home and from those to whom the individual is attached. But no separation is more pervasive in this age of anxiety than our disconnection from the natural world." Roszak challenged the psychiatric profession, saying it's time "for an environmentally based definition of mental health."[9]

Around the time Roszak was writing about the mental distress that might be caused from isolation from nature, other voices from the field of philosophy began to join in the discussion. The term *ecological self* was coined by the deep ecologist and philosopher Arne Næss. The deep ecologists realized that as long as people viewed nature in instrumental terms, they would continue to regard other species merely as resources that fulfilled utilitarian desires. Objectifying our fellow creatures would forever prohibit the human psyche from identifying with them as unique beings not unlike ourselves and therefore imbued with intrinsic value and worthy of being treated as ends, not means. The deep ecologists were particularly hard on many conventional environmentalists for championing a conservation ethic based on stewarding natural resources strictly for human enjoyment.

Næss and other deep ecologists, whom I have personally known and come to admire, nonetheless fall short when it comes to the way they perceive their relationship to individual animals. While they express a personal regard for other creatures, their relationship is often more cognitive than affective. Joanna Macy, another pioneer in ecophilosophy, argues that by rediscovering our emotional connection to other creatures, we expand our sense of self from the personal to the ecological. It is by the act of empathy with the particular plight of individual creatures that we are able to transcend our mental isolation and become reattached to our animal roots. We come to emotionally identify with other creatures *as if* they were us, and begin to regard them as part of our extended evolutionary family. By our empathic extension we become an extended self.

This emotional identification extends not only to other lifeforms but also to ecosystems and the biosphere itself.[10] Environmental activist John Seed perhaps best described the reawakening of a biophilia connection. Pondering the fate of the rainforest, he says, "I try to remember that it's not me, John Seed, trying to protect the rainforest. Rather, I am part of the rainforest protecting itself. I am part of the rainforest recently emerged into human thinking."[11] The idea of a self-conscious, extended ecological self actively choosing to reengage in the myriad interdependent relationships that make up the living biosphere is exactly what Barfield had in mind when he talked about the third stage of human development.

Preparing our children to think as extended ecological selves—to have biosphere consciousness—will be the critical test of our age and might well determine whether we will be able to create a new, sustainable relationship with the Earth in time to slow climate change and prevent our own extinction.

Aware of the perilous times ahead, educators are beginning to ask the question of whether simply becoming economically productive ought to be the primary mission of education. Shouldn't we place at least as much attention on developing our youngsters' innate empathic drives and biophilia connections so that we can ready them to think and act as part of a universal family that includes not only all of our fellow human beings but our fellow creatures as well?

THE DISTRIBUTED AND COLLABORATIVE CLASSROOM

A new generation of educators is beginning to deconstruct the classroom learning processes that accompanied the First and Second Industrial Revolutions and reconstitute the educational experience along lines designed to encourage an extended, ecological self, imbued with biosphere consciousness. The dominant, top-down approach to teaching, the aim of which is to create a competitive, autonomous being, is beginning to give way to a distributed and collaborative educational experience with an eye to instilling a sense of the social nature of knowledge. Intelligence, in the new way of thinking, is not something one inherits or a resource one accumulates but, rather, a shared experience distributed among people.

The new approach to learning mirrors the way a younger generation learns and shares information, ideas, and experiences on the Internet in open-source learning spaces and social media sites. Distributed and collaborative learning also prepares the workforce of the twenty-first century for a Third Industrial Revolution economy that operates on the same set of principles.

More important, by learning to think and act in a distributed and collaborative fashion, students come to see themselves as empathic beings, enmeshed in webs of shared relationships, in ever more inclusive communities, that eventually extend to the entirety of the biosphere.

The distributed and collaborative perspective starts with the assumption that learning is always a deeply social experience. We learn by participation. While our conventional education encourages the notion that learning is a private experience, in reality, "thinking occurs as much among as within individuals."[12] Although we all enjoy moments of private reflection, even then, the substance of our thoughts is ultimately connected, in one way or another, to our former shared experiences with others, from which we internalize shared meanings. The new education reformers emphasize breaking down the walls and engaging diverse others in more distributed and collaborative learning communities, both in virtual and real space.

The proliferation of social networks and collaborative forms of participation on the Internet are taking education beyond the confines of the classroom to a global learning environment in cyberspace. Students are connecting with distant peers in virtual classrooms through Yahoo! and Skype technology. When students from very different cultures participate in joint academic assignments and class projects in real time in virtual space, learning is transformed into a lateral experience that stretches around the world.

Students at Brooklyn High School of Telecommunications and Lee School in Winterthur, Switzerland, were involved in a joint virtual-classroom project during the Iraq war, exploring how their different cultures viewed the war in the Middle East and other global conflicts and peace initiatives. The students exchanged points of view, questioned one another, and collaborated on virtual class assignments via online chat rooms, videoconferences, and bulletin boards.

In one exchange, a Swiss student expressed the belief that most Americans supported the war, which elicited fast responses from two American students, the first of whom had an uncle serving in the armed forces in Iraq, and another, whose parents were of Palestinian descent. During the online virtual classroom discussions, students were often just as curious about conflicts closer to home. One of the American students asked a Swiss student if young people in his city can buy knives and guns as easily as in New York City.[13]

The extension of the classroom exposes young people to their cohorts in widely different cultures, allowing empathic sensibility to expand and deepen. Education becomes a truly planetary experience, hastening the shift to biosphere consciousness.

The global extension of learning environments in cyberspace is being matched by the local extension of learning environments in school neighborhoods. The traditional barrier separating the classroom and community is beginning to give way as learning becomes a distributed exercise involving both formal and informal modes of education in broader, more diverse social spaces in the civil society.

In the past twenty-five years, American secondary schools and colleges have introduced service-learning programs into the curriculum—a deeply empathic collaborative teaching model that has altered the educational experience for millions of young people. As part of the requirements for graduation, students are expected to volunteer in neighborhood nonprofit organizations and in community initiatives designed to help those in need and improve the well-being of their communities. According to the US Department of Education, four out of every five millennials have been involved in community service while in high school.[14]

The Memory Bridge Initiative in Chicago trains students from some of the poorest neighborhoods in the city's south side to serve as aids to Alzheimer's patients in nursing homes. What makes the Chicago program so unique is that many of the students come from broken homes and have grown up in a world of abject poverty, where drug addiction, rampant criminality, and violence is a way of life and hardened behavior is a survival strategy. Assisting with helpless seniors, who struggle to perform the simplest tasks, awakens an empathic connection within the students, allowing them to come out of themselves and nurture long-repressed drives for communion.[15]

Performing service in food kitchens, health clinics, environmental projects, tutoring programs, counseling centers, and hundreds of other neighborhood nonprofit activities has transformed the learning experience. The exposure to diverse people from various walks of life has spurred an empathic surge among many of the nation's young people. Studies indicate that many students experience a deep maturing of empathic sensibility by being thrust into unfamiliar environments where they are called on to reach out and assist others. These experiences are often life-changing, affecting their sense of what gives their life meaning. School systems in other countries are beginning to implement their own service-learning curricula.

Some school systems and universities are elevating service learning by embedding it into the rest of the academic curriculum. Subject areas come alive by direct involvement. Students learn about sociology, political science, psychology, biology, mathematics, music, the arts, literature, and the like both in the classroom and in direct participation with others through service in the community.

For example, the students working with senior citizens might bring their service-learning experience to bear in social studies classes in discussions around federal and state budget priorities and the question of a younger generation's obligation to care for the elderly in an increasingly aging society. How much financial sacrifice should youth be expected to make to the elderly in their waning years, especially if it means foreclosing opportunities for optimizing their own future lives? Classroom discussion becomes far more relevant, immediate, and expansive when students' own experiences with others in the larger community provide perspective.

LATERAL LEARNING

Distributed and collaborative education flows from the idea that when people reason together, their combined experience is more likely to achieve the desired results than when people reason alone.

The first academic to stumble across the great value of lateral learning was L. J. Abercrombie at the University Hospital, University of London.

In research conducted in the 1950s, Abercrombie noted the rather curious fact that when medical students accompanied a doctor on his rounds of hospital patients together as a group, and collaborated in their assessment of the condition of the patient, they came to a more accurate diagnosis than if they each accompanied the doctor alone. The group interaction allowed the medical students the opportunity to challenge each other's hypotheses, offer individual insights and build on each other's observations, finally leading to a group consensus of the likely state of the patient under review.

We are so accustomed to conventional learning environments that we rarely step back and ask critical questions about the nature of the learning process. We simply take for granted that the way we are being taught is the fundamental way knowledge is passed on. What we are really learning, however, is a way of structuring our reality and organizing our relationships to the world around us. Kenneth Bruffee, professor of English at Brooklyn College, City University of New York, reviews the key operating assumptions of the contemporary learning process, describing the significant role they play in creating the modern frame of mind.

Bruffee begins with the teacher, whose responsibility is to transfer knowledge into the minds of the students. He does this by creating an authoritative relationship with each student. That is, he calls on individuals and asks each to recite or provide an answer to a directed question. Each student is expected to perform strictly for the teacher, by recitation or by written exam. The relationship is always top-down and one-to-one. Students are discouraged from interacting with each other, whether by posing questions to one another, or assisting each other. Such behavior would breach the authority of the teacher and create an alternative pattern of authority that would be lateral and interactive. Thinking together would be considered cheating. Each student, in turn, is individually evaluated and graded.

Students are made to believe that knowledge is an objective phenomenon that exists in the form of bits of information and facts, and that the teacher's role is to implant those bits of impartial knowledge into each head. Students quickly come to understand that there are right and wrong answers to every question by the approving or disapproving response of the teacher. They are often discouraged, even penalized, for offering their own subjective thoughts on the subject matter before the class and severely reprimanded for questioning the views of the teacher.

Bruffee summarizes the educational experience this way: "A student's responsibility according to these foundational classroom conventions is to 'absorb' what the professor in one way or another imparts. The professor's responsibility is to impart knowledge to students and evaluate their retention of it."[16]

Lateral learning starts from a completely different assumption about the nature of learning. Knowledge is not regarded as objective, autonomous phenomena but, rather, the explanations we make about the common experiences that we share with each other. To seek the truth is to understand how everything relates and we discover those relationships by our deep participation with others. The more diverse our experiences and interrelationships, the closer we come to understanding reality itself and how each of us fits into the bigger picture of existence.

Knowledge, according to Bruffee and other educational reformers, is a social construct, a consensus among the members of a learning community.[17] If knowledge is something that exists between people and comes out of their shared experiences, then the way our educational process is set up is inimical to deep learning. Our schooling is often little more than a stimulus-response process, a robotic affair in which students are programmed to respond to the instructions fed into them—much like the standard operating procedures of scientific management that created the workers of the First and Second Industrial Revolutions.

Peer-to-peer learning shifts the focus from the lone self to the interdependent group. Learning ceases to be an isolated experience between an authority figure and student and is transformed into a community experience.[18]

Students are dividing up into small working groups and tasked with specific assignments. Once the teacher sets out the assignment, she removes herself, allowing students to organize their own knowledge community. Students are expected to exchange ideas, question one another, critique each other's analysis, build off each other's contributions, and negotiate a consensus.[19]

Often, the group will be further divided, and each individual tasked with becoming an expert on one of the subtopics relevant to the assignment. Each expert is expected to share his or her knowledge with the group and become a guide to the discussion when it touches on his or her area of expertise. In this way students teach each other and learn how to lead without commandeering the conversation. Students become adept at social facilitation and dispute resolution.[20]

The groups then come back together in a plenary session to share their findings. The teacher's role is to act as facilitator of the conversation. While she is expected to share the knowledge of the academic discipline of which she is a part, including an appraisal of the differences of opinion that exist within the discipline as well as the agreements or differences that exist between the discipline and other knowledge communities, these are meant to be contributions to the conversation. Bruffee cautions that "professors must resist reverting to the hierarchical authority of traditional classrooms, in which students believe that when teachers begin talking they are going to tell them what the answer *really* is."[21]

In lateral learning, the role of students is transformed from passive recipients of knowledge to active participants in their own education. The goal is to encourage students to think rather than perform. The collaborative nature of the learning process reinforces the notion that gaining knowledge is never a solitary act but a community affair.

Lateral learning redirects the fulcrum of power and authority in the classroom from hierarchical, centralized, and top-down to reciprocal, democratic, and networked. Students learn that they are each responsible for one another's education. Being responsible means being attuned to each other's thoughts, open to different perspectives and points of view, able to listen to criticism, eager to come to one another's assistance, and willingness to take responsibility for the learning community as a whole. These are the very same qualities so essential to the maturation of empathy.

Lateral learning fosters empathic sensibility by encouraging students to walk in another's shoes and experience that person's feelings and thoughts as if it were their own. The test to tell when a community of scholars has really come together and gelled is when each of the members of the cohort group deeply resonates with the struggle of his or her peers to flourish, and experiences the group as an extension of his or her being.

Needless to say, the new learning favors interdisciplinary teaching and multicultural studies. Academia is experiencing a transformation from autonomous disciplines with well-defined academic borders, to collaborative networks whose participants come from various fields, but share knowledge in a distributed manner. The more traditional reductionist approach to the study of phenomena is beginning to give way to the systemic pursuit of big-picture questions about the nature of reality and the meaning of existence—which requires a more interdisciplinary perspective.

Cross-disciplinary academic associations, journals, and curricula have proliferated in recent years, reflecting the burgeoning interest in the interconnectedness of knowledge. A younger generation of academics is beginning to cross over traditional academic categories to create a more integrated approach to research. Several hundred interdisciplinary fields like behavioral economics, ecopsychology, social history, ecophilosophy, biomedical ethics, social entrepreneurship, and holistic health are shaking up the academy and portend a paradigm shift in the educational process.

Meanwhile, the globalization of education has brought together people from diverse cultures, each having his or her own anthropological point of reference, offering up a plethora of fresh, new ways of studying phenomena that are shaped by a different cultural history and narrative.

By approaching a study area from a number of academic disciplines and cultural perspectives, students learn to be more open-minded. The early evaluations of distributed and collaborative educational reform programs are encouraging. Schools report a marked reduction in aggression, violence, and other antisocial behavior, a decrease in disciplinary actions, greater cooperation among students, more pro-social behavior, more focused attention in the classroom, a greater desire to learn, and improvement in critical thinking skills.

THE BIOSPHERE BECOMES THE LEARNING ENVIRONMENT

Collaborative learning helps students extend their sense of self to diverse others and fosters deep participation in more interdependent communities. It enlarges the empathic boundary. Yet, if we are to prepare our children for life in a biosphere era, our educational system will need to advance distributed learning beyond the human domain to include our fellow creatures and the broad swath of nature. Schools and universities have only just begun to explore pedagogy and learning practices that would help extend the self to include the ecological self.

Sadly, today children in the United States between the ages of eight and eighteen spend six and a half hours per day interacting with electronic media—television, computers, video games, and the like. In just the short period between 1997 and 2003, there was a 50 percent drop in the proportion of children nine to twelve who spent time outdoors engaged in hiking, walking, gardening, and beach play. Less than 8 percent of young people now spend time in these traditional outdoors activities.[22]

Richard Louv, in his book *Last Child in the Woods,* says that we are raising a generation of children who suffer from what he calls "nature-deficit disorder"—kids who have virtually no exposure to or interaction with natural wilderness. They are no longer playing outdoors where they might come in contact, even on the most superficial level, with other creatures, whether in local vacant lots, nearby parks, creeks, ponds, meadows, or woods. He recounts the remark from a young fourth-grade student who said, "I like to play indoors better, 'cause that's where all the electrical outlets are."[23]

Children today are taught by parents to distrust the outdoors as a dangerous place where bad people lurk, rabid or otherwise diseased wild animals wander, and disabling accidents of all kinds await them around every turn. Add to this all of the local codes and ordinances that prohibit unsupervised play outdoors for fear of lawsuits and we get a pretty bleak picture of nature. No wonder parents discourage unstructured, outdoor play.

Researchers are beginning to catalogue a range of health issues associated with nature-deficit disorder, including higher incidences of depression and other mental illness as well as physical illnesses caused by sedentary behavior. Some researchers are even beginning to look at the possible link between some forms of attention deficit hyperactivity disorder (ADHD) and nature-deficit disorder.[24]

Robert Michael Pyle, a writer and lepidopterist, goes a step further, suggesting that our children's increasing isolation from nature is leading to "the extinction of experience," by which he means a steady erosion of contact of any kind with the natural world and, with it, a complete alienation from nature, including our own. The loss of experience with the rest of the life force of the planet has a subconscious impact on the human psyche. We become increasingly disaffected from the rest of nature and uncaring about the plight of the Earth. We also become more isolated and lonely, and come to feel like aliens on our own planet. Simulated experiences, regardless of how "real life" they seem, can never replace the affiliations we once felt for all the living beings to whom we are related. Pyle writes:

Simply stated, the loss of neighborhood species endangers our experience of nature. . . . [D]irect personal contact with living things affects us in vital ways that vicarious experiences can never replace. I believe that one of the greatest causes of the ecological crisis is the state of personal alienation from nature in which many people live. We lack a widespread sense of intimacy with the living world. . . . The extinction of experience . . . implies a cycle of disaffection that can have disastrous consequences.[25]

A growing number of educators are engaged in the process of revolutionizing curricula and pedagogy to reestablish a biophilia connection in the educational process. E. O. Wilson argues that the natural world is the most information-rich environment that exists on Earth.[26] Thomas Berry, the Catholic priest and historian, concurs and asks us to imagine how the human race could ever have developed metaphors so critical for creating human narratives and consciousness were our species to have been domiciled from its earliest origins on the moon where there are no other life forms. We would have, therefore, no ability to imagine the life of the other *as if* it were applicable, in some way, to our own experience—which is the very basis of metaphoric thinking and cognitive development.

Anthropologist Elizabeth Lawrence, who coined the term *cognitive biophilia,* observes that the natural world has long been the primary source on which human beings have called to create symbols and images for human cognitive development.[27] New research findings suggest that greater experiential exposure to nature has a significant impact on a child's cognitive development during middle childhood and adolescence.

Sociologist Stephen Kellert brings up the rarely considered point that interaction with nature is essential to critical thinking. The child's developing mind is continuously observing natural phenomena and attempting to understand how it affects the world he is growing up in. Why does rain fall down from the sky, and the sun rise every day? Why do plants bloom at certain times of the year and cats chase mice and eat them? What are shadows? Where does the wind come from? Why do I sweat when it's hot? When we talk about the creation of consciousness, what we are really alluding to is how a child makes connections between phenomena and establishes predictable relationships, all of which help him place himself in the world. Limited exposure to nature diminishes the possibilities of understanding what we mean by existence. Kellert concludes that "few areas of life provide young people with as much opportunity as the natural world for critical thinking, creative inquiry, problem solving, and intellectual development."[28] Nature is the source of awe and wonder without which human imagination could not exist, and without human imagination, consciousness would atrophy.

I find it interesting that one of the most often used words among American youth is *awesome*. Virtually every other sentence is punctuated with this refrain. Is it possible that its overuse might be a projection of a vast deficit brought on by growing up in a world devoid of the wonders of nature and where reality is technologically simulated in pixels on tiny computer screens? In miniaturizing all of existence to fit a three-inch BlackBerry screen, do we risk the inflation of ego and the loss of a sense of awe? If a generation's gaze is continually looking down on a flat, two-dimensional screen rather than up toward the stars, how likely is it that it will be awed by existence rather than bored by technological overstimulation?

Rachel Carson mused on this subject when the television screen was beginning to draw millions of children in from the backyard in the early evening. For 175,000 years, children would scan the stars in the night sky wondering about the deep mysteries of an infinite universe. Now that reality was suddenly narrowed by sitting in front of a lighted box, peering at tiny figures darting across the screen.

Carson wrote:

> A child's world is fresh and new and beautiful, full of wonder and excitement. . . . What is the value of preserving and strengthening this sense of awe and wonder, this recognition of something beyond the boundaries of human existence? Is the exploration of the natural world just a pleasant way to pass the golden hours of childhood or is there something deeper? I am sure there is something deeper, something lasting and significant. . . . Those who contemplate the beauty of the earth find reserves of strength that will endure as long as life lasts.[29]

What the new biophilia educators are saying is that in the rush to embrace artificial reality, we may be losing touch with our intimate connection to nature, with troubling consequences for the future evolution of human consciousness.

Studies of school yards in the United States, Canada, Australia, and Sweden add credence to Carson's concerns. Researchers noted a marked difference in how children played in manufactured play areas versus green areas. In the artificial settings children organized themselves in social hier-archies based on physical attributes. In green playgrounds, by contrast, the social organization was more egalitarian and children were far more likely to engage in fantasy and make-believe and express wonder. Their social standing depended less on physical attributes and more on creativity. Researchers at the Human Environment Research Laboratory at the University of Illinois say that an evaluation of many such studies makes it clear that "green space supports healthy child development."[30]

Yet despite numerous studies that have found that play outside in nat-ural settings stimulates wonder, imagination, and creativity, the Alliance for a Healthier Generation reports that nearly one-third of US elementary schools don't schedule recess on a regular basis and 25 percent of children do not take part in any physical activity during free time. Only seven states require elementary schools to have a qualified physical education teacher on staff.[31]

This might be changing. Educators are growing increasingly alarmed by the loss of attention span and the rise in ADHD diagnoses and suspect that part of the reason might be the physiological loss of connection with the nat-ural rhythms and cycles of nature to which our species has been biologically conditioned over eons of evolutionary history, and the substitution of in-creasingly artificial rhythms over the past century and, especially, the last two decades. Young people growing up in a world highly mediated by electronic stimulation of all kinds and constantly bombarded by a stream of informa-tion are losing the ability to focus, according to countless studies conducted in recent years. In classrooms, where multitasking has become the norm and distractions are the rule, the ability to reflect, organize one's thoughts, and pursue an idea to its conclusion becomes ever more elusive. Many kids are overloaded and burned out by the time they reach middle school.

ADHD has become widespread in the very communities and countries where the new information and communications technologies are the most pervasive. And everywhere schools are reporting a drop in classroom per-formance because of what educators call "attention fatigue." Up to now, the only palliative offered has been medication. Today millions of young-sters in the United States and other high-tech countries are on Ritalin and other pharmaceutical drugs in an effort to hold the crisis at bay. But it's not abating. It's only growing in magnitude.

How can we expect present and future generations to attend to the long-term stewardship of the biosphere, which requires focused attention and patience stretched out over lifetimes of commitment, when they are so easily distracted from moment to moment by a blur of signals, images, and data screaming out for their immediate attention. The well-being of the biosphere is measured over millennia of history and necessitates a human consciousness that can reflect and project along a similar time table.

How do we stretch our sense of time to include an awareness of our ancient past and anticipation of a far-off future? Some educators say that the answer is to immerse students, at least for extended periods of time, in natural environments and the rhythms of the natural world with its recurring seasonal cycles. Environmental psychologists Stephen and Rachel Kaplan, at the University of Michigan, conducted a nine-year study of young people who participated in Outward Bound–type wilderness programs. After two weeks of immersion in the wild, participants reported a greater sense of personal peace and calm and an ability to think more clearly.

A similar study by Terry A. Hartig, a psychology professor at the Institute for Housing and Urban Research at Uppsala University in Sweden, tested a random group of individuals, asking them to carry out a forty-minute sequence of tasks designed to exhaust their "directed attention capacity." He then instructed participants to spend forty minutes either "walking in a local nature preserve, walking in an urban area, or sitting quietly while reading magazines and listening to music." He found that "after this period, those who had walked in the nature preserve performed better than the other participants on a standard proofreading task. They also reported more positive emotions and less anger."[32] Other studies of children suffering from ADHD show that the greater their exposure to outdoor activity in green spaces or even exposure to greenery through windows, the better able they were to focus their attention.[33]

So what are educators doing to reintegrate students into nature, recapture the biophilia connection, and improve their empathic sensibility and critical thinking abilities? Richard Louv reports on the remarkable approach to schooling in the Finland education system. According to a 2003 review by the Organization of Economic Cooperation and Development (OECD), Finland ranked first in literacy and in the top five in math and science among thirty-one OECD nations. (The United States ranked far behind in the middle of the OECD nations). Finland accomplished this feat in a most unorthodox fashion. First, students don't go to school until they're seven years old. Second, the Finish school system puts a significant emphasis on balancing directed attention in the classroom with open play in the school yard. Every forty-five minutes, the students take to the school yard for a fifteen-minute play break. Third, the Finish classroom extends out into the community. Classes are conducted in various natural settings in the surrounding environment. Finland's Ministry of Social Affairs and Health says that the country's educational philosophy is centered around the belief that "the core of learning is not in the information . . . being predigested from the outside, but in the interaction between a child and the environment."[34]

A number of school experiments are underway in the United States to prepare students for biosphere consciousness. Environmentally based education, experiential education, and place-based and community-oriented schooling are among the many educational reform movements currently underway. A report compiled by the State Education and Environmental Roundtable of the performance of forty biosphere-directed schools, showed dramatic improvement across the academic fields in standardized test scores.[35]

Schools in Europe and America are also greening schoolyards. One-third of Great Britain's thirty thousand schoolyards have been transformed into green spaces in its "learning through landscapes" program.[36] Similar programs are underway in Sweden, Canada, and the United States.

NATURE ISN'T PIXILATED

School systems are also beginning to establish formal partnerships with local arboretums, zoos, park systems, wildlife rehabilitation centers, animal sanctuaries, humane societies, environmental organizations, and university research centers to create classrooms in the community where students can learn their subject matter by hands-on involvement and active service with their fellow creatures.

What all these educational efforts have in common is a new lateral approach to learning that focuses on extending the self by immersing students in the many ecological communities of which they are a part and that make up the biosphere.

Educators realize that creating biosphere consciousness is no easy task, especially since over half of the world's human population now lives in dense urban or suburban environments that were designed to be isolated and walled-off from nature. Rewilding urban landscapes—bringing nature back into our lives—has become a central theme among urban land planners and architects.

We forget that even the most sterile urban environments abound with wildlife—birds, insects, rodents, rabbits, raccoons, opossums, even deer, fox, coyotes, and abundant flora. Instead of fencing wildlife out, or killing them off, urban planners and an increasing number of civic organizations are finding new, creative ways to revitalize urban biospheres by reestablishing ecological niches scattered across metropolitan regions. The debate over rewilding urban and suburban spaces is often contentious. As existing wildlife habitats shrink in the face of suburban development, more wildlife is migrating into urban areas to eke out a survival. This sudden crossing of the line between "wild" and "civilized" is a welcome tonic for some and a frightening omen for other urban and suburban dwellers.[37]

Wildlife incursion in residential neighborhoods and commercial areas frequently engenders lawsuits over wildlife-related injuries and prompt calls for efforts like culling local deer populations.[38] Many urban jurisdictions are beginning to wrestle with the problem by accommodating both urban life and wildlife.

A growing empathic regard for other creatures has sparked a rethinking of what we mean by "urban life." Landscape urbanism and green urbanism are among the new efforts to rethink urban planning. Localities are creating woodlands, wetlands, urban canyons, and other wildlife habitats in an effort to integrate wildlife into the life of the cities and suburbs. The new emphasis is on leaving untouched previously open spaces, natural habitats, and migratory routes, and building around them to create an integrated environment in which humans can coexist with their fellow creatures.

The United States and Europe have very different urban and rural land patterns, and very different approaches to revitalizing their swath of the biosphere. We recognized this early on when we prepared our first master plans for the cities of San Antonio and Rome. American urban cores have extended out, with suburban enclaves meeting rural areas at their edges. In Europe, urban areas are denser and often limited by the medieval walls that once surrounded them. The countryside tends to come right up to the city gates. These very different realities call for new approaches to envisioning and remaking urban regions as biospheres. Ben Breedlove, an American urban designer, is cautiously optimistic about creating environments where people and wildlife can coexist. Breedlove notes that "The largest unmanaged ecosystem in America is suburbia," which is a counterintuitive notion that strikes a chord.[39]

In Europe, metropolitan areas are far advanced of the United States and other parts of the world in re-wilding urban regions and establishing an urban biosphere consciousness. Many European cities have devoted half their space or more to open green areas, forests, and agriculture. They have also made sure to maintain or reclaim creeks, small clumps of forests, and meadows inside or close to the urban cores. For example, one quarter of Zurich, Switzerland, remains forested.

Fortunately, in many European cities, the forestlands of former royal estates were kept off limits from developers and were either preserved for wildlife or transformed into public parks where local populations can commingle with wildlife. Timothy Beatley, author of *Green Urbanism: Learning from European Cities,* observes that many European communities eschew "the historic opposition of things urban and natural" and prefer to live in urban areas that "are fundamentally embedded in natural environments."[40]

In 1890, the US Census Bureau announced the official closing off of the American frontier. Today a new generation of educators and urban designers is asking us to tear down some of the fences and take up a new relationship with the wild—this time in a caring manner—so that we can step back into nature and learn to live in a more sustainable, ecologically sensitive way. E. O. Wilson urges educators to bring out students' natural inclination to explore new frontiers by shifting curiosity from the barren reaches of outer space to our still largely "unexplored planet." He believes that "the creative potential is not going to be met by sending a handful of people to Mars. It's going to be fulfilled by the exploration of this planet, by the constant celebration and deepening of knowledge of life around each one of us, on both the scientific and popular levels."[41]

Re-wilding urban areas provides students with the opportunity to experience nature up close, rekindle the biophilia connection, understand their relationship to their evolutionary kin, and develop biosphere consciousness. That's why in our TIR master plans we have reconceptualized metropolitan areas like Rome as urban biospheres. If biosphere consciousness is the ultimate aim of education, then every urban environment needs to be embedded into the biosphere so that the students' classroom becomes the biosphere itself—the place where students participate in and learn about their relationship to and responsibility for our planet.

By transforming education into an empathic experience and a distributed and collaborative learning process that extends to the whole of the biosphere, we nurture the critical thinking skills and consciousness that will accompany a Third Industrial Revolution paradigm that operates by the same logic.

Skeptics will likely recoil in disbelief at the idea of revolutionizing the educational system of the world to create biosphere consciousness, and scoff at the idea that we can prepare a Third Industrial Revolution work-force in less than half a century. They need to be reminded that the Enlight-enment ideas about human consciousness, and human nature, and the kind of educational system that needed to be put in place to accompany the First Industrial Revolution was institutionalized in roughly the same amount of time in Europe and America. Why should we expect anything less?

CHAPTER NINE

MORPHING FROM THE INDUSTRIAL TO THE COLLABORATIVE ERA

anguished for months over the title of this book, wondering who is going to cozy up to a work with the word *industrial* splashed on the cover. It seemed so retro. Isn't *industrial* something only engineers and trade union leaders care about? *Industrial* conjures up visions of worker drones spaced along assembly lines, mindlessly attaching small parts to a product as it speeds down the conveyor belt. Didn't we leave all of that behind when we connected to the Internet and joined Facebook? Yes and no.

The Third Industrial Revolution is the last stage of the great industrial saga and the first stage of the emerging collaborative era rolled together. It represents an interregnum between two periods of economic history—the first characterized by industrious behavior and the second by collaborative behavior.

If the industrial era emphasized the values of discipline and hard work, the top-down flow of authority, the importance of financial capital, the workings of the marketplace, and private property relations, the collaborative era is more about creative play, peer-to-peer interactivity, social capital, participation in open commons, and access to global networks.

The Third Industrial Revolution will move apace over the next several decades, probably peaking around 2050, and plateau in the second half of the twenty-first century. Already, in the shadow of its ascending bell curve, we can see a new economic era that will take us beyond the *industrious* mode that characterized the last two centuries of economic development and into a *collaborative* way of life. The metamorphosis from an industrial to a collaborative revolution represents one of the great turning points in economic history. To understand the momentous change that this represents, we need to revisit a last remaining tenet of classical economic theory, the paradox of which sets the context for this transformation.

DOES SUPPLY CREATE ITS OWN DEMAND?

Jean-Baptise Say, a classical French economist of the early nineteenth century, like Adam Smith, picked up on the Newtonian metaphor, arguing that supply continuously generates its own demand like a kind of perpetual motion machine. He wrote, "a product is no sooner created than it, from that instant, affords a market for other products to the full extent of its own value. . . . The creation of one product immediately opens up a vent for other products."[1] Later, neoclassical economists refined Say's use of the Newtonian metaphor, suggesting that economic forces, once set in motion, remain in motion, unless acted on by an outside force. According to the argument, new labor-saving technologies increase productivity, allowing suppliers to produce more goods at a cheaper cost per unit. The increased supply of cheaper goods then creates its own demand. Greater demand, in turn, stimulates additional production, fueling demand again, in a never-ending cycle of expanding production and consumption.

The increased value of goods being sold will assure that any initial loss of employment brought about by technological improvements will quickly be compensated by additional hiring to meet the expanded production levels. In addition, lower prices from technological innovation and rising productivity will mean consumers have extra money left over to buy other products, further stimulating productivity and increased employment in other parts of the economy.

A corollary to this argument states that even if workers are displaced by new technologies, the problem of unemployment will invariably resolve itself. The rising number of unemployed will eventually bid down wages. Cheaper wages will entice employers to hire additional workers rather than purchase more expensive capital equipment, thereby moderating the impact of technology on employment.

This central assumption of classical economic theory—that supply creates its own demand—has come up against new realities that cast serious doubt on its continued validity.

Economists are finding, much to their chagrin, that increases in productivity over time have not automatically led to increases in consumer demand and more employment but, in some instances, have had the opposite effect—the loss of jobs and purchasing power. I first reported on this phenomenon in *The End of Work*, published in 1995.

Researchers tracking economic growth and employment over the past fifty years have taken notice of a disturbing trend—that each period of economic expansion in the United States over the past half century has been accompanied by weaker job growth. In the economic expansion of the 1950s, 1960s, and 1970s, private sector jobs increased by 3.5 percent, while economic expansions in the 1980s and 1990s saw only a 2.4 percent increase in employment, and in the expansions of the first decade of the twenty-first century, job growth actually declined by 0.9 percent per year.[2] Economists now talk about "jobless recoveries," a phenomena that would have been considered laughable a half century earlier.

While some observers are quick to place the blame on the outsourcing of jobs overseas, the more important culprit is often productivity itself, which goes against everything we believe about how the economic system functions. In industry after industry, from factory production to banking services, companies have experienced dramatic increases in productivity, which allow them to produce more output with fewer workers. Companies have been shedding workers at a record pace. Janet L. Yellen, the president of the Federal Reserve Bank of San Francisco, took note of the trend, pointing out that the GDP remained unchanged in the four quarters of 2009, but payrolls declined by 4 percent. In other words, companies increased their output per worker by 4 percent.[3] New efficiencies in supply chain management accounted for much of this increase in productivity.

Nowhere is the disconnect between productivity gains and job losses greater than in manufacturing. In the period between 1995 and 2002, more than thirty-one million manufacturing jobs disappeared in the twenty largest economies, while productivity rose by 4.3 percent and global industrial production increased by 30 percent.[4] The reality is that manufacturers can produce more goods with fewer workers. Even China eliminated fifteen million factory jobs during the time period, or 15 percent of its entire workforce, while dramatically increasing output with the introduction of new, automated smart technologies. Manufacturing jobs declined by 16 percent, in the same period, in the other major economies and by more than 11 percent in the United States.[5] By 2010, manufacturing workers in the United States were producing 38 percent more output per hour than in 2000. While manufacturing output has remained fairly stable over the decade, because it takes fewer workers to produce the same output, employment has declined by more than 32 percent.[6]

The steel industry is a good example of the trend. In the period between 1982 and 2002, US steel production grew from 75 million tons to 102 million tons, while the number of steel workers declined from 289,000 to 74,000.[7] This kind of dramatic productivity gain is reverberating across the manufacturing sector as intelligent technology replaces mass human labor on the factory floor. Even in the poorest countries, the cheapest workers are not as cheap or as efficient as the intelligent technology replacing them.

If the current trend continues—and it's likely only to accelerate with even more efficient technology displacement—global manufacturing employment is estimated to decrease from 163 million workers to just a few million workers by 2040, eliminating most factory jobs around the world.[8]

White-collar and service industries are experiencing similar dramatic gains in productivity and shedding record numbers of workers in the process. Secretaries, file clerks, bookkeepers, telephone operators, and bank tellers are among the scores of traditional white-collar jobs that have become virtually extinct with the introduction of intelligent technology.

The retail sector is in the midst of the same shift. Automatic checkout lines have replaced cashiers and automated shipping departments have replaced the need for human labor in the back room. Similarly, the travel industry is increasingly employing voice recognition technology that can converse with customers in real time and book travel and hotel accommodations without any need of human intervention. Even hospitals are making the transition to intelligent technology, with robots performing routine tasks ranging from simple surgeries and medical diagnostics to cleaning and maintenance. Intelligent technology is taking over a multitude of jobs once performed by human beings, from operating light rail and automated weapon systems to buying and selling on the stock exchange.

A new generation of robots will soon be coming online that have the mobility of humans, are equipped with emotional and cognitive skills, and have the ability to reflect and respond to human queries and directions with increasing agility and resourcefulness.

To date, manufacturing, finance, and the wholesale and retail sectors account for most of the recent productivity gains. But as intelligent technology, as well as renewable energies, become more agile and cheaper, the United States is likely to see similar productivity gains spread to the remaining sectors of the economy where productivity has remained relatively flat for the last thirty years.

The conundrum is that if productivity advances brought on by the application of intelligent technologies, robotics, and automation continue to push more and more workers to marginal employment or unemployment around the world, the diminishing purchasing power is likely to stifle further economic growth. In other words, if smart tech replaces more and more workers, leaving people without income, who is going to buy all of the products being produced and services being offered?

Intelligent technology is only just beginning to impact the world economy. In the next several decades, tens of millions of workers across every industry and sector are likely going to be displaced by machine intelligence. Ray Kurzweil at MIT observes that "the pace of change of our human-created technology is accelerating and its powers are expanding at an exponential pace."[9] Kurzweil calculates that at the current rate of technological change, by the end of the twenty-first century "we will witness on the order of twenty thousand years of progress (again measured by *today's* rate of progress), or about one thousand times greater than what we achieved in the twentieth century." Or, to put it another way, because we're doubling the rate of progress every decade, we are likely to experience "the equivalent of a century of progress—*at today's rate*—in only twenty-five calendar days."[10]

Kurzweil and other scientists ask us to try and imagine what the effect on human society might be considering that before the end of the century our smart technology will be "trillions of trillions of times more powerful than unaided human intelligence."[11]

The implications for human work—professional, technical, and vocational—are staggering. Just as the industrial age ended slave labor, the collaborative age is likely to end mass wage labor. Virtually all of the global companies I work with foresee intelligent technologies replacing mass human labor over the course of the next several decades. While the nineteenth and twentieth centuries were characterized by mass labor operating machines, the twenty-first century is characterized by boutique, high-tech, professional workforces programming and monitoring intelligent technology systems. All of which begs the question of how to keep hundreds of millions of people employed as we move further into the century.

The Third Industrial Revolution is likely the last opportunity in history to create millions of conventional mass wage labor jobs—that is, short of a catastrophic series of events that derails technological progress for decades or even centuries. While the Third Industrial Revolution establishes the infrastructure for a transition into a distributed and collaborative era, signaling the end to the industrial age and the mass labor force that accompanied it, the laying down of the critical infrastructure over the course of the next forty years will require a final surge of mass labor power.

Transforming the global energy system to renewable electricity, converting hundreds of millions of buildings into mini power plants, introducing hydrogen and other storage technology across the global infrastructure, rewiring the world's power grid and power lines with digital technologies and intelligent utility networks, and revolutionizing transport with the introduction of electric plug-in and hydrogen fuel cell vehicles will necessitate high-tech, boutique planning teams working side by side with a highly skilled mass industrial workforce. The irony is that the conventional industrial workforce of the first half of the twenty-first century is going to help erect an intelligent infrastructure for a new economic system that in the second half of the twenty-first century will eliminate the very industrial jobs that built it.

A full global commitment to establishing a five-pillar Third Industrial Revolution infrastructure will create hundreds of thousands of new businesses and hundreds of millions of new jobs. If current projections hold, a juvenile Third Industrial Revolution infrastructure should be in place on most continents by 2040 to 2050, at which time the industrial workforce will peak and plateau. By then, the synergies created by the new TIR infrastructure will have moved the global economy to a historical turning point, with the collaborative age eclipsing the Third Industrial Revolution in many parts of the world. The way we live will have been fundamentally changed, just as it did when our ancestors transitioned from a forager-hunter existence to a centralized, hydraulic agricultural way of life and, more recently, from an agricultural age to an industrial civilization.

I'm reminded that much of the world's human population metamorphosed from an agricultural to an industrial mode and from a rural to an urban existence in less than one hundred years. This time, the transition from an industrial to a collaborative era is likely going to unfold in half of that time or less, as Kurzweil and others are forecasting.

We will need to be prepared by readying the human race to shift out of an industrial existence and into a collaborative future just as our great-grandparents made the shift from an agricultural and rural existence to an industrial and urban way of life.

RETHINKING WORK

The transformation in how we think about work is going to be more challenging this time around. When agriculture began replacing human labor with mechanical and chemical surrogates, millions of displaced workers were able to migrate to the cities to find skilled and unskilled employment in the factories. And, again, when the factories began to automate production, millions of blue-collar workers changed shirts, skilled up, and became part of the white-collar workforce in the burgeoning service industries. Similarly, when the service industries began to replace mass labor with intelligent technology, the workforce migrated to the caring industries and experiential fields, such as health care, social work, entertainment, and travel and tourism.

Today, however, all four sectors—agricultural, industrial, service, and caring and experiential—are replacing mass wage labor with boutique, high-tech workforces and increasingly sophisticated and agile smart technology systems. This raises the question of what happens to the millions of mass wage earners of the industrial age as the world careens past the infrastructure stage of the Third Industrial Revolution to the fully distributed collaborative era. In a sense, rethinking work this time around is more akin to the great upheaval that ensued when millions of serfs were released from their indenture in a feudal system and forced to become free agents and wage earners in a market economy.

The issue, then, becomes more of how we reenvision what we mean by work rather than just how we retrain the workforce. There are four areas where people can engage in work: the market, the government, the informal economy, and the civil society. Market employment, however, is going to continue to shrink with the introduction of intelligent technology systems. Governments around the world are also culling their workforces and introducing intelligent technology in areas as diverse as tax collection and military service. The informal economy, which includes household production, barter, and at the extreme end, black-market and criminal economic activity, is also likely to diminish as traditional economies transition into high-tech societies.

This leaves us with the civil society as a means of employment. This arena is often referred to as the "third sector," to suggest that it is of less importance than either the market or government. Organizations within the sector are similarly referred to in demeaning terms. "Not-for-profit" and "nongovernmental organizations" indentify them by what they are not.

The civil society is where human beings create social capital, and is made up of a wide range of interests—religious and cultural organizations, education, research, health care, social services, sports, environmental groups, recreational activity, and a host of advocacy organizations whose purpose is to create social bonds.

While the civil society is often relegated to the back tier of social life, and regarded as of marginal importance in comparison to the economy and government, it is the primary arena in which civilization unfolds. There are no examples that I know of in history where a people first set up markets and governments, and then later created a culture. Rather, markets and governments are extensions of culture. That's because culture is where we create the social narratives that bind us together as a people, allowing us to empathize with one another as an extended, fictional family. By sharing a common heritage, we come to think of ourselves as a community and accumulate the trust without which markets and governments would be impossible to establish and maintain. The civil society is where we generate the social capital—which is really accumulated trust—that is invested in markets and governance. If markets or governments destroy the social trust vested in them, people will eventually withdraw their support or force a reorganization of the other two sectors.

The civil society is also an emerging economic force. A 2010 economic analysis done by the Johns Hopkins Center for Civil Society Studies surveying more than forty nations, reported that the third sector accounts for $2.2 trillion in operating expenditures. In the eight countries in which data has already been completed—the United States, Canada, France, Japan, Australia, the Czech Republic, Belgium, and New Zealand—the third sector represents, on average, 5 percent of the GDP. This means that the nonprofit sector's contribution to the GDP in these countries now exceeds the GDP of utilities, including electricity, gas, and water and, incredibly, is equal to the GDP of construction (5.1 percent), and approaches the GDP of banks, insurance companies, and financial services (5.6 percent). The nonprofit sector is also closing in on the GDP contribution from transport, storage, and communications, which averages 7 percent of the GDP.[12]

It may come as a surprise, but the "Third Sector" also accounts for a significant amount of the employment in many countries. Although millions of people volunteer their talents, resources, skills, and time in civil society organizations (CSOs), millions of others work as paid employees in CSOs.

Nonprofits employ nearly 56 million full-time equivalent workers or an average of 5.6 percent of the economically active populations in 42 counties surveyed.[13] The nonprofit workforce now exceeds the workforce in each of the traditional market sectors in the nations studied, including construction, transport, utilities, communications, and most of the industrial manufacturing industries. The growth in the nonprofit sector is highest in Europe, which now even exceeds the United States. An impressive 15.9 percent of the paid employment in the Netherlands is now in the nonprofit sector. In Belgium, 13.1 percent of all workers are in the nonprofit field, while in the United Kingdom it is 11 percent, in Ireland 10.9 percent, and in France 9 percent of total employment. In the United States, 9.2 percent of the employment is in the not-for-profit sector, and in Canada, it is 12.3 percent.[14]

Even more interesting, the third sector is the fastest growing employment sector in many parts of the world. In France, Germany, the Netherlands, and the UK, the nonprofit sector accounted for 40 percent of total employment growth—or 3.8 million jobs between 1990 and 2000.[15]

There is a widespread misconception that the third sector is totally dependent on private and corporate charitable donations and government grants for its survival, and therefore unable to function on its own, much less generate millions of jobs. The reality, however, is that fees for services and products account for approximately 50 percent of the aggregate revenue in the third sector in the forty-two countries surveyed, while government support makes up 36 percent of the revenue and private philanthropy constitutes only 14 percent of the revenue.[16]

Many of the best and brightest young people around the planet are eschewing traditional employment in the marketplace and government in favor of working in the not-for-profit third sector. The reason is that the distributed and collaborative nature of the third sector makes it a more attractive alternative for a generation that has grown up on the Internet and engaged in similar distributed and collaborative social spaces. Like the open-source commons that make up the very sinew of virtual space, the third sector is a commons as well, where people share their talents and lives with one another for the sheer joy of social connectivity. And like the Internet, the core assumption in civil society is that giving oneself to the larger networked community optimizes the value of the group as well as its individual members.

Unlike the market, where relationships between people are predominantly instrumental and a means to an end—optimizing each person's material self-interest—in the third sector, the relationships are an end in themselves, and are therefore imbued with intrinsic value rather than mere utility value.

The civil society is likely to become as significant a source of employment as the market sector by mid-century, for the simple reason that creating social capital relies on human interactivity, whereas creating market capital increasingly relies on intelligent technology. Growing employment in the civil society, however, will provide an increasing percentage of the consumer income necessary to purchase goods and services in an ever more intelligent and automated global economy.

Just as the industrial revolutions of the nineteenth and twentieth centuries freed people from serfdom, slavery, and indentured labor, the Third Industrial Revolution and the collaborative era to which it gives rise frees human beings from mechanized labor to engage in deep play—which is what sociability is all about. I use the term *deep play* because what I'm talking about is not frivolous entertainment but, rather, empathic engagement with one's fellow human beings. Deep play is the way we experience the other, transcend ourselves, and connect to broader, ever more inclusive communities of life in our common search for universality. The third sector is where we participate, even on the simplest of levels, in the most important journey of life—the exploration of the meaning of our existence.

In his essay "On the Aesthetic Education of Man," written in 1795, at the dawn of the market era, Friedrich Schiller observed that "man plays only when he is in the fullest sense of the word a human being, and he is fully a human being only when he plays."[17]

In the nineteenth and twentieth centuries, being industrious was the mark of a man and becoming a productive worker the goal in life. Generations of human beings were transformed into machines in the relentless pursuit of material wealth: *We lived to work*. The Third Industrial Revolution and the collaborative era offer humanity the opportunity to liberate itself from the grip of a mechanized life cocooned inside a utilitarian world and breathe in the exhilaration of being free: *We live to play*. The French philosopher Jean-Paul Sartre captured the close kinship between freedom and play. He wrote "as man apprehends himself as free and wishes to use his freedom . . . then his activity is to play."[18] To which I might add, does anyone ever feel more free than when engaged in play?

The next forty years buys us some precious time. The millennial generation and their children will need to be educated to work and live in both an industrial and collaborative economy. Their children, however, will be increasingly employed in the civil society, creating social capital while intelligent technology will substitute for much—but not all—of human labor in the commercial arena.

The prospect of freeing up the human race from the drudgery of securing its economic survival has long been the dream of philosophers. Allowing the human spirit to soar and roam the vast unexplored social frontier in the age-old spiritual quest to understand the meaning of existence and our place in the grand scheme of things is the most precious gift bestowed on every human being born into this world. For too long we have had to spend an inordinate amount of our limited time on Earth eking out the minimum comforts of survival, leaving little time for deep play in the transcendent realm—making for a less examined life.

The possibility of shifting more of our time and attention to advancing the civil society and the creation of social capital is naturally appealing, and is quickly emerging in developed countries around the world. Yet we can't escape the fact that 40 percent of the human race is still making $2 a day or less and barely able to survive. This tragic reality is compounded by the frightening volatility in prices of everything from basic food commodities and construction materials to petrol for transport, and the even more terrifying real-time impacts of climate change on worldwide agriculture as we enter the long endgame of the Second Industrial Revolution.

The Third Industrial Revolution offers the prospect, at least, that the poorest countries on Earth, who were virtually left out of both the First and Second Industrial Revolutions, could leapfrog into the new era of distributed capitalism over the course of the next half century. Still, no one, myself included, doubts the enormity of the challenge ahead. Assuring that 40 percent of the human race reaches the level of material comfort necessary to free themselves from the shackles of backbreaking and often mindless toil in the marketplace and informal economy, so they can be free to engage in deep play in the pursuit of social capital is a daunting task—made all the more difficult by the need to reorganize economic life to mitigate industrially induced climate change. Yet, for the first time in history, we are close enough to at least imagine such a possibility, which makes me guardedly hopeful that we might succeed.

CIVILIZATIONS THROUGHOUT HISTORY have experienced critical moments of reckoning where they have been forced to radically change course to meet a new future or face the prospect of demise. Some were able to transform themselves in time; others were not. But in the past, the consequences of the collapse of civilizations have been limited in space and in duration, and have not affected the species as whole. What makes this period different is a growing probability of a qualitative change in the temperature and chemistry of the Earth, brought on by climate change, that could trigger the beginning of a mass extinction of animal and plant species and, with it, the very real possibility of a wholesale die-off of our own species.

The critical task at hand is to harness the public capital, market capital, and especially the social capital of the human race to the mission of transitioning the world into a Third Industrial Revolution economy and post-carbon era. A transformation of this scale will require a concomitant leap to biosphere consciousness. Only when we begin to think as an extended global family, that not only includes our own species but all of our fellow travelers in the evolutionary sojourn on Earth, will we be able to save our common biosphere community and renew the planet for future generations.

NOTES

CHAPTER 1

1. Yergin, Daniel. (1992). *The Prize: The Epic Quest for Oil, Money and Power*. New York: Simon & Schuster, p. 625.
2. Trillin, Calvin. (1974, January 21). U.S. Journal: Boston Parallels. *New Yorker*. p. 67.
3. Mouawad, J. (2009, July 10). One Year After Oil's Price Peak: Volatility. *Green* (blog). *New York Times*. Retrieved from http://green.blogs.nytimes.com/2009/07/10/one-year -after-oils-price-peak-volatility/.
4. Weekly All Countries Spot Price FOB Weighted by Estimated Export Volume (Dollars per Barrel). (March 9, 2011). *U.S. Energy Information Administration (EIA) Independent Statistics and Analysis*. Retrieved from http://www.eia.doe.gov/dnav/pet/hist/Leaf Handler.ashx?n=PET&s=WTOTWORLD&f=W.
5. Ibid.
6. Diouf, J. (2009, October 14). Opening statement by the director-general, address presented at Committee on World Food Security, 35th Session, Rome.
7. Meyers, W. H., & Meyer, S. (2008, December 8). Causes and Implications of the Food Price Surge, Food and Agricultural Policy Research Institute (FAPRI), University of Missouri-Columbia, December 2008. Rep. No. FAPRI-MU A. Comparison based on 2003 levels.
8. U.S. Field Production of Crude Oil (Thousand Barrels per Day). (2010, July 29). *U.S. Energy Information Administration*. Retrieved from http://tonto.eia.doe.gov/dnav/pet /hist/LeafHandler.ashx?n=PET&s=MCRFPUS2&f=A.
9. International Energy Agency. (2010). *World Energy Outlook 2010: Executive Summary*. Paris: Author, p. 6.
10. Inman, M. (2010, November 9). Has the World Already Passed "Peak Oil"? *National Geographic News*. Retrieved from http://news.nationalgeographic.com/news /energy/2010/11/101109-peak-oil-iea-world-energy-outlook/.
11. BP Amoco Statistical Review of World Energy 2000. (2000, June 21). *BP Global*. Retrieved from http://www.bp.com/genericarticle.do?categoryId=2012968&contentId=20 01815.
12. GDP Growth (Annual %). (n.d.). *World Bank*. Retrieved from http://data.worldbank .org/indicator/NY.GDP.MKTP.KD.ZG.
13. Blair, D. (2010, December 9). Oil Price Rise Puts Pressure on OPEC. *Financial Times*. http://www.ft.com/cms/s/0/cf79bac8-03bc-11e0-8c3f-00144feabdc0 .html#axzz1IagH4LTi.
14. Pfeifer, S. (2011, January 4). Rising Oil Price Threatens Fragile Recovery *Financial Times*. http://www.ft.com/cms/s/0/056db69c-1836-11e0-88c9-00144feab49a .html#axzz1IagH4LTi.
15. Ibid.

16. Wolf, M. (2011, January 4). In the Grip of a Great Convergence. *Financial Times.* http://www.ft.com/cms/s/0/072c87e6-1841-11e0-88c9-00144feab49a.html#axzz1IagH4LTi.

17. Ibid.

18. Ibid.

19. Edwards, J. (2002, March 14). [E-mail message to Jeremy Rifkin]; Edwards, John D. Twenty-First Century Energy: transition from Fossil Fuels to Renewable, Non-polluting Energy Sources. University of Colorado, Department of Geological Sciences—EMARC. April 2001.

20. Rich, M., Rampell, C., & Streitfeld, D., (2011, February 25). Rising Oil Prices Pose New Threat to U.S. Economy. *New York Times,* p. A1.

21. Farchy, J., & Hook, L., (2011, February 25). Supply Fears and Parallels with Gulf War Spook Market. *Financial Times,* p. 3.

22. Su, B. W. (2001). Employment Outlook: 2000-10 *The U.S. Economy to 2010:* Washington, DC: Bureau of Labor Statistics, http://www.bls.gov/opub/mlr/2001/11/art1full.pdf.

23. Annual U.S. Bankruptcy Filings by District 1990–1994. (n.d.). *American Bankruptcy Institute.* Retrieved from http://www.abiworld.org/AM/AMTemplate.cfm?Section=Home&TEMPLATE=/CM/ContentDisplay.cfm&CONTENTID=35484.

24. Annual U.S. Bankruptcy Filings by District 2001–2004. (n.d.). *American Bankruptcy Institute.* Retrieved from http://www.abiworld.org/AM/AMTemplate.cfm?Section=Home&TEMPLATE=/CM/ContentDisplay.cfm&CONTENTID=35453.

25. United States Census Bureau. (n.d.). *Median and Average Sales Prices of New Homes Sold in United States.* Retrieved from http://www.census.gov/const/uspriceann.pdf.

26. Bureau of Labor Statistics. (2010, January 8). *The Employment Situation—December 2009* [Press release]. http://www.bls.gov/news.release/archives/empsit_01082010.pdf.

27. United States Federal Reserve. (2008, December 11). *Flow of Funds Accounts of the United States: Flow and Outstandings Third Quarter 2008.* Washington, DC: Author.

28. Krugman, P. (2010, December 12). Block Those Metaphors. *New York Times P. A25.*

29. RealtyTrac. (2011, January 12). *Record 2.9 Million U.S. Properties Receive Foreclosure Filings in 2010 Despite 30-Month Low in December* [Press release]. Retrieved from http://www.realtytrac.com/content/press-releases/record-29-million-us-properties-receive-foreclosure-filings-in-2010-despite-30-month-low-in-december-6309.

30. Peck, D. (2010, March). How a New Jobless Era Will Transform America. *Atlantic,* p. 44.

31. Wolf, M. (2008, September 23). Paulson's Plan Was Not a True Solution to the Crisis. *Financial Times.* Retrieved from http://us.ft.com/ftgateway/superpage.ft?news_id=fto092320081447402080.

32. Parker, K. (2010, December 5). Can the City on a Hill Survive? *Washington Post,* p. A23.

33. Jarraud, M., & Steiner, A. (2007, November 17). Foreword. *Climate Change 2007: Synthesis Report.* Valencia, Spain: Intergovernmental Panel on Climate Change. Retrieved from http://www.ipcc.ch/publications_and_data/ar4/syr/en/frontmattersforeword.html.

34. Solomon, S., et al. (2007). *Climate Change 2007: The Physical Science Basis. Contribution of Working Group I to the Fourth Assessment Report of the Intergovernmental Panel on Climate Change.* Cambridge: Cambridge University Press. Retrieved from http://www.ipcc.ch/publications_and_data/publications_ipcc_fourth_assessment_report_wg1_report_the_physical_science_basis.htm.

35. Bernstein, L., Bosch, P., Canziani, O., Chen, Z., Christ, R., Davidson, O., Yohe, G. (2007, November 17). *Climate Change 2007: Synthesis Report.* Valencia, Spain: Intergovernmental Panel on Climate Change. Retrieved from http://www.ipcc.ch/pdf/assessment-report/ar4/syr/ar4_syr.pdf.

36. Raup, D. M., & Sepkoski, J. J. (1982). Mass Extinction in the Marine Fossil Record. *Science, 215* (4539), 1501–1503.

37. Whitty, J. (2007, May/June). Gone: Mass Extinction and the Hazards of Earth's Vanishing Biodiversity. *Mother Jones.* Retrieved from http://motherjones.com/environment/2007/05/gone.

38. Houghton, J. (1997). *Global Warming: The Complete Briefing* (2nd ed.). Cambridge: Cambridge University Press, p. 127.

39. Beardsley, T. (1998, October). In the Heat of the Night. *Scientific American,* 279 (4), p. 20.

40. Solomon, S., Qin, D., Manning, M., Marquis, M., Averyt, K., Tignor, M., Chen, Z. (2007). Observations: Surface and Atmospheric Change. In *Climate Change 2007: The Physical Science Basis. Contribution of Working Group I to the Fourth Assessment Report of the Intergovernmental Panel on Climate Change.* Cambridge: Cambridge University Press, p. 254. Retrieved from http://www.ipcc.ch/pdf/assessment-report/ar4/wg1/ar4-wg1-chapter3.pdf

41. Bernstein, L., Bosch, P., Canziani, O., Chen, Z., Christ, R., Davidson, O., Yohe, G. (2007, November 17). Observed Changes in Climate and Their Effects. In *Climate Change 2007: Synthesis Report.* Valencia, Spain: Intergovernmental Panel on Climate Change, p. 32. Retrieved from http://www.ipcc.ch/pdf/assessment-report/ar4/syr/ar4_syr.pdf.

42. Webster, P., Holland, G., Curry, J., & Chang, H. (2005). Changes in Tropical Cyclone Number, Duration, and Intensity in Warming Environment. *Science,* 309 (5742), 1844–1846.

43. Schneeberger, C., Blatter, H., Abe-Ouchi, A., & Wild, M. (2003). Modeling Changes in the Mass Balance of Glaciers of the Northern Hemisphere for a Transient $2xCO_2$ Scenario. *Journal of Hydrology,* 282 pp. 145–163.

44. Bernstein, L., Bosch, P., Canziani, O., Chen, Z., Christ, R., Davidson, O., Yohe, G. (2007, November 17). *Climate Change 2007: Synthesis Report.* Valencia, Spain: Intergovernmental Panel on Climate Change, p. 49.

45. Parry, M., Canziani, O., Palutikof, J., van der Linden, P., & Hanson, C. (2007). Polar Regions (Arctic and Antarctic). In *Climate Change 2007: Impacts, Adaptation and Vulnerability. Contribution of Working Group II to the Fourth Assessment Report of the Intergovernmental Panel on Climate Change.* Cambridge: Cambridge University Press, p. 676. Retrieved from http://www.ipcc.ch/publications_and_data/ar4/wg2/en/ch15.html; Instanes, A. (2005). Infrastructure: Buildings, Support Systems, and Industrial Facilities. In *Arctic Climate Impact Assessment.* Cambridge: Cambridge University Press. Retrieved from http://www.acia.uaf.edu/PDFs/ACIA_Science_Chapters_Final/ACIA_Ch16_Final.pdf.

46. Lean, G. (2008, August 31). For the First Time in Human History, the North Pole Can Be Circumnavigated. *The Independent.* Retrieved from http://www.independent.co.uk/environment/climate-change/for-the-first-time-in-human-history-the-north-pole-can-be-circumnavigated-913924.html.

47. Walter, K. M., Zimov, S. A., Chanton, J. P., Verbyla, D., & Chaplin, F. S. (2006). Methane Bubbling from Siberian Thaw Lakes as a Positive Feedback to Climate Warming. *Nature,* 443 (7), pp. 71–75; Walter, K. M., Smith, L. C., & Chapin, F. S. (2007). Methane Bubbling from Northern Lakes: Present and Future Contributions to the Global Methane Budget. *Philosophical Transactions of the Royal Society, 365,* pp. 1657–1676; Mascarelli, A. (2009, March 5). A Sleeping Giant? *Nature Reports Climate Change.* Retrieved from http://www.nature.com/climate/2009/0904/full/climate.2009.24.html.

48. Hansen, J., Sato, M., Kharecha, P., Beerling, D., Berner, R., Masson-Delmotte, V., Zachos, J. C. (2008). Target Atmospheric CO_2: Where Should Humanity Aim? *Open Atmospheric Science Journal,* 2 (1), p. 217.

49. Achenbach, J., & Fahrenthold, D. A. (2010, August 3). Oil Spill Dumped 4.9 Million Barrels into Gulf of Mexico, Latest Measure Shows. *Washington Post.* Retrieved from http://www.washingtonpost.com/wp-dyn/content/article/2010/08/02/AR2010080204695.html.

50. CNN Political Unit. (2011, April 19). CNN Poll: Support for Increased Offshore Oil Drilling On Rise. *CNN Political Ticker.* Retrieved April 19, 2011, from http://politicalticker.blogs.cnn.com/2011/04/19/cnn-poll-support-for-increased-offshore-oil-drilling-on-rise/.

51. Crooks, E. (2011, January 4). US Oil Groups Seek Easing of Drilling Curbs. *Financial Times.* Retrieved from http://www.ft.com/cms/s/0/f313329c-1835-11e0-88c9-00144feab49a.html#axzz1IagH4LTi.

52. Crude Oil and Total Petroleum Imports Top 15 Countries. (February 25, 2011). *U.S. Energy Information Administration*. Retrieved from http://www.eia.doe.gov/pub/oil_gas/petroleum/data_publications/company_level_imports/current/import.html.

53. Graves, S. W. (2009, September 1). The Contract from America. *Contract from America*. Retrieved from http://www.thecontract.org/the-contract-from-america/.

CHAPTER 2

1. Getting to $787 Billion. (2009, February 17). *Wall Street Journal*. Retrieved from http://online.wsj.com/public/resources/documents/STIMULUS_FINAL_0217.html.

2. Rankin, J. (2010, September 30). EU "Must Spend €1 Trillion" on Electricity Grid. *European Voice*. Retrieved from http://www.europeanvoice.com/article/2010/09/electricity-grid-system-needs-1-trillion-investment-/69073.aspx.

3. European Photovoltaic Industry Association (EPIA). (2009). *Solar Photovoltaic Electricity: A Mainstream Power Source in Europe by 2020*. (Set for 2020 report). Retrieved from http://www.setfor2020.eu/uploads/executivesummary/SET%20For%202020%20Executive%20Summary%20final.pdf.

4. Global Prospects of the Solar Power Station Market: Harness the Sun's Energy. (2010). Q-Cells. Retrieved from http://www.q-cells.com/en/sytems/market_potential/index.html.

5. Stevens, H., & Pettey, C. (2008, June 23). Gartner Says More Than 1 Billion PCs in Use Worldwide and Headed to 2 Billion Units by 2014. *Gartner*. Retrieved from http://www.gartner.com/it/page.jsp?id=703807.

6. Wollman, D. (2010, October 10). Internet Users to Surpass 2 Billion in 2010: UN Report. *Huffington Post*. Retrieved from http://www.huffingtonpost.com/2010/10/20/internet-users-to-surpass_n_770405.html.

7. European Photovoltaic Industry Association (EPIA). (2009, April). *Global Market Outlook for Photovoltaics until 2013*. Brussels, Belgium: Author, pp. 3–4; Global Wind Energy Council (GWEC). (2009). *Global Wind 2008 Report*. Brussels, Belgium: Author, p. 10.

8. Lewis, N. S., & Nocera, D. G. (2006). Powering the Planet: Chemical Challenges in Solar Energy Utilization [Abstract]. *Proceedings of the National Academy of Sciences of the United States of America,* 103 (43).

9. European Photovoltaic Industry Association (EPIA). (2010, June 23). Roofs Could Technically Generate Up to 40% of EU's Electricity Demand by 2020 [Press release]. Retrieved from http://www.epia.org/fileadmin/EPIA_docs/public/100623_PR_BIPV_EN.pdf.

10. Zweibel, K., Mason, J., & Fthenakis, V. (2007, December 16). A Solar Grand Plan. *Scientific American,* pp. 64–73.

11. European Photovoltaic Industry Association (EPIA). (2010, May). *Global Market Outlook for Photovoltaics until 2014*. Brussels, Belgium: Author. Retrieved from http://www.epia.org/fileadmin/EPIA_docs/public/Global_Market_Outlook_for_Photovoltaics_until_2014.pdf.

12. EWEA: Factsheets. (2010). *European Wind Energy Association*. Retrieved March 14, 2011, from http://www.ewea.org/index.php?id=1611.

13. United States Department of Energy, Office of Energy Efficiency and Renewable Energy. (May, 2010). Wind and Water Program: Building a New Energy Future with Wind Power [Brochure]. Retrieved from http://www1.eere.energy.gov/windandhydro/pdfs/eere_wind_water.pdf.

14. Wald, M. L. (2010, October 12). Offshore Wind Power Line Wins Praise and Backing. *New York Times,* pp. 1–A3.

15. Archer, C. L., & Jacobson, M. Z. (2005). Evaluation of Global Wind Power. *Journal of Geophysical Research, 110* (D12110).

16. Dixon, D. (2007). *Assessment of Waterpower Potential and Development Needs*. Palo Alto, CA: Electric Power Research Institute.

17. Green, B. D., & Nix, R. J., (November, 2006) *Geothermal—The Energy Under Our Feet* National Renewable Energy Laboratory Technical Report (Report No. NREL/TP-840-40665), p. 3. Retrieved from http://www1.eere.energy.gov/geothermal/pdfs/40665.pdf.

18. The Geothermal Energy Association. (2010). Geothermal Energy in 2010. *PennEnergy*. Retrieved from http://www.pennenergy.com/index/power/display/8301455971/articles/power-engineering/volume-114/Issue_7/departments/View-on-Renewables/Geothermal_Energy_in_2010.html.

19. MIT. (2006). *The Future of Geothermal Energy: Impact of Enhanced Geothermal Systems (EGS) on the United States in the 21st Century.* Idaho Falls, ID: U.S. Department of Energy. Retrieved from http://www1.eere.energy.gov/geothermal/future_geothermal.html.

20. World Bio Energy Association (2009, November). WBA Position Paper on Global Potential of Sustainable Biomass for Energy [Press release]. Retrieved from http://www.worldbioenergy.org/system/files/file/WBA_PP1_Final%202009-11-30.pdf.

21. Appleyard, D. (2010, June 1). The Big Question: Could Bioenergy Power the World? *Renewable Energy World*. Retrieved from http://www.renewableenergyworld.com/rea/news/article/2010/06/the-big-question-could-bioenergy-power-the-world.

22. Renewable Energy for America: Biomass. (n.d.). Natural Resources Defense Council. Retrieved from http://www.nrdc.org/energy/renewables/biomass.asp#note3.

23. Pimentel, D., & Patzek, T. W. (2005). Ethanol Production Using Corn, Switchgrass, and Wood; Biodiesel Production Using Soybean and Sunflower [Abstract]. *Natural Resources Research, 14* (1), 65–76.

24. Tob, P., & Wheelock, C. (2010, Fall). *Executive Summary: Waste-to-Energy Technology Markets.* Retrieved from https://www.pikeresearch.com/wordpress/wp-content/uploads/2010/12/WTE-10-Executive-Summary.pdf.

25. Renewable Energy World, "Feed-In Tariffs Go Global." (July-August 2009). Retrieved from http://www.earthscan.co.uk/Portals/0/pdfs/Mendonca_Jacobs_REW.pdf/.

26. Rifkin, J., Easley, N., & Laitner, J. A. "Skip" (2009). *San Antonio: Leading the Way Forward to the Third Industrial Revolution–Recommendations* (Rep.) p. 26.

27. Ibid.

28. Ekhart, M. T. (2010, December 3). Standing Up for Clean Energy. *Washington Post*. Retrieved from http://www.washingtonpost.com/wp-dyn/content/article/2010/12/03/AR2010120305574.html; Yildiz, O. (2010, November 23). Electric Power Annual. *U.S. Energy Information Administration*. Retrieved from http://www.eia.doe.gov/cneaf/electricity/epa/epa_sum.html.

29. Report Calls for Boost to Industry through Open Markets. (2010, October 13). *European Parliament*. Construction Statistics. Retrieved March 18 from http://www.europarl.europa.eu/news/public/story_page/052-86235-281-10-41-909-20101008STO86176-2010-08-10-2010/default_en.htm.

30. Warren, A. (2009, May 17). If we don't know how many buildings are out there, how can we plan cuts in emissions? *Click Green*. Retrieved April 4, 2011, from http://www.clickgreen.org.uk/opinion/opinion/12171-if-we-don%E2%80%99t-know-how-many-buildings-are-out-there,-how-can-we-plan-cuts-in-emissions.html.

31. Martin, A. (2007, November 15). In Eco-Friendly Factory, Low-Guilt Potato Chips. *New York Times*. Retrieved from http://www.nytimes.com/2007/11/15/business/15plant.html.

32. Camus, M. (2008, July 8). World's Largest Rooftop Solar Power Station Being Built in Zaragoza. *GM Media Online*. Retrieved from http://archives.media.gm.com/archive/documents/domain_138/docId_46878_pr.html.

33. Bouygues Construction. (n.d.). First Positive-Energy Building [Press release]. Retrieved from http://www.bouygues-construction.com/667i/sustainable-development/news/first-positive-energy-building.html&.

34. Morales, A. (2010, November 2). Huhne Says Nuclear, Wind at Heart of U.K.'s "Green Revolution." *BusinessWeek*. Retrieved from http://www.businessweek.com/news/2010-11-02/huhne-says-nuclear-wind-at-heart-of-u-k-s-green-revolution-.html.

35. CETRI-TIRES, Sviluppo Italia Sicilia, and Universita' Degli Studi Di Palermo–Facolta' Di Ingegneria. Ipotesi Di Piano Di Valorizzazione Energetica, Capacity Building per Tecnologie E Potenziale Del Fotovoltaico Sui Tetti Siciliani. Tech. Palermo, 2010.

36. Wei, M., Patadia, S., & Kammen, D. M. (2009). Putting Renewables and Energy Efficiency to Work: How Many Jobs Can the Clean Energy Industry Generate in the US? *Energy Policy*, 38, p. 1. Retrieved from http://rael.berkeley.edu/sites/default/files/Wei PatadiaKammen_CleanEnergyJobs_EPolicy2010_0.pdf.

37. PRODI, R. (JUNE 16, 2003). "The Energy Vector of the Future." Retrieved from ftp:// ftp.cordis.lu/pub/sustdev/docs/energy/sustdev_h2_keynote_prodi.pdf.

38. European Parliament Committee on Industry, Research and Energy. (2008). *Draft Report on the Proposal for a Council Regulation Setting up the Fuel Cells and Hydrogen Joint Undertaking*. Brussels: European Parliament, p. 38.

39. LaMonica, M. (2009, May 18). Cisco: Smart Grid Will Eclipse Size of Internet. *CNET News*. Retrieved from http://news.cnet.com/8301-11128_3-10241102-54.html.

40. *The US Smart Grid Revolution, KEMA's Perspectives for Job Creation*. (2008, December 23). Retrieved from KEMA. http://www.kema.com/services/consulting/utility -future/job-report.aspx.

41. Rankin, J. (2010, September 30). EU "Must Spend €1 Trillion" on Electricity Grid. *European Voice*. Retrieved from http://www.europeanvoice.com/article/2010/09/electricity -grid-system-needs-1-trillion-investment-/69073.aspx.

42. Borbely, A., & Kreider, J. F. (2001). *Distributed Generation the Power Paradigm for the New Millennium*. Washington, DC: CRC Press, p. 47.

43. Interview with EU Competition Commissioner Neelie Kroes on energy. (2006, March 22). *EurActiv*. Retrieved from http://www.euractiv.com/en/energy/interview-eu-competition -commissioner-neelie-kroes-energy/article-153617/.

44. Ibid.

45. Ibid.

46. Nuclear Power in France. (2010, December 17). *World Nuclear Association*. Retrieved from http://world-nuclear.org/info/default.aspx?id=330&terms=france.

47. Kamenetz, A. (2009, July 1). Why the Microgrid Could Be the Answer to Our Energy Crisis. *Fast Company*. Retrieved from http://www.fastcompany.com/magazine/137 /beyond-the-grid.html.

48. Litos Strategic Communication. (n.d.). *What the Smart Grid Means to America's Future*. U.S. Department of Energy, p. 5.

49. The White House, Department of Energy. (2009, March 19). *President Obama Announces $2.4 Billion in Funding to Support Next Generation Electric Vehicles* [Press release]. Retrieved from http://www.whitehouse.gov/briefing-room/Statements-and -Releases/2009/03?page=5.

50. Ramsey, M. (2011, February 24). GE, Siemens Set Challenge to Car Charger Start-Ups. *Wall Street Journal*. Retrieved from http://online.wsj.com/article/SB100014240527487 03775704576162552192684150.html.

51. PRTM. (2009, December 10). PRTM Analysis Shows Worldwide Electric Vehicle Value Chain to Reach $300B+ by 2020, Creating More than 1 Million Jobs [Press release]. Retrieved from http://www.prtm.com/NewsItem.aspx?id=3609&langtype=1033.

52. Ibid.

53. Lovins, A. B. and Williams, B. D. (2000). "From Fuel Cells to a Hydrogen-Based Economy." *Public Utilities Fortnightly* 25: 552.

54. Initiative "H2 Mobility"—Major Companies Sign Up to Hydrogen Infrastructure Built-up Plan in Germany. (2009, September 10). *Daimler*. Retrieved from http://www .daimler.com/dccom/0-5-658451-1-1236356-1-0-0-0-0-0-13-7165-0-0-0-0-0-0-0.html.

55. The World Factbook. (2011). *Central Intelligence Agency*. Retrieved from https://www .cia.gov/library/publications/the-world-factbook/.

56. European Parliament. (2007, May 14). *Written Declaration Pursuant to Rule 116 of the Rules of Procedure on Establishing a Green Hydrogen Economy and a Third Industrial Revolution in Europe through a Partnership with Committed Regions and Cities, SMEs*

and Civil Society Organisations. Retrieved from http://hyfleetcute.com/data/MEP%20 Green%20H2%20Declaration.pdf.

CHAPTER 3

1. Nasa Temp Data. (2010, December 22). E-mail message to J. Rothwell.
2. U.S. Energy Information Administration (2008, December). Annual Energy Outlook 2009 Early Release: Tables 2, 4, 5, and 18. Retrieved from http://www.eia.doe.gov/oiaf /aeo/aeoref_tab.html.
3. UN-Habitat. (2008). *State of the World's Cities 2008/2009: Harmonious Cities.* London: Earthscan.
4. The Principal Agglomerations of the World. (2011, January 1). *City Population.* Retrieved from http://www.citypopulation.de/world/Agglomerations.html.
5. World Vital Events Per Time Unit: 2011. (2011). *U.S. Census Bureau.* Retrieved from http://www.census.gov/cgi-bin/ipc/pcwe.
6. Imhoff, M. L., Bounoua, L., Ricketts, T., Loucks, C., Harriss, R., & Lawrence, W. T. (2004). Global Patterns in Human Consumption of Net Primary Production. *Nature,* 429, p. 870–873.
7. World Population: 1950–2050. (2010, December 28). *U.S. Census Bureau.* Retrieved from http://www.census.gov/ipc/www/idb/worldpopgraph.php.
8. Tainter, J. A. (1988). *The Collapse of Complex Societies.* Cambridge: Cambridge University Press, p. 133.
9. Ibid., p. 145.
10. Harl, K. (2001). Early Medieval and Byzantine Civilization: Constantine to Crusades. *Encarta Online Encyclopedia.* Retrieved from www.tulane.edu/~august/h303/byzantine .html.
11. ICF Consulting. (2005, July). *Alamo Regional Industry Cluster Analysis.* San Francisco: Author; Laitner, S., & Goldberg, M. (1996). *Planning for Success: An Economic Development Guide for Small Communities.* Washington, DC: American Public Power Association.
12. ICF Consulting. (2005, July). *Alamo Regional Industry Cluster Analysis.* San Francisco: Author.
13. Laitner, J. A., & Goldberg, M. (1996). *Planning for Success: An Economic Development Guide for Small Communities.* Washington, DC: American Public Power Association.
14. Ibid., p. 12.
15. Ibid.
16. Ibid., p. 13.
17. Clinton, B. (2010, September 19). *Face the Nation* [Transcript, television broadcast]. CBS Broadcasting Inc.
18. Rifkin, J., Easley, N., & Laitner, J. A. "Skip." (2009). *San Antonio: Leading the Way Forward to the Third Industrial Revolution,* p. 59.
19. Harman, G. (2010, January 6). Operation: CPS. *San Antonio Current.* Retrieved from http://www.sacurrent.com/.
20. Ibid.
21. South Texas Nuclear Project—The Record. (n.d.). *Public Citizen.* Retrieved from http:// www.citizen.org/Page.aspx?pid=2178.
22. Rifkin, J., Easley, N., & Laitner, J. A. "Skip." (2009). *San Antonio: Leading the Way Forward to the Third Industrial Revolution,* p. 56.
23. Ibid.
24. Harman, G. (2010, January 6). Operation: CPS. *San Antonio Current.* Retrieved from http://www.sacurrent.com/news/story.asp?id=70826.
25. Smith, R. (2010, February 18). Small Reactors Generate Big Hopes. *Wall Street Journal. Retrieved from* http://online.wsj.com/article/SB10001424052748703444804575507140 2124482176.html.

26. Negin, E. (2010, July 23). Renewable Energy Would Create More Jobs Than Nuclear Power. *Statesman.com.* Retrieved from http://www.statesman.com/opinion/negin -renewable-energy-would-create-more-jobs-than-819936.html.

27. Schlissel, D., & Biewald, B. (2008). *Nuclear Power Plant Construction Costs.* Cambridge, MA: Synapse Energy Economics.

28. Rifkin, J., Easley, N., & Laitner, J. A. "Skip." (2009). *San Antonio: Leading the Way Forward to the Third Industrial Revolution,* p. 55.

29. Smith, R. (2009, August 12). Electricity Prices Plummet. *Wall Street Journal.* Retrieved from http://online.wsj.com/article/SB125003563550224269.html?KEYWORDS=electri city+prices+plummet.

30. CPS Energy. (2010, May 10). *Vision 2020 Plan: Board of Trustees Forward* [Slide presentation].

31. Admin. (2010, July 2). GM Expands Initial Volt Launch Market. *IVeho.* Retrieved from http://www.iveho.com/2010/07/02/gm-expands-initial-volt-launch-market-2/#more -1064.

32. Our History: Honorary Members. (n.d.). *The International SeaKeepers Society.* Retrieved from http://www.seakeepers.org/history-honorary.php.

33. *Monaco en Chiffres.* (2010). Principauté de Monaco, p. 143.

34. Jeremy Rifkin Enterprises. (2009). *Climate Change Master Plan Report for Monaco.*

35. Ibid.

36. Ibid.

37. Ibid.

38. Monaco, Principauté de Monaco, Département de l'Equipement, de l'Environnement et de l'Urbanisme & Direction de l'Environnement. (2010). *Plan Énergie Climat de la Principauté de Monaco.* Retrieved from http://www.paca.developpement-durable .gouv.fr/IMG/pdf/Grandes_Lignes_du_plan_d_actions_de_la_Principaute_de_Monaco _cle7da677.pdf.

CHAPTER 4

1. Patterns of Railroad Finance, 1830–1850. (1954, September). *Business History Review,* 28: 248–263.

2. Chandler, A. D., Jr. (1977). *The Visible Hand: The Managerial Revolution in American Business.* Cambridge, MA: Belknap Press, p. 91.

3. Burgess, G. H., & Kennedy, M. (1940). *Centennial History of the Pennsylvania Railroad Company.* Philadelphia: Ayer Company, p. 807; U.S. Bureau of Statistics (1894) *Statistical Abstract of the United States 1893. Bureau of the Census Library,* pp. 718, 721.

4. Stover, J. F. (1961). *American Railroads.* Chicago: University of Chicago Press, p. 135; Ripley, W. Z. (1912). Chapters 14–15. In *Railroads: Rates and Regulations.* New York: Longmans, Green, and Co.

5. Chandler, A. D., Jr. (1977). Revolution in Transportation and Communication. In *The Visible Hand: The Managerial Revolution in American Business.* Cambridge, MA: Belknap Press, p. 120.

6. Malone, D. (1946). *Dictionary of American Biography* (Vol. VII). New York: Ch. Scribner's Sons, p. 461; Burgess, G. H., Kennedy M. C., "Centennial History of the Pennsylvania Railroad 1846–1946" (1949), The Pennsylvania Railroad Company, Philadelphia, pp. 514–515.

7. Taylor, F. (1947). *The Principles of Scientific Management.* New York: W. W. Norton, pp. 235–236.

8. Ibid.

9. Anderson, R. O. (1984). *Fundamentals of the Petroleum Industry.* Norman: University of Oklahoma Press, p. 20.

10. Ibid., pp. 29–30.

11. Annual Energy Review 2009. (2010, August 19). *U.S. Energy Information Administration.* Retrieved from http://www.eia.doe.gov/aer/eh/eh.html.

12. A Brief History: The Bell System. (2010). *AT&T*. Retrieved from http://www.corp.att
.com/history/history3.html.

13. DLC: The World's Top 50 Economies: 44 Countries, Six Firms. (2010, July 14). *Democratic Leadership Council*. Retrieved from http://www.dlc.org/ndol_ci.cfm?contentid=2
55173&kaid=108&subid=900003.

14. Armed Forces: Engine Charlie. (1961, October 6). *TIME*. Retrieved from http://www
.time.com/time/magazine/article/0,9171,827790,00.html.

15. The Dramatic Story of Oil's Influence on the World. (1993). *Oregon Focus*. pp. 10–11.

16. Kristof, N. D. (2010, November 6). Our Banana Republic. *New York Times*. Retrieved
from http://www.nytimes.com/2010/11/07/opinion/07kristof.html?_r=1&ref=nicholas
dkristof.

17. Rich, F. (2010, November 13). Who Will Stand Up to the Superrich? *New York Times*.
Retrieved from http://www.nytimes.com/2010/11/14/opinion/14rich.html?src=twrhp.

18. Wikipedia: Size Comparisons. (2011, March 31). *Wikipedia*. Retrieved from http://
en.wikipedia.org/wiki/Wikipedia:Size_comparisons.

19. Wikipedia.org Site Info. (n.d.). *Alexa the Web Information Company*. Retrieved from
http://www.alexa.com/siteinfo/wikipedia.org.

20. 3D printing: The Printed World [Editorial]. (2011, February 10). *The Economist*.
Retrieved March 29, 2011, from http://www.economist.com/node/18114221?story
_id=18114221.

21. Ibid.

22. Etsy Lets Artists Create a Living. (2008, July 1). *Rare Bird, Inc.* Retrieved from http://
www.rarebirdinc.com/news/articles/etsy.html.

23. Botsman, R., & Rogers, R. (2010). From Generation Me to Generation We. In *What's
Mine Is Yours: The Rise of Collaborative Consumption*. New York: HarperBusiness,
p. 49; Kalin, R. (2011, March 28). Etsy—Speaking Engagement Request [E-mail to the
author].

24. Microfinance and Financial Inclusion. (2010, December 19). *Financial Times*. Retrieved from http://www.ft.com/cms/s/0/cc076c20-0b99-11e0-a313-00144feabdc0.html
#axzz1EoWZY7ga.

25. At a Glance, December, 2010. (n.d.). *Grameen Shakti*. Retrieved from http://www
.gshakti.org/index.php?option=com_content&view=article&id=140:ataglancedecember
,2010&Itemid=78.

26. About Us. (n.d.). *Kiva*. Retrieved from http://www.kiva.org/about.

27. Ibid.

28. Facts & History. (n.d.). *Kiva*. Retrieved from http://www.kiva.org/about/facts.

29. Community Supported Agriculture. (n.d.). *Local Harvest*. Retrieved from http://www
.localharvest.org/csa/.

30. Keegan, P. (2009, August 27). Car-Rental, Auto Industry React to Zipcar's Growing Appeal. *CNNMoney*. Retrieved from http://money.cnn.com/2009/08/26/news/companies
/zipcar_car_rentals.fortune; Green Benefits. (2011). *Zipcar*. Retrieved from http://www
.zipcar.com/is-it/greenbenefits.

31. Ibid.

32. Fenton, C. (n.d.). Guiding Principles. *CouchSurfing*. Retrieved from http://www.couch
surfing.org/about.html/guiding.

33. Statistics. (n.d.). *CouchSurfing*. Retrieved from http://www.couchsurfing.org/statistics
.html.

34. British Have Smallest Homes in Europe. (2002, May 3). *The Move Channel*. Retrieved
from www.themovechannel.com; Housing Vacancy Survey—Annual 2002. (2002). *U.S.
Census Bureau*. Retrieved from http://www.census.gov/; Summers, A. A., Cheshire, P.
C., & Senn, L. (1993). *Urban Change in the United States and Western Europe: Comparative Analysis and Policy*. Washington, DC: Urban Institute Press, p. 517.

35. Weingroff, R. F., "Federal-Aid Highway Act of 1956, Creating the Interstate System."
(1996). Retrieved from http://www.nationalatlas.gov/articles/transportation/a_highway
.html; McNichol, D., (2006). *The Roads that Built America: The Incredible Story of the
U.S. Interstate System*. New York: Sterling Publishing Co., pp. 112–114.

36. William Haycraft [Interview by D. McNichol]. (2003, January 14). As cited in Mc-Nichol, D. (2006). *The Roads that Built America,* p. 127.

37. Anthony Caserta, FHWA tunnel engineer [Interview by D. McNichol]. (2003, April); FHWA Bridge Table, December 2002 as cited in McNichol, D. (2006). *The Roads that Built America,* p. 11.

38. Pernick, Ron and Wilder, Clint (2007). *The Clean Tech Revolution: The Next Big Growth and Investment Opportunity,* p. 280.

39. DeSanctis, G., & Fulk, J. (1999). *Shaping Organization Form: Communication, Connection, and Community.* Thousand Oaks, CA: Sage, p. 105.

CHAPTER 5

1. Mallet, V. (2011, March 27). Spain: Indignant in Iberia. *Financial Times.* Retrieved from http://www.ft.com/intl/cms/s/0/13d1f2b4-8895-11e0-afe1-00144feabdc0.html#axzz 1NwtWYrhu.

2. Ibid.

3. Nuclear power plants, worldwide. (n.d.). *European Nuclear Society.* Retrieved April 18, 2011, from http://www.euronuclear.org/info/encyclopedia/n/nuclear-power-plant-world-wide.htm; Schlissel, D., & Biewald, B. (2008). *Nuclear Power Plant Construction Costs* (Rep.). Cambridge, MA: Synapse Energy Economics; International Energy Agency. (2010). *Key World Energy Statistics,* p. 6 (Rep.). Paris: IEA.

4. Chris Huhne, Speech to LSE: Green Growth: The Transition to a Sustainable Economy. (2010, November 2). *Department of Energy and Climate Change.* Retrieved April 18, 2011, from http://www.decc.gov.uk/en/content/cms/news/lse_chspeech/lse_chspeech .aspx.

5. Private Secretary to Gregory Barker MP. (2011, January 11). RE: Follow up on December Telephone Conference [E-mail to the author].

6. About Coops Europe. (2010). *Cooperatives Europe.* Retrieved from http://www.coops europe.coop/spip.php?rubrique18.

7. Office of the Governor of Massachusetts. (2010, July 12). Governor Patrick Announces Ambitious Region-Wide Energy Efficiency and Renewable Energy Goals [Press release]. Retrieved from http://www.mass.gov/?pageID=gov3pressrelease&L=1&L0=Home&sid =Agov3&b=pressrelease&f=100712_energy_efficiency_goals&csid=Agov3.

8. Behr, P. (2010, February 26). Battle Lines Harden over New Transmission Policy in Rumbles. *New York Times.* http://www.nytimes.com/cwire/2010/02/26/26climatewire-battle-lines-harden-over-new-transmission-po-77427.html.

9. Wald, M. L. (2009, July 14). Debate on Clean Energy Leads to Regional Divide. *New York Times.* http://www.nytimes.com/2009/07/14/science/earth/14grid.html.

10. Eggen, D., & Kindy, K. (2010, July 22). Three of Every Four Oil and Gas Lobbyists Worked for Federal Government. *Washington Post,* p. A01.

11. Ibid.

12. Fisher, N. (2011, February 14). Cutting Fossil Fuel Subsidies: Third Time's the Charm? Americans for Energy Leadership. Retrieved from http://leadenergy.org/2011/02/cutting -fossil-fuel-subsidies-third-times-the-charm/.

13. Broder, J. M. (2010, October 20). Climate Change Doubt Is Tea Party Article of Faith. *New York Times.* Retrieved from http://feeds.nytimes.com/click.phdo?i=1ec15f84f5c15 c237ad33c5311cd0955.

14. Ibid.

15. Ibid.

16. Callahan, D. (2010, August 8). As the Green Economy Grows, the "Dirty Rich" Are Fading Away. *Washington Post,* B01.

CHAPTER 6

1. Browne, P. (2010, March 17). More Firms Join Desertec Solar Project. *Green* (blog). *New York Times.* Retrieved from http://green.blogs.nytimes.com/2010/03/17/more -firms-join-desertec-solar-project/?pagemode=print.

2. Humber, Y., & Cook, B. (2007, April 18). Russia Plans World's Longest Tunnel, A Link to Alaska. *Bloomberg*. Retrieved from http://www.bloomberg.com/apps/news?pid=new sarchive&sid=a0bsMii8oKXw.

3. Alfred, R. (2008, April 25). April 25, 1859: Big Dig Starts for Suez Canal. *Wired.com*. Retrieved from http://www.wired.com/science/discoveries/news/2008/04/dayintech_0425.

4. Interesting Facts. (n.d.). *Panama Canal Museum*. Retrieved from http://panamacanal museum.org/index.php/history/interesting_facts/.

5. Bangkok Declaration (1967). (n.d.). *The Official Website of the Association of Southeast Asian Nations*. Retrieved from http://www.aseansec.org/1212.htm.

6. Cebu Declaration on the Acceleration of the Establishment of an ASEAN Community by 2015, Cebu, Philippines, 13 January 2007. (n.d.). *The Official Website of the Association of Southeast Asian Nations*. Retrieved April 8, 2011, from http://www.aseansec .org/19260.htm.

7. Overview. (n.d.). *The Official Website of the Association of Southeast Asian Nations*. Retrieved from http://www.aseansec.org/64.htm.

8. ASEAN Nuclear Power Frameworks and Debates. (2009, April 15). *Nautilus Institute*. Retrieved from http://gc.nautilus.org/Nautilus/australia/reframing/aust-ind-nuclear/ind -np/asean-nuclear-power/asean-framework.

9. Cebu Declaration on East Asian Energy Security, Cebu, Philippines. *The Official Website of the Association of Southeast Asian Nations*. 15 January 2007 (date of declaration). Retrieved from http://www.aseansec.org/19319.htm.

10. ASEAN Plan of Action for Energy Cooperation (APAEC) 2010–2015. (2010, November 8). *Asean Centre for Energy*. Retrieved April 19, 2011, from http://www.aseanenergy .org/index.php/about/work-programmes.

11. Ibid.

12. Ibid.

13. Ibid.

14. Country Comparison: GDP (Purchasing Power Parity). (n.d.). *Central Intelligence Agency*. Retrieved from https://www.cia.gov/library/publications/the-world-factbook/ rankorder/2001rank.html.

15. African Union in a Nutshell. (n.d.). *African Union*. Retrieved from http://www.africa -union.org/root/au/AboutAu/au_in_a_nutshell_en.htm.

16. Access to Electricity. (2009). *World Energy Outlook*. Retrieved from http://www .worldenergyoutlook.com/electricity.asp.

17. Africa-EU Energy Partnership. (n.d.). *Africa-EU Renewable Energy Cooperation Programme*. Brussels, Belgium: European Union Energy Initiative (EUEI), p. 2.; *Joint Africa EU Strategy Action Plan 2011–2013*. (November 30, 2010.). Council of the European Union: Brussels, Belgium.

18. Africa-EU Energy Partnership. (n.d.). *Africa-EU Renewable Energy Cooperation Programme*. Brussels, Belgium: European Union Energy Initiative (EUEI), p. 2.

19. First Steps to Bring Saharan Solar to Europe. (2010, February 22). *European Union Information Website*. Retrieved April 8, 2011, from http://www.euractiv.com/en/energy /steps-bring-saharan-solar-europe/article-184274.

20. Pfeiffer, T. (2009, August 23). Europe's Saharan Power Plan: Miracle or Mirage? *Reuters*. Retrieved from http://www.reuters.com/article/idUSTRE57N00920090824.

21. Ryan, Y. (2010, May). Should the Sahara's Solar Energy Power Europe? *Take Part* (blog). Retrieved from http://www.takepart.com/news/2010/05/14/harnessing-the -saharas-energy-for-europe.

22. Ibid.

23. Rosenthal, E. (2010, December 24). African Huts Far From the Grid Glow with Renewable Power. *African Huts Far From the Grid Glow with Renewable Power*. Retrieved from http://www.nytimes.com/2010/12/25/science/earth/25fossil.html.

24. Declaration of Margarita: Building the Energy Integration of the South. (2007, April 17). *Comunidad Andina*. Retrieved from http://www.comunidadandina.org/ingles /documentos/documents/unasur17-4-07.htm.

25. Energy Information Administration. (2011). *Country Analysis Briefs: Brazil*. US Department of Energy: Washington, DC, pp. 4–8.

26. International Energy Data and Analysis for Brazil. (2011, January). *U.S. Energy Information Administration.* Retrieved from http://eia.gov/countries/?fips=BR#.
27. South America: Venezuela. (n.d.). *Central Intelligence Agency.* Retrieved from https://www.cia.gov/library/publications/the-world-factbook/geos/ve.html.
28. Romero, S. (2006, September 17). From a Literary Lion in Caracas, Advice on Must-Reads. *New York Times.* Retrieved from http://query.nytimes.com/gst/fullpage.html?res=950DE1DB1331F934A2575AC0A9609C8B63.
29. Carter, Jimmy. (1979, July 15.) "The Crisis of Confidence." Speech. Presidential Public Address. Retrieved from http://www.pbs.org/wgbh/americanexperience/features/primary-resources/carter-crisis/.
30. Ibid.
31. Canada-U.S. Relations: A Unique and Vital Relationship. (n.d.). *Government of Canada.* Retrieved from http://www.canadainternational.gc.ca/can-am/offices-bureaux/welcome-bienvenue.aspx?lang=eng&menu_id=146&menu=L.
32. Canada-U.S. Energy Relations. (2009, April 14). *Government of Canada.* Retrieved from http://www.canadainternational.gc.ca/washington/bilat_can/energy-energie.aspx?lang=eng.
33. Imports, Exports and Trade Balance of Goods on a Balance-of-Payments Basis, by Country or Country Grouping. (2010, June 10). *Statistics Canada.* Retrieved from http://www40.statcan.gc.ca/l01/cst01/gblec02a-eng.htm.
34. Rifkin, J. (2005, March). Continentalism of a Different Stripe: Are Canadian Provinces and the Blue States in the U.S. Quietly Forging a Radical New North American Union? This American Says, "Yes." *The Walrus.* Retrieved from http://www.walrusmagazine.com/articles/2005.03-politics-north-american-union/.
35. Region, N. E. (n.d.). Pacific Northwest Economic Region: About Us—Background. *Pacific Northwest Economic Region.* Retrieved from http://www.pnwer.org/AboutUs/Background.aspx.
36. Cernetig, M. (2007, April 14). Cascadia: More Than a Dream. *Discovery Institute.* Retrieved from http://www.discovery.org.
37. Du Houx, R. (2008, November/December). New England Governors, Eastern Canadian Premiers Establish Working Partnerships at Conference. *Maine Democrat.* Retrieved from http://www.polarbearandco.com/mainedem/agc.html.
38. Ibid.
39. Office of the Governor of Massachusetts Deval L. Patrick. (2010, July 12). Governor Patrick Announces Ambitious Region-Wide Energy Efficiency and Renewable Energy Goals [Press release]. Retrieved from http://www.mass.gov/?pageID=gov3pressrelease&L=1&L0=Home&sid=Agov3&b=pressrelease&f=100712_energy_efficiency_goals&csid=Agov3.

CHAPTER 7

1. Randall, J. H. (1976). *The Making of the Modern Mind: A Survey of the Intellectual Background of the Present Age.* New York: Columbia University Press, p. 259.
2. Smith Adam. *The Essays of Adam Smith.* 1776. p. 384. Retrieved from http://books.google.com/books?id=keEURjQkAW8C&printsec=frontcover&dq=Smith+Adam.+The+Essays+of+Adam+Smith&hl=en&ei=j6WcTZ-1LsLJ0QHp853mAg&sa=X&oi=book_result&ct=result&resnum=3&ved=0CDoQ6AEwAg#v=onepage&q=%22the%20greatest%20discovery%22&f=false.
3. Whitehead, A. N. (1952). *Science and the Modern World.* New York: New American Library, p. 50.
4. Miller, G. T. (1971). *Energetics, Kinetics, and Life: An Ecological Approach.* Belmont, CA: Wadsworth, p. 46.
5. Soddy, F. (1911). *Matter and Energy* New York: H. Holt and Co., pp. 10–11.
6. Canterbery, E. R. (2003). Isaac Newton and the Economics Paradigm: Newton, Natural Law and Adam Smith. In *The Making of Economics.* River Edge, NJ: World Scientific Pub, p. 75.

7. Laslett, P. (1967). Second Treatise. In *John Locke: Two Treatises of Government* Cambridge: Cambridge University Press, p. 312.

8. Schrödinger, E. (1947). *What Is Life?* New York: Macmillan, pp. 72–75.

9. Miller, G. T. (1971). *Energetics, Kinetics and Life: An Ecological Approach.* Belmont, CA: Wadsworth, p. 291.

10. Ibid.

11. Ensminger, M. E. (1991). *Animal Science.* Danville, IL: Interstate.

12. Quoted in Doyle, J. (1985). *Altered Harvest: Agriculture, Genetics, and the Fate of the World's Food Supply.* New York: Viking.

13. Brown, Lester, et al., *State of the World 1990.* New York: Norton, p. 5, table 1-1.

14. Cattle Feeding Concentrates in Fewer, Larger Lots, *Farmline,* June 1990, 2.

15. Steinfeld, H., Gerber, P., Wassenaar, T., Castel, V., Rosales, M., & De Haan, C. (2006). *Livestock's Long Shadow,* p. xxi (Rep.). Rome: FAO.

16. de Condorcet, Marquis. (1795). *Outlines of an Historical View of the Progress of the Human Mind.* London: J Johnson, pp. 4–5.

17. Ayres, R. U., & Ayres, E. (2010). *Crossing the Energy Divide: Moving from Fossil Fuel Dependence to a Clean-Energy Future* (p. 11). Upper Saddle River, NJ: Wharton School Pub.

18. Ibid., pp. 12–13, 205–206.

19. Ibid., pp. 13–14.

20. Ortega Coba and Luis Antonio, email with the author, April 27, 2011.

21. The American Physical Society Panel on Public Affairs, & The Materials Research Society. (2011). *Energy Critical Elements: Securing Materials for Emerging Technologies.* Washington, DC: American Physical Society, p. 1.

22. Reeve, A. (1986). *Property.* London: Macmillan, p. 124; Schlatter, R. 1973; *Private Property: The History of an Idea.* New York: Russel & Russel, p. 154.

23. Eckert, P., & Blanchard, B. (2010, January 21). Clinton Urges Internet Freedom, Condemns Cyber Attacks. *Reuters India.* Retrieved from http://in.reuters.com/article/idINIndia-45574120100121.

24. Diehl, J. (2010, October 25). Time to Reboot Our Push for Global Internet Freedom. *Washington Post,* p. A19.

25. Dobb, M. M. (1947). *Studies in the Development of Capitalism.* New York: International Publishers, p. 143.

26. Internet Usage Statistics. (n.d.). *Internet World Stats.* Retrieved from http://www.internetworldstats.com/stats.htm.

27. Levine, M. (2009, March 8). Share My Ride. *New York Times,* p. MM36.

28. Kuznets, S. (1934). "National Income, 1929–1932." 73rd US Congress, 2nd Session, Senate document no. 124, p. 7. Retrieved from http://library.bea.gov/cdm4/document.php?CISOROOT=/SOD&CISOPTR=888.

29. Kuznets, S. (1962, October 20). How to Judge Quality. *New Republic,* pp. 29–32.

30. Orme, J. (1978). Time: Psychological Aspects: Time, Rhythms, and Behavior. In T. Carlstein, D. Parkes, & N. J. Thrift (Eds.), *Making Sense of Time.* New York: J. Wiley, p. 67.

31. Hammer, K. (1966). Experimental Evidence for the Biological Clock. In J. T. Fraser (Ed.), *The Voices of Time: A Cooperative Survey of Man's Views of Time as Expressed by the Sciences and by the Humanities.* New York: G. Braziller; Meerloo, J. A. (1970). *Along the Fourth Dimension: Man's Sense of Time and History.* New York: John Day Company, p. 67; Sharp, S. (1981–1982). Biological Rhythms and the Timing of Death. *Omega Journal of Death and Dying,* 12, pp. 15–23.

CHAPTER 8

1. Barringer, F. (2010, November 26). In California, Carports that Can Generate Electricity. *New York Times,* p. A23.

2. Ibid.

3. Zeller, T., Jr. (2010, December 29). Utilities Seek Fresh Talent for Smart Grids. *New York Times.* Retrieved from http://www.nytimes.com/2010/12/30/business/energy-environment/30utility.html?src=busln.

4. Gruchow, P. (1995). *Grass Roots: The Universe of Home*. Minneapolis, MN: Milkweed Editions.

5. Ulrich, R. (1984). View through a Window May Influence Recovery from Surgery. *Science*, 224, p. 421.

6. Barfield, O. (1965). *Saving the Appearances: A Study in Idolatry*. New York: Harcourt, Brace & World.

7. Arousing Biophilia: A Conversation with E. O. Wilson. *Orion*, Winter 1991. Retrieved from http://arts.envirolink.org/interviews_and_conversations/EOWilson.html.

8. Roszak, T. (1996, January 1). The Nature of Sanity. *Psychology Today*. Retrieved March 9, 2011, from http://www.psychologytoday.com/articles/199601/the-nature-sanity.

9. Roszak, T. (1992). *The Voice of the Earth*. New York: Simon & Schuster.

10. Bragg, E. A. (1996). Towards Ecological Self: Deep Ecology Meets Constructionist Self-Theory. *Journal of Environmental Psychology*, 16, pp. 93–108.

11. Ibid.

12. Salomon, G. (1993). Chapter 1. In *Distributed Cognitions: Psychological and Educational Considerations*. Cambridge, England: Cambridge University Press, p. 43.

13. Virtual Classroom Discusses War And Peace. (2003, March 26). *Swissinfo*. Retrieved from http://www.swissinfo.ch/eng/index/Virtual_classroom_discusses_war_and_peace.html?cid=3235036.

14. Winograd, M., & Hais, M. D. (2008). *Millennial Makeover: MySpace, YouTube, and the Future of American Politics*. New Brunswick, NJ: Rutgers University Press.

15. Memory Bridge Classroom Experience. (n.d.). *Memory Bridge: The Foundation for Alzheimer's and Cultural Memory*. Retrieved from http://memorybridge.org.

16. Bruffee, K. A. (1999). *Collaborative Learning: Interdependence and the Authority of Knowledge, 2nd Edition*. Baltimore, MD: John Hopkins University Press, p. 66.

17. Ibid., p. XIV.

18. Brown, A. L., Ash, D., Rutherford, M., Nakagawa, K., Gordon, A., & Campione, J. C. (1993). Distributed Expertise in the Classroom. In G. Salomon (Ed.), *Distributed Cognitions: Psychological and Educational Considerations*. Cambridge: Cambridge University Press.

19. Ibid.

20. Ibid.

21. Bruffee, K. A. (1999). *Collaborative Learning: Higher Education, Interdependence, and the Authority of Knowledge, 2nd Edition*. Baltimore, MD: John Hopkins University Press.

22. St. George, D. (2007, June 19). Getting Lost in the Great Outdoors. *Washington Post*. Retrieved from http://www.washingtonpost.com/wp-dyn/content/article/2007/06/18/AR2007061801808.html.

23. Louv, R. (2005). *Last Child in the Woods: Saving Our Children from Nature-Deficit Disorder*. Chapel Hill, NC: Algonquin Books of Chapel Hill, p. 10.

24. Ibid., pp. 34–50.

25. Pyle, R. M. (1993). *The Thunder Tree: Lessons from an Urban Wildland*. Boston, MA: Houghton Mifflin.

26. Wilson, E. O. (1993). Biophilia and the Conservation Ethic. In S. R. Kellert & E. O. Wilson (Eds.), *The Biophilia Hypothesis*. Washington, DC: Island Press.

27. Lawrence, E. (1993). The Sacred Bee, the Filthy Pig, and the Bat out of Hell: Animal Symbolism as Cognitive Biophilia. In S. R. Kellert & E. O. Wilson (Eds.), *The Biophilia Hypothesis*. Washington, DC: Island Press.

28. Kellert, S. R. (2002). Experiencing Nature: Affective, Cognitive, and Evaluative Development in Children. In P. H. Kahn & S. R. Kellert (Eds.), *Children and Nature: Psychological, Sociocultural, and Evolutionary Investigations*. Cambridge, MA: MIT Press, pp. 124–125.

29. Carson, R., & Kelsh, N. (1998). *The Sense of Wonder*. New York: HarperCollins, pp. 54, 100.

30. Taylor, A. F., Wiley, A., Kuo, F., & Sullivan, W. (1998). Growing Up in the Inner City: Green Spaces as Places to Grow. *Environment and Behavior*, 30 (1), pp. 3–27.

31. Physical Activity and Education. (2009). *Alliance for a Healthier Generation*. Retrieved from http://healthiergeneration.org/schools.aspx?id=3302.

32. Clay, R. A. (2001). Green Is Good for You. *Monitor on Psychology, 32* (4), p. 40.

33. Faber Taylor, A., Kuo, F. E., & Sullivan, W. C. (2002, February). Views of Nature and Self-Discipline: Evidence from Inner City Children. *Journal of Environmental Psychology*, pp. 46–63; Taylor, A. F., Kuo, F. E., & Sullivan, W. C. (2001, January). Coping with ADD: The Surprising Connection to Green Play Settings. *Environment and Behavior, 33* (1), pp. 54–77.

34. Louv, R. (2005). *Last Child in the Woods*, p. 203.

35. Lieberman, G. A., & Hoody, L. L. (1998). *Closing the Achievement Gap: Using the Environment as an Integrating Context for Learning*. Poway, CA: Science Wizards.

36. National Wildlife Federation. (n.d.). *Be Out There: Schoolyard Habitats How-to-Guide* [Brochure]. Reston, VA.

37. Wolch, J., Gullo, A., & Lassiter, U. (1997). Changing Attitudes Toward California's Cougars. *Society & Animals, 5*, pp. 95–116.

38. Ibid.

39. Louv, R. (2005). Wonder Land: Opening the Fourth Frontier. In *Last Child in the Woods: Saving Our Children from Nature-Deficit Disorder*. Chapel Hill, NC: Algonquin Books of Chapel Hill, p. 243.

40. Beatley, T. (2000). *Green Urbanism: Learning from European Cities*. Washington, DC: Island Press, p. 197.

41. Arousing Biophilia: A Conversation with E. O. Wilson. *Orion*, Winter 1991. Retrieved from http://arts.envirolink.org/interviews_and_conversations/EOWilson.html.

CHAPTER 9

1. Bell, J. F. (1985). *A History of Economic Thought*. New York: Ronald Press, pp. 285–286.

2. Goodman, P. S. (2010, February 21). Despite Signs of Recovery, Chronic Joblessness Rises. *New York Times*, p. 1.

3. Yellen, J. L. (2010, February 22). *The Outlook for the Economy and Monetary Policy*. Speech presented at Presentation to the Burnham-Moores Center for Real Estate School of Business Administration, University of San Diego, San Diego, CA.

4. Carson, J. G. (2003, October 24). U.S. Weekly Economic Update: Manufacturing Payrolls Declining Globally: The Untold Story (Part 2). *AllianceBernstein*. Retrieved from https://www.alliancebernstein.com.

5. Carson, J. G. (2003, October 24). U.S. Weekly Economic Update: Manufacturing Payrolls Declining Globally: The Untold Story (Part 2). *AllianceBernstein*. Retrieved from https://www.alliancebernstein.com.

6. Sherk, J. (2010, October 12). Technology Explains Drop in Manufacturing Jobs. *The Heritage Foundation*. Retrieved from http://www.heritage.org/research/reports/2010/10/technology-explains-drop-in-manufacturing-jobs.

7. Schwartz, N. D. (2003, November 24). Will "Made in USA" Fade Away? Yes, We'll Still Have Factories, and Great Ones Too. We Just Might Not Have Many Factory Workers. Why Those Jobs Are Never Coming Back. *CNNMoney.com*. Retrieved from http://money.cnn.com/magazines/fortune/fortune_archive/2003/11/24/353800/index.htm.

8. Carson, J. G. (2003, October 24). U.S. Weekly Economic Update: Manufacturing Payrolls Declining Globally: The Untold Story (Part 2). *AllianceBernstein*. Retrieved from https://www.alliancebernstein.com; Carson, J. G. (2003, October 10). U.S. Weekly Economic Update: Manufacturing Payrolls Declining Globally: The Untold Story. *AllianceBernstein*. Retrieved from https://www.alliancebernstein.com.

9. Kurzweil, R. (2005). The Six Epochs. In *The Singularity Is Near: When Humans Transcend Biology*. New York: Viking, pp. 7–8.

10. Ibid., p. 11.

11. Ibid., p. 9.

12. Ibid., pp. 198–200.

13. Salamon, L. M. (2010). Putting the Civil Society Sector on the Economic Map of the World. *Annals of Public and Cooperative Economics,* 81 (2), p. 187.
14. Ibid., p. 188.
15. Salamon, L. M., Anheier, H., List, R., Toepler, S., & Sokolowski, W. S. (1999). *Global Civil Society: Dimension of the Nonprofit Sector* (Comparative Nonprofit Sector Project, The John Hopkins Center for Civil Society Studies). Retrieved from www.jhu.edu/~ccss/pubs/books/gcs.
16. Ibid., p. 189.
17. Schiller, F. In E. M. Wilkinson & L. A. Willoughby (Trans.). *On the Aesthetic Education of Man, In a Series of Letters.* Oxford: Clarendon Press, 1967.
18. Sartre, J. (1974). *The Writings of Jean-Paul Sartre* (Vol. 2). Evanston, IL: Northwestern University Press.

INDEX